796.962
B

BaT   11/07
88

# The Unwritten Rules
# of Fighting and Retaliation
# in the NHL

ROSS BERNSTEIN

TRIUMPH
BOOKS

Library of Congress Cataloging-in-Publication Data

Bernstein, Ross.

The code : the unwritten rules of fighting and retaliation in the NHL / Ross Bernstein.

    p. cm.

Includes bibliographical references.

ISBN-13: 978-1-57243-756-2 (alk. paper)

ISBN-10: 1-57243-756-1 (alk. paper)

1. Hockey—Miscellanea. 2. National Hockey League—Miscellanea. I. Title.

GV847.B45 2006

796.962'64—dc22

2006014188

This book is available in quantity at special discounts for your group or organization. For further information, contact:

**Triumph Books**

542 South Dearborn Street

Suite 750

Chicago, Illinois 60605

(312) 939-3330

Fax (312) 663-3557

Printed in U.S.A.

ISBN-13: 978-1-57243-756-2

ISBN-10: 1-57243-756-1

Design by Sue Knopf

Photos courtesy of AP/Wide World Photos unless otherwise indicated. Page 1 photo courtesy of Ross Bernstein.

"The first rule of Fight Club is…you do not talk about Fight Club. The second rule of Fight Club is… YOU DO NOT TALK ABOUT FIGHT CLUB. Third rule of Fight Club: if someone yells Stop!, goes limp, or taps out, the fight is over. Fourth rule: only two guys to a fight. Fifth rule: one fight at a time, fellas. Sixth rule: no shirt, no shoes. Seventh rule: fights will go on as long as they have to. And the eighth and final rule: if this is your first night at Fight Club, you HAVE to fight."

—from the 1999 movie *Fight Club*

# Contents

## Section I: The History of Fighting in the NHL

## Section II: Defining the Code

## Section III: The Enforcer and His Impact on the Game

# Foreword by Marty McSorley

I remember being a kid and dreaming of playing in the National Hockey League. To finally see that dream come true was so gratifying for me. I grew up on a farm in Canada with six brothers, and we had to answer for what we did. That made us pretty tough, no question. There was no running back to Mommy when things didn't go our way, so we had to stand up for ourselves and be accountable. Respect was earned in my family; it wasn't just given to any of us. Certainly that attitude and work ethic helped me in my professional career.

I was lucky to play as long as I did and with so many great teammates. I owe everything I have to hockey, and for that I will be forever grateful. To get the opportunity to play the game at its highest level was so special. I got my name on Lord Stanley's Cup twice; I got to play against the Soviet Red Army team; I got to play with the greatest player of all time in Wayne Gretzky—I just had a ball doing what I loved best, playing hockey.

There is great satisfaction in knowing that you accomplished so many of the things that you set out to do in life. I am not going to lose any sleep worrying about what other people remember about me. I know that I did my best and that my teammates respected me. That is really all that matters to me. My old teammate with the Kings, Kelly Hrudey, told me something one time after a tough game that I really took to heart as a great, great compliment. He said, "Marty, we are certainly never going to get cheated on your effort." That meant a great deal to me because that is how I felt as a player, that I never wanted to cheat my teammates out of anything. I gave it my all every time I laced 'em up, and that, more than anything, is how I hope to be remembered when I am long gone.

As for the code, to me it was what we, as hockey players, lived by. The code was a living, breathing thing among us. It changed and evolved as the rules changed and evolved, and it took on a life of its own. The basic premise of the code is that you have to answer for your actions on the ice. You learn it pretty early on in your hockey career, and it doesn't take very long to figure out just how important it is. The code says that you play hard and physically in order to get yourself more space out on the ice, but you don't take advantage of guys who aren't in a position to defend themselves along the way. I enjoyed playing the game very physically. I was always under the assumption that you stood up for your teammates no matter what, but it wasn't so much about intimidation for me as it was about just playing honest.

The most important aspects of the code, bar none, are honesty and respect. Because without those things it's the Wild West out there, which is no good for anybody. If players don't play honestly and with respect, then there is a price to pay in this game. That is just the way it is. Hockey is a game that polices itself, and there is a lot of honor behind that. It is something we as players take very, very seriously. As an enforcer, it was my job to make sure that my teammates had space out on the ice and could play the game honestly. If opposing players wanted to take liberties with my guys, then they would have to answer to me. That kept things honest, and that is the basis of the code in its purest sense.

Most fans will be shocked to hear this, but it's true: almost every time two heavyweights get into a fight, they didn't start it. No way. It escalated from something way down the line and finally wound up in their laps. Maybe a rookie was trying to show he belongs by doing something stupid, or an agitator was carrying his stick too high. It could be anything really. And everybody on both benches knows it's coming, too. That is just the way it is. A series of events led up to that point, and the enforcers would have to end it so that the game could calm down again. That's how the code works. And when the fight was over, it would have a sobering effect on the guys back on the bench, who could then get back to playing good, clean hockey. So, that is what we did: we made sure guys played clean because if they didn't, things were going to get ugly.

I think that the toughest thing about fighting was that your hands and body would get so beat up, and then you would have to go out there and try to play a hockey game. It is tough enough to do one or the other, but to combine them night in and night out—that was a constant battle for sure. Sometimes you were just so exhausted, both mentally and physically, and it could have an effect on how you played the game. You know, I was lucky: I got a regular shift, and I prided myself on being a well-rounded hockey player. I could do a lot more than just fight. That is not the case for a lot of fighters in this league, and being able to contribute meant a lot to me. I took it very seriously and wanted to be the best player I could for my teammates.

So, why do we do what we do? We are hockey players, and we all have roles to play. Not everybody can be Wayne Gretzky; that is just a fact of life. Football teams need offensive linemen, and hockey teams need enforcers. That is how teams win, with role players. Some guys fight out of fear; some guys fight out of insecurity; some guys fight because it is the right thing to do at that time; and some guys fight because they just like to fight. Whatever the reason, fighting in hockey is a necessary evil and something that actually protects the game's best players from injury and acts of disrespect.

You know, hockey enforcers are typically the nicest guys on their teams. They are the most approachable and the most fun to hang around with, too. They usually accepted that role because they care about their teammates so much. In fact, it might just be the most selfless job in all of professional sports. They are good people. They are like the cop on the beat or a protective father looking out for those who might not be able to look out for themselves. Some people like to paint horns on them and call them animals, but when you get to know most of them you will see that it couldn't be further from the truth.

---

Old school. That may be the best way to describe Marty McSorley, one of the most respected heavyweights ever to play in the National Hockey League. Marty grew up one of seven boys and three girls on a 720-acre farm outside of Hamilton, Ontario. He grew up tough, and that toughness would lead him to an illustrious 17-year NHL career from 1983 to 2000, which included stops with the Pittsburgh Penguins, Edmonton Oilers, Los Angeles Kings, San Jose Sharks, New York Rangers, and Boston Bruins. During that time Marty tallied 108 goals and 251 assists for a total of 359 points. He also accumulated a whopping 3,381 penalty minutes, garnering a reputation as one of the top enforcers of all time. Marty's unselfish attitude endeared him not only to his teammates but also to hockey fans everywhere. He played the game the right way, as a true professional, and led by example, epitomizing the very code of honor by which he lived.

# Foreword by Tony Twist

What's it like to be a fighter in the NHL? Well, imagine yourself as a kid in school, having to worry about going to class and getting good grades, but then knowing in the back of your mind that at 3:00, every day, you were going to have to fight the biggest, baddest bully on campus, and in front of the entire student body. Now magnify that by 20,000 screaming fans and another half million watching on TV, and that is what it was like to be an NHL enforcer. And by the way, in addition to all of that stress and anxiety, you still have to play a hockey game. Did I mention that you might have a broken hand to boot? Or that your shoulder was separated? It doesn't matter because when that bell rings you have to go, no matter what. You have to be an asset in this business, not a liability, or you are out of work. Welcome to my world.

I think the secret to my success on the ice was that my level of intimidation came from another place. I fought with malice, meaning I didn't fight just to fight. I fought to win, and I wanted to hurt my opponent. My objective was to put my fist through the back of that guy's skull. Period. Most of the guys who fought me understood that. And I wasn't afraid to take a punch, either. In fact, I was more than happy to take two or three shots in exchange for my one big one. I was willing to do whatever it took to beat that guy and give my teammates a lift—that was my job. You know, I wasn't ever nervous to fight. For me it was more about eager anticipation. I mean, if you didn't have butterflies of some sort before you dropped the gloves, there was a good chance you were going to get cleaned up. Take a guy in this league too lightly and you could get killed—literally.

Was I a student of the game? Absolutely. I probably have 700 fight tapes at my house right now, if that is any indication of how much I did my homework. Sure, I studied guys and I wanted to prepare myself as best I could. It would be stupid not to. Any one of those guys could kill you if you weren't properly prepared out there. It didn't matter much, though, because I wasn't going to change my style for anybody. I watched them for enjoyment more than anything. They got me really fired up to do my job. As for me, my tape was easy to study. I was an open book. Guys knew exactly what they were going to get from me; there were no secrets about my style. I was coming at you, and I was coming hard. I was going to grab you with my left hand and then bash you with my right one until you went down. It was pretty basic but very effective.

When it came to sticking up for my teammates, no matter who they were, the greater interest was always served. It didn't matter if I didn't like a certain guy on my team or if I didn't agree with what I was fighting over. If we were wearing the same color sweater, then I was going to defend him no matter what. That is what the code says. I had their backs, and I knew that they had mine. Hey, that was my job. If everybody on the team does his job then you will have success. I remember screaming at Brett Hull one time when he got in a fight. I said, "What the hell are you doing putting your hands up? That is my job. You do your job. You score goals and leave that to me. You're cheating the rest of us when you do stuff like that." What if he got hurt punching a guy? Then he couldn't score goals and we wouldn't win games. The trickle-down effect for every man's actions forces each player to be accountable for himself.

My teammate Craig MacTavish paid me a great compliment one time when he told me that I had become so good at my job that after a while they didn't even need me anymore. He said that they just needed to put a cardboard cutout of me down on the end of our bench like a scarecrow. That was enough for the opposition to behave, he said. That was very gratifying to hear. You know, sometimes I felt like I was a victim of my own success in that I had earned such a reputation as a fighter that very few guys were even willing to fight me. As a result, our guys got tons of space out on the ice and we won a lot of games.

But because I wasn't fighting, I also wasn't getting much ice time, which was terrible for me. Even though I prided myself on being a great fighter, I still wanted to play the game and take a regular shift. All fighters want that. We don't want to just come off the bench for a fight. We want to score goals and celebrate with our teammates at center ice. That is what hockey is all about. Don't get me wrong, I knew what my role was. I wasn't going to be sent out there to score the tying goal in a playoff game or anything, but ice time was a nice perk. If I only got two or three shifts per game, then I was going to make the most of them. My coach, Mike Keenan, was very up front with me about my role and about the minutes I got, and he never short-shifted me. He always gave me an opportunity to do my job, so I have a lot of respect for him for that reason.

Al MacInnis used to tell me that he could really tell the difference between when I was in a game and when I wasn't. He said he would never get run when I was out there, and even when I was on the bench he would get another foot or two to move around. As an enforcer you take that as a great compliment, too.

My philosophy was pretty straightforward. I never turned anybody down and always gave guys a shot who wanted to fight me; I never jumped anybody; and I was always up front and center with them. It wasn't personal with me, it was just business. I tried to be respectful of my opponents and tried not to do anything to break the code, like going after a guy at the end of his shift. Stuff like that was bullshit. The true heavyweights, the toughest guys in the league, would never do something like that. You addressed guys when they were fresh, or you waited. If you knew that you were going to go with a guy and he was a minute into his shift, then you skated by and said, "No worries, I'll catch you next time. You're a little short of breath." That is what the code is all about, civilized insanity.

All in all, I enjoyed a good scrap. I enjoyed every aspect of it. It was one of my favorite things in the world. I could take all my pent-up energy from the week and just release it on somebody during a game. And hey, it was legal. I mean, to get a charge from 20,000 screaming fans who are all rooting for you at the same time, it was the greatest rush you could ever imagine. To hear them chanting your name and pounding on the glass, it was like you were in slow motion out there. The next day your picture would be in the paper and people would talk about you like you were some kind of superhero. You tell me, what is not to like about that?

I loved it because I was really good at it. I hated to lose and I rarely did. Just to be able to play at this level was a thrill of a lifetime. To go up against the top players in the world, stay at fine hotels, eat great food, hang out with great friends, get treated like a rock star wherever you went—it was truly the best of times. Then, on top of that, on the first and 15th of every month they paid me millions of dollars. Are you kidding me? I felt like I should be paying them!

Do I miss the game? Yes, I miss it terribly. I had to leave the game as the result of a bad motorcycle accident in which I broke my pelvis and my leg and also blew out my knee. I was done. I didn't get to leave the game on my own terms, and that really sucked for me. That was one of the saddest days of my life, for sure. But I have no regrets because I played every game like it was my last. I retired after 10 years in the league and went out at the absolute top of my game. I can honestly say that for the last five years I played, nobody could beat me. Nobody. I take great pride in that, and that is something they can never take away from me.

As for my legacy, I would hope to be remembered as a guy who did anything for his club, day in and day out, no matter what it was. And that I did my job well and with enthusiasm. Hey, I just loved to play the game.

---

To say that Tony Twist was tough might be the understatement of the century. "Twister," as he is affectionately known, may very well have been the most feared fighter ever to lace 'em up in NHL history. The son of a Royal Canadian Mounted Police Officer and the grandson of a former welterweight boxing champion, Twist came from a thoroughbred stock of authority and strength to be sure. An accomplished amateur kickboxer, the Prince George, British Columbia, native would go on to spend 10 illustrious seasons in the NHL from 1989 to 1999, both with the Quebec Nordiques and the St. Louis Blues, racking up 1,121 penalty minutes along the way. Despite the fact that the gritty winger's career was sadly cut short as the result of a motorcycle accident, he is still regarded by most as the toughest heavyweight of all time. His love of life and what he did out on the ice made him not only a huge fan favorite, but also the ultimate teammate.

# Introduction

I will never forget watching *SportsCenter* one evening in early March 2000 and seeing the highlights of an otherwise meaningless game between the Boston Bruins and Vancouver Canucks. The highlight reel was playing in slow motion over and over, and it focused on one play, a vicious hit by Bruins enforcer Marty McSorley on fellow tough guy Donald Brashear. It was in the final moments of the game, and McSorley had apparently hit Brashear on the side of the face with his stick in order to goad him into a fight. Like everybody, I was shocked and appalled. To see Brashear, this chiseled hulking warrior lying on the ice, out cold, was almost surreal. Was this just another hockey fight, or was this something deeper? I wondered. Immediately, McSorley was vilified by the media, which claimed that he had done something even more egregious than the act itself: he had broken "the code."

Code? What code? I had been playing hockey my entire life and I had never heard of any code. As I listened more closely and dug a little deeper in the days and weeks that ensued, a clearer picture emerged of just what they had been talking about. The code, I learned, was in fact a living, breathing entity among those lucky enough to call themselves members of the National Hockey League. The code was hockey's sacred covenant, its unwritten rules of engagement that had been handed down from generation to generation. There was, as I learned, a mysterious chain of accountability that dealt with the issues of violence and fighting. It was no wonder I hadn't ever heard of it, because "it" is usually not spoken of by those who live by it.

As a former college hockey walk-on who didn't have the goods to make it, I never got far enough up the ladder to fully grasp the roles of honor, courage, intimidation, and retaliation in the game. Heck, I had enough trouble just trying to skate from one end of the rink to the other without tripping over myself. Nevertheless, I was intrigued by the code and started to watch the pro game a little differently. As the years went by I saw the triumphant return of professional hockey to Minnesota up close and personal when an expansion team, the Wild, hit the ice. I started to look at fighting not just as entertainment for the fans, but as a strategic tactic. I saw how players protected one another, and I saw how there was accountability on the ice by those who took liberties with others. I saw how every player had a role. It was truly eye-opening.

Then, in 2004, another "incident" occurred, this time between Vancouver Canucks star forward Todd Bertuzzi and Colorado Avalanche forward Steve Moore. While the news clip of Bertuzzi sucker-punching Moore from behind, followed by him then driving Moore's head to the ice, played over and over on TV, this time the situation was different. This time it was not about two heavyweights; it was about one player, Bertuzzi, seeking justice for his team captain whom he felt had been wronged several games earlier by Moore with a questionable hit. Again, I heard talk of "the code" and about how Bertuzzi had broken it.

As a journalist and a hockey nut, I wanted to dig deeper into the Steve Moore story. What I found was amazing. I found a story line complete with a thickening plot, suspense, drama, and a tragic ending. No, this was not a Tom Clancy novel I was reading, it was the play-by-play of the accounts that led up to the event. Again, all that the common fan saw on TV were the last few seconds of a miniseries of events that had been playing out for a very long time. Moore, who suffered a potentially career-ending neck injury in the attack, was clearly the victim, but not without fault with regards to the events that led up to the incident.

With that, I decided that this "code" thing was worth really looking into. So, I dug much deeper and decided to write a book about it. What started in 2004 got sidetracked that year when the NHL decided to lock out its players and cancel its season. While I was devastated at first, upon further review I was thrilled. Not only was hockey going to get its financial house in order by virtue of having a salary cap, but it was also going to change its rule book to "open up the game" and cut down on all the dreaded obstruction, which had slowed it down to a snail's pace in recent years. Then I wondered how all of these events would affect the code and how my book would invariably be altered.

To my surprise, my book changed a great deal over that year, but all in a positive way. I now had perspective—a before and an after. It gave me more time to research, reflect, and interview players who were enjoying some rare down time. It turned out to be a truly fascinating journey. In fact, of the more than 30 books I have written, this was by far the most interesting and fun. I spoke to more than 50 current and former players for the project, from enforcers to agitators to lightweights. I wanted to get everyone's take on the code because it affects everyone on the ice equally. I did a lot of listening, too, because these guys love to tell stories.

I learned about roles and role players. I remember having lunch one day with my buddy Tom Chorske, a speedy winger who played in the NHL for 11 seasons during the late 1980s and 1990s. I asked him about his most memorable fight in the "show," and what it was like. I was expecting a crazy answer, like some sort of wild bench-clearing brawl. Instead, he told me about the time he wound up squaring off against a bigger guy who had tried to take some liberties with him in a game. Normally, a tough guy would do that for him, but Tom wanted to stand up for himself and prove to his teammates that he was tough. He didn't win the fight, but he held his own; he "showed up," as they say, and figured his boys would be proud of him. Most were, except for his team enforcer, who was really upset. Afterward the enforcer took him aside and told him never to do that again.

He explained to Tom that fighting that guy out there was his job, and that if Tom didn't allow him to do his job, then he may not have a job. He explained that while Tom's contract was measured by goals and assists, his was judged by other factors, such as penalty minutes. He also explained that if the other teams knew that Tom was now going to fight them and be undisciplined, then they would do so as a tactic for getting him off the ice. He explained the repercussions of his actions not just for that game but for future games as well. He also said that he couldn't do Tom's job, to score goals, so Tom shouldn't try to do his job either, to fight agitators who are doing their job by goading goal scorers into doing something they normally wouldn't do. Hearing how the code worked in that situation, about the psychology behind how the players perform their roles, and when and why they retaliate was an eye-opening experience for me.

One of the first guys I interviewed was Marty McSorley, because I wanted to hear his side of what really went down that night in Vancouver. I was shocked. Just as there had been a complex story line to the Bertuzzi incident, so too was there a chronology with that one. It made me wonder about not only every fight I saw, but about every hit, every high stick, every glare that happens on the ice at professional hockey games. I wanted to know how and why the game polices itself. I wanted to learn all I could about these unspoken rules. I was on a mission.

What I learned changed my life. It had a profound impact not only on the way I view hockey, but also on how I view all sports. As I dug deeper I wanted to honor these enforcers—all of them—for what they do for their teammates in their quest for Lord Stanley's Cup. I didn't want to do another "fighting" book; that has been done to death. I wanted to go behind the scenes and really figure out what it takes to be an NHL player who lives by the code of honor. The code is so much more than just fighting. It is about players sacrificing their bodies to block shots; about getting stitched up between shifts, not periods; about standing up for one another no matter what—even if that means having to square off against a former teammate or best friend.

I learned that the code, for the most part, is learned first by kids playing minor and junior hockey in Canada, who then carry it forward to the NHL. They learn what is acceptable and what isn't by trial and error. It doesn't take long for them to figure it out, either. If they get a guy with a cheap shot, they are going to have to pay for it. As soon as they get smacked upside the head a few times, they realize that they should avoid cheap shots. This basic premise cleans up the game and lets the players police themselves. Those who think that hockey is simply about scoring goals aren't following the game closely enough. Hockey is about the toughness, intimidation, and threshold of pain that go into scoring goals. There is a big difference.

Believe it or not, the fans see a very different game from the one the players are monitoring from their bench. The fans see goals and assists and checks and passes. The players see those things, too, but they also see every little act of disrespect, every little insult, every subtle cheap shot, every excessive celebration after a goal, and every bit of obstruction out in the slot. They see it all, and when the time is right, they will react to each act with varying degrees of intensity and passion. That is the code. Violate it, and you will pay. It is the theory that retribution, and the threat of retribution, prevents further dirty play down the road.

Hockey's rules of engagement are all about protection, intimidation, and solidarity among teammates. If a player challenges another player over an issue he deems as disrespectful, that player must answer the bell or risk the humiliation of being considered a coward. Or, worse yet, if that player refuses to right what was wronged right then and there, he risks having that incident escalate to another level, involving other teammates. Before long the wheels of retaliation are in motion, and someone will have to be held accountable.

The code keeps people at all levels of the game honest and forces them to keep their heads on a swivel. It makes them think twice about carrying their sticks high, running a player from behind, or cross-checking the wrong guy. It is intimidation based on the theory that a good offense can be established by having a good defense. Hockey is a character game. It is all about one team trying to get its opponent to play out of character, to be undisciplined and take stupid penalties that put them at a disadvantage. There are many ways of going about this, and the code has rules for all of them.

You know, when a fight breaks out in pro hockey, it doesn't matter where you are or what you are doing, you stop and you watch. Period. It is like time stands still. Just two gladiators going toe-to-toe out there in front of 20,000 screaming fans, and everyone just waits in nervous anticipation for what will happen. It is like that proverbial car wreck along the side of the road: you don't want to look, but you have to slow down and just take a peek. It's the voyeur in all of us. It is living vicariously through those two tough SOBs out on the ice, hoping quietly that the opposing player gets knocked out cold, thus swinging the momentum of the game.

Hockey is a crazy game. Once it gets in your blood, it stays there for a very long time, both as a player and as a fan. It's been in me since I was a little kid, and luckily it remains to this day. I have played the game my entire life, and after writing this book, I can honestly say that I now see it in a completely different light. As a kid, watching my beloved North Stars, I rooted for tough guys like Jack Carlson, Willi Plett, and Basil McRae, who kept the peace at the old Met Center. Back then, when there was a fight, I just stood and cheered. I had no idea what had led up to it or why they were even doing it. I think many casual hockey fans would concur. Now, after spending the better part of two years immersing my life in their craft, I have been enlightened. That new knowledge has opened my eyes, and the game is much, much more exciting to watch now.

As for the purpose of this book, first and foremost the point is to have fun. Beyond that, hopefully it will make the game much more enjoyable for you to watch. The intent is to celebrate not only the honor and courage behind players protecting their teammates, but also the overall toughness that is synonymous with the sport of hockey. The book delves into the history of fighting and violence in pro hockey and lets you formulate your own opinions. It will also give you a great perspective into how the new rule changes imposed by the league in 2005 have changed the game.

As for my personal feelings toward fighting? I am torn. Believe it or not, I have never been in a fight in my entire life. Ever. Either on or off the ice. But this book is not about encouraging violence in hockey—especially for kids. It is about celebrating the honor and courage behind the way hockey players go about their business as professionals. It is also about getting into the heads of those who use violence, aggression, physical intimidation, and tribal retribution as a means of conflict resolution. Hockey is a tough game played by tough people with an unyielding determination to win. This book honors those people and hopefully gives you, the reader, a window into their amazing world. Enjoy!

# The History of Fighting in the NHL

"The code to me is 100 percent about respect. It is about the respect the players have for the game; the respect the players have for their peers; the respect the players have for the Stanley Cup; the respect the players have for the players who played before them and paved the way; and the respect the players have for the history of the game. It is also about playing hurt and doing whatever it takes to help your team win. There is so much honor in that, and that makes me really proud to be a part of this great game.

"You know hockey is such a passion for people in Canada; it is our national pastime. So, you are immersed into the game at a very early age and you just grow up with it. Every kid dreams of playing in the NHL and hoisting Lord Stanley's Cup one day, and that is what drives all of us who play the game at this level. You learn the code early on and you learn about the right way to play the game, with respect. That is what the code is all about. You just don't want to cheat the game; it's too special to all of us. There is so much history and passion for it, and I just really appreciate it."

—WILLIE MITCHELL
seven-year NHL defenseman,
currently with Vancouver Canucks

# 1

# A Look Back at the History of Fighting and Violence in Professional Hockey

The game of hockey has roots that run deep all the way from its birthplace in Canada. Hockey, as many historians view it, is an amalgam of several different ice games that were popular among the native peoples of Canada, as well as the Europeans who migrated there in the early 1800s. Sticks, skates, and pucks were fashioned out of almost everything you could imagine, including branches for sticks and buffalo chips for pucks. As the game evolved, soccer, rugby, and lacrosse were thrown into the mix, and out came what we now know and love as ice hockey. By the turn of the 20th century the game was pretty well established from coast to coast, with the rules being defined and refined on a regular basis so as to grow its popularity among the masses.

As one looks back at the early documented accounts, however, a common denominator comes glaring through like a Brett Hull slap shot: toughness, retaliation, and, yes, fighting, have been around this game since day one. The theories behind this are plentiful. Among them is the timeless realization that checking is an integral aspect of the game and "boys will be boys." Others include the idea that hockey, as well as lacrosse, made for great training methods in preparing young men for the battlefield. Whatever the reason, blood has been spilling onto the ice for more than a century—with no signs of slowing.

The National Hockey League came into being in 1917, and with it came a whole new brand of toughness. The early days of the Wild West were just that—wild. In fact, the game during the 1910s and '20s was probably more like rugby on skates than it was modern hockey. The rules were much different then, which led to much more rough play and dangerous stick work. For instance, the two blue lines were first introduced in 1918, and with them came the advent of forward passing. Passing was only permitted in the neutral zone, however, which meant that the players had to stickhandle through a gauntlet of flailing fists and elbows, high sticks, and outstretched legs, ready to kick or trip them as they skated by. If they made it through that, and the body checks that ensued, they would then try to make a lateral pass like in rugby. This "phone booth" style of hockey, where the players are in tight quarters, contributed to extremely brutal play, complete with lots of injuries and illegal stick work.

Jack Adams, a former winger who would go on to coach in the NHL, described how players dealt with injuries during those days: "Did these targets go to the dressing room for repairs during the game? No, they stayed on the ice. When you got cut in those days, you skated to the boards and the trainer sloshed off the blood with a sponge he kept in a bucket. Then he patched you up with a slice of adhesive tape."

Once, after a game, Adams went to the hospital to get stitched up. When he got there, however, he was so bloody that his sister, who worked there as a nurse, didn't even recognize him. This sort of brutality was typical of those days, and the toughest SOB of this era was Sprague Cleghorn, who played pro hockey from 1910 to 1928. Red Dutton, who fought Cleghorn on many occasions and would go on to become the president of the NHL, later commented on his old nemesis: "If some of the longhairs I see on the ice these days [the 1970s] met Sprague Cleghorn, he'd shave them to the skull. Jesus, he was mean. If you fell in front of Cleg, he'd kick your balls off."

The NHL could have banned this type of violence altogether, but it chose to keep it as a part of the game. In fact, in 1922 Rule 56 was introduced, which regulated but did not ban "fisticuffs," instead giving the guilty party a five-minute penalty rather than a suspension or expulsion. The owners saw how much the fans loved the violence and saw dollar signs. Fighting and hockey were now officially joined at the hip.

A few years later professional hockey came to the Big Apple. Promoter Tex Rickard ran Madison Square Garden in those days and figured hockey fans to be much like the blood-thirsty folks who came to his boxing and wrestling matches. He was right. So, old Tex hired fleets of ambulances to speed through the streets of Manhattan on game day with their lights and sirens blaring, inciting curious onlookers to come see what it was all about. Then, while the fans were lined up outside the Garden waiting to get in, the ambulances would pull up and park out front—seemingly waiting to pick up their would-be battered and bruised patients who would undoubtedly be needing a lift to the hospital shortly after the game got started.

Perhaps Rickard's most clever promotion came about when legendary brawler Eddie Shore and his Boston Bruins came to town to do battle against the hometown Rangers. Rickard had "WANTED: DEAD OR ALIVE" posters made up with Shore's picture on them and plastered them across the streets of New York. It was brilliant. Shore didn't disappoint either. "Old Blood and Guts," as he was known, was one of the toughest, meanest hombres ever to lace 'em up. Included on his list of career injuries are nearly 1,000 stitches, 14 broken noses, 12 broken collarbones, and five broken jaws, not to mention a broken back and hip.

In 1939, John Lardner wrote of Shore: "For 20 years, man and boy, this evil fellow has been punching people, hitting them over the head with his stick, chewing their ears, butting, gouging, shoving and generally bedeviling his fellow men and always for handsome fees. No one has ever made malevolence pay better money. … [He has] developed the role of Villain to such an extent that professional wrestlers gnash their teeth with envy."

Of all the bone-crushing hits that Shore dished out over the years, however, there is one that stands out far above the others. Not only would it be a hit that would make Shore infamous, but it would also serve as a defining moment for the sport of hockey and its tolerance for violence and retaliation. It happened on December 12, 1933, in Toronto, when Shore's Boston Bruins were in town to face the Maple Leafs. Shore was rushing the puck up the ice and was thumped at the blue line by Toronto's King Clancy. When no penalty was called, an irate Shore exacted revenge by plowing into Leaf winger Ace Bailey with a vicious hit from behind. Bailey, a future Hall of Famer known for his speed and stickhandling, was sent crashing headfirst onto the ice, where he suffered a severely fractured skull at both temples.

Bailey fell into a coma and for more than two weeks his life hung in the balance. Two brain surgeries later, he recovered—only to learn that he would never play hockey again. A short while later an All-Star benefit game was held for him to help raise money for his family. Showing that there were no hard feelings over his unjustified career-ending assault, Bailey forgave Shore by shaking his hand at center ice before the emotionally charged opening faceoff. "It's all right," he would say, "it's all part of the game." The game would become an annual affair, morphing into what we now know as the NHL All-Star Game, featuring the league's top players who exemplify good play and good sportsmanship.

## The Evolution of Violence

As the years went by, professional hockey's popularity grew. With that, however, came the pressure to keep the fans interested as well as entertained. Hockey, after all, was a business and as such had to account for its bottom line. While the vast majority of fans loved the speed, finesse, and excitement of the game, many others loved the hard-hitting checks along with the brawls that often ensued. Revenge, intimidation, and retaliation soon became the norm, and hockey's elite knew that without tough guys patrolling the ice, they would have no room to operate. With just six teams (the NHL's original six: Boston, Chicago, Detroit, Montreal, New York, and Toronto) in the league, rivalries were intense, and none was more intense than Chicago versus Detroit.

One of the most notorious tough guys of the 1940s was Chicago Blackhawks defenseman John Mariucci, who knew his role well: protect the Bentley brothers at all costs. If someone decided to take liberties with Doug or Max Bentley, then the Windy City's most famous hatchet man would be there to settle the score. The resident enforcer for the Detroit Red Wings, meanwhile, was Black Jack Stewart. Together, they would spend quite a bit of time in the penalty box. In fact, they still hold the record for the NHL's longest fight, lasting nearly 20 minutes. While Mariucci and Stewart were archrivals to the core, not many people knew it but they also enjoyed having a beer with each other after a game. That's what is so interesting about hockey brawlers: for many of them, it wasn't personal; it was just a job.

Former Minnesota North Stars coach Glen Sonmor, one of Mariucci's best friends, recalled:

> You know, when I was playing with New York I got to know the Bentley brothers, who played for years with Mariucci in Chicago. John was the ultimate warrior out on the ice. He knew his role and

he loved it. He knew that he wasn't there to score 50 goals, he was there to play solid hockey and to protect his teammates. So, one time I asked those Bentley brothers about what it was like to play hockey with John Mariucci. They said that playing with John made hockey fun for them again. Before John got there [Chicago] other players used to intimidate them and make runs at them because they were the stars of the team.

Well, when John got there it took just one trip around the league for every team to learn not to even look funny at the Bentley brothers. They left them alone after that because anybody from that point on knew that if they tried anything with those guys, John was coming to get them. And back then you didn't have any of the penalties or rules about coming off the bench to mix it up. I remember Max [Bentley] saying, "Anybody who tried to intimidate us had to have some pretty big balls because as soon as they went after us they would have to turn around and get ready for big John, who would come flying off the bench in a hurry. And there wasn't any doubt as to why he was coming either, because he left his stick and gloves back on the bench!"

John used to love beating the crap out of guys, and he was pretty darn good at it. Those Bentleys told me that after that no one would mess with them with the exception of one guy, Black Jack Stewart. They said that Black Jack would get bored out there sometimes, so to make it interesting he would take a shot at one of the Bentleys just so John would come after him. Those two used to love brawling with each other, and then they would go out and have beers together after the game. It was crazy, but that was the kind of guy John was: he would knock you down and then pick you back up.

By the 1950s hockey was flourishing and the fans were coming out in droves to see it. Not only did they love the action and playmaking from the game's top stars, but they also loved the toughness the players displayed. Sometimes the players' passions got too heated, however, and that is when all hell would break loose. Case in point, on March 13, 1955, when Montreal's Maurice "Rocket" Richard tomahawked Boston's Hal Laycoe over the head after being high-sticked, and then proceeded to punch the linesman for good measure. Richard, a future Hall of Famer, was suspended for the rest of the season by then league president Clarence Campbell. The Habs fans were so upset that the next season during a game between the Canadiens and Detroit at the Montreal Forum, the fans started pelting Campbell, who was in attendance, with eggs. A riot ensued, causing more than a half million dollars in damage, and the game was forfeited.

In the mid-1960s the league finally got smart and unveiled separate penalty boxes at its arenas. Incredibly, up until that time opposing players shared the same cozy bench, with just a brave official sitting between them. Brawls in the box were commonplace, but it finally came to a halt following a particularly ugly scuffle between Toronto's Bob Pulford and Montreal's Terry Harper back in October of 1963.

In 1967 the league expanded from six teams to 12, doubling the number of jobs for hungry players. While it was essential for the growth of the game, it also diluted the talent pool considerably. All of a sudden, there was work for less-skilled players who excelled at being thugs. As a result, the incidences of dirty play, including stick fighting, soared.

Stick fighters, or surgeons, as they were known, were the most feared and dangerous players on the ice. One of the most legendary stick-fighting duels took place in 1968 between Philadelphia's Larry Zeidel and Boston's Eddie Shack. The two got into it when Shack took a butt-end in the ribs from Zeidel and retaliated with his stick. Before long the two were apparently chasing each other around the ice like a pair of insane lumberjacks, swinging their sticks likes axes at each other's heads. At first the crowd cheered, but then they got eerily silent as they watched in horror. As the two battled for nearly five minutes, all the fans could hear was the sound of stick on bone as they exchanged blows. The officials had to stand back, so the two kept at it until they ran out of steam. It was a bloody mess.

Another notorious stick-swinging incident happened the next year between St. Louis' Wayne Maki and Boston's "Terrible" Ted Green during a preseason game. The play started with a couple of hard hits and quickly escalated into a slash and a spear, followed by Maki clubbing Green over the head and severely fracturing his skull. Green nearly died in the incident and needed three major surgeries, including a steel plate in his head, to save his life. Both players were suspended and later acquitted of assault charges—earning the distinction of becoming the first players ever charged for such a crime during a game.

Violent assaults aren't reserved for fighting or stick swinging, though. They also include slashing. Arguably the most infamous slash of all time came two years later in the pivotal Game 6 of the 1972 Summit Series, when Team Canada's Bobby Clarke, of Philadelphia, deliberately took out Soviet superstar Valeri Kharlamov's ankle. Knowing that his ankle was sore, Clarke, at the urging of assistant coach John Ferguson, dished out a vicious blow that many contend swung the momentum of the game. As cheap and dirty as it was, the attack proved to be just the wake-up call Team Canada needed to rally back and win the emotional series. When asked about the incident years later Clarke replied: "If I hadn't learned to lay on a two-hander once in a while, I'd never have left Flin Flon."

Another stick-swinging incident made national news a few years later when Detroit's Dan Maloney tomahawked Toronto's Brian Glennie on the head on November 5, 1975. Maloney was charged for assault in an Ontario court and pleaded no-contest. He wound up doing some community service work and was also banned from playing in Toronto for two seasons.

## Hockey Violence and the U.S. Courts

While Maki and Maloney were the first players brought to court in Canada for an act that occurred in competition, Boston Bruins forward Dave Forbes was the first to be charged in the United States, over an incident that happened that same year, 1975. Forbes was charged with aggravated assault with a deadly weapon when he maliciously butt-ended Minnesota North Stars winger Henry Boucha in the eye. The two had been in a scrum moments earlier with Boucha apparently getting the better of Forbes. After serving seven minutes apiece for roughing and fighting, they left the penalty box to head back to their respective benches. That's when Forbes assaulted Boucha. Boucha went straight down in a pool of blood, writhing in agony. Forbes then dove on Boucha and began punching him until Minnesota's goalie, Cesare Maniago, as well as Murray Oliver, Tommy Reid, and Bill Goldsworthy, sped over and drug him off. A huge mêlée ensued with both benches emptying shortly thereafter.

Boucha remembers the incident:

> We had an altercation in the corner and wound up fighting. He had been shadowing me all game and cheap-shotting me, so I finally decided that I had had enough. I got the better of him and we wound up having words together in the box afterward. While we were in there, Bobby Orr got a penalty too, so they were in there talking. We were in there for a total of 15 minutes by the time it was all said and done. Finally, there was a stoppage of play and we each left the penalty box to skate back to our benches. I looked over to him to see if he was going to do anything, and apparently he had calmed down after 15

minutes and had had enough. So, I looked over to our bench, and just as I looked back he came over and threw a punch with the butt-end of his stick and smashed the orbital bone above my right eye, as well as my cheekbone. Blood squirted out as far as eight feet onto the ice after that, and I went straight down. He knew I was in bad shape and tried to cover up, but he still had the audacity to jump on my back, grab my long hair, and keep punching me in the back of the head. It was really scary. I was out of it at that point.

Boucha, a Native American from Warroad, Minnesota, who was a rising star in the NHL, was then carried off on a stretcher and taken to the hospital where he received 30 stitches to sew up his eye. He later had multiple surgeries to repair his fractured eye socket and cheekbone. He would return to the ice some 19 games later, but he was never the same player due to recurring vision problems from the injury. His promising career was ultimately cut short after a few more seasons and he was forced to retire at the age of just 25. As for the legal fallout, a criminal suit was filed by Hennepin County.

Boucha continued:

Their reasoning was if somebody hit you on the street with a stick to your eye, it would be attempted murder or aggravated assault. So, they came and took pictures of me as evidence and everything. Their big thing was the fact that there were thousands of kids who saw the incident at the game and they didn't want them to think that behavior like that was acceptable. Ironically, there was a promotion at the arena that night called Minnesota Judges Night, so all of these lawyers and judges saw the entire thing from just behind the penalty box. Anyway, the county waited to see what the league was going to do and when they suspended Forbes for only 10 games, they decided to press charges and take it to trial. They wanted to set an example, so they made it a criminal case. That summer the jury heard the case, and it resulted in a hung jury, which meant that Forbes had been acquitted. His lawyer argued that it [the attack] was the fault of hockey's culture of violence, not Forbes'.

It was an unprovoked attack, a completely gutless cheap shot. He clearly broke the code; it was way over the line. Not only did he sucker me when I wasn't looking, he used his stick as a weapon. He sat there for 15 minutes thinking about what he was going to do to me. I don't know how that could even be conceivable as a player.

I was so stunned because I was not expecting it at all. You know it was not a gut reaction where you knew you were going to get hit

## Glen Sonmor on Playing by the Code in the 1950s

"We learned the code as kids up in Canada and we then brought it with us to the National Hockey League. They were our rules for how we were going to conduct ourselves above and beyond the official rules of what the officials would enforce. It was a marvelous system based on honor and accountability. If you did something dishonorable or disrespectful toward another player, then you were going to have to answer to that by fighting. In fact, if you used your stick on a guy in those days, you were going to be taken to task not only by your opponents but also by your own teammates. They too would make you stand up and take your medicine.

"The code even went further than that, though, for the absolute superb players, who you almost couldn't even touch at all. You just didn't mess with the top guys in those days. That was a privilege that those elite few had earned. I remember one time when Pat Quinn absolutely leveled Bobby Orr on a beautiful open-ice check, nothing dirty about it at all, and then had to face the entire 'Big Bad Bruins' team that came after him. Even Quinn's teammates were slow to come to his aid because when you nailed a guy like Orr, a superstar, then you had to be accountable for it. And of course when I was coaching the North Stars I also found it difficult to get my guys to even check Gretzky out there because they knew that as soon as they did they were going to have to turn around and face his bodyguards, McSorley or [Dave] Semenko."

and were bracing yourself for it. Amazingly, there is no video footage of the event either because the network was on a commercial time-out. So I have never seen it, believe it or not. I can kind of remember the incident, but it is more of a foggy dream. Forbes did call me afterward in the hospital to apologize and wish me the best. I was pretty drugged up at that point and just said thanks. I have never spoken to him since. I have tried to put it behind me and have tried to just look forward. It is incredible to think that it has been more than 30 years now, but I still think about it a lot. In my mind justice was never really served.

I was able to return to the game, but my eyesight was never the same. I had extreme double vision because the muscles around my eye had been so damaged. My eye wouldn't move properly and I had no depth perception. The North Stars pretty much guilted me into playing the last few games of the year because they didn't want to end up in the league cellar, and that was a terrible decision to do so on my part. I was basically blind in one eye out there.

The other bad part about it was the fact that I had just been offered a very lucrative five-year deal with the North Stars and was about to sign a new contract. I had a lot of bargaining power at that point because I was only 23 years old and I was scoring a lot of goals. Then, after the incident, they came back with only a one-year offer worth a lot less money. So, I wound up signing with the WHA's franchise in Minnesota, the Fighting Saints, instead. From there, I bounced around with Kansas City and finally Colorado that next year. I worked hard to rehab it at the Mayo Clinic and everything, but there was simply too much damage that had been done. After only a few games with the Rockies, I just couldn't see the puck out of that eye and had to call it a career. It was one of the saddest days of my life.

Boucha later sued Forbes, the Bruins, and the NHL, ultimately settling the case in 1980 for monetary damages.

"As for the legacy of it all," said Boucha, "I guess I am happy that it brought more attention to what can happen as the result of a dirty, malicious act in sports. And I am also glad to see that more kids wear protection over their eyes now with the visors. You just never know in this game. Every time you lace 'em up it could be your last."

In 1976 four Philadelphia Flyers players were charged criminally after a brawl with several Toronto Maple Leaf players spilled into the crowd during a playoff game. Mel Bridgman was charged with assault causing bodily harm, and Don Saleski was charged with possession of a dangerous weapon, a stick. While both got off with stays, Bob Kelly and Joe Watson each pleaded guilty to assault and were fined $750 apiece.

Two years later Detroit center Dennis Polonich got into a scuffle with Colorado Rockies winger Wilf Paiement and wound up with a busted nose, a concussion, and some pretty nasty lacerations. The league suspended Paiement for 15 games, but Polonich wound up suing Paiement in the league's first civil case. Polonich cited nasal problems, which resulted in a loss of taste and smell, and claimed the injuries negatively affected his quality of life. A U.S. federal court agreed and awarded Polonich a whopping $850,000.

Over the next three decades there were many more ugly incidents that warranted severe penalties and suspensions by the league. Among the numerous suspensions was a 10-game suspension for Winnipeg's Jimmy Mann for sucker punching Pittsburgh's Paul Gardner in January 1982; a 20-game suspension to Chicago's Tom Lysiak for intentionally tripping a linesman in October 1983; a 15-game suspension to Philadelphia's Dave Brown for cross-checking New York's Tomas Sandstrom across the face in November 1987; a 12-game suspension to New York's David Shaw for high-sticking Pittsburgh's Mario Lemieux in October 1988; a 12-game suspension to Philadelphia goalie Ron Hextall for attacking Montreal's Chris Chelios during a playoff game in May 1989; a 21-game suspension to Washington's Dale Hunter for a blindside hit on New York Islander's winger Pierre Turgeon during the 1993 playoffs; a 15-game suspension to Los Angeles's Tony Granato for slashing Pittsburgh's Neil Wilkinson in February 1994; a 12-game suspension to Los Angeles's Matt Johnson for attacking New York's Jeff Beukeboom in November 1998; a 12-game suspension to San Jose's Brantt Myhres for leaving the bench to go after Los Angeles's Mattias Norstrom in February 1999; and a 10-game suspension to Anaheim's Ruslan Salei for hitting Dallas's Mike Modano from behind in October 1999. The two most notorious incidents, however, were yet to come as the new millennium was about to be ushered in.

## The McSorley Incident

An ugly incident occurred on the night of February 21, 2000, that had a profound impact on how hockey violence was going to be dealt with by the legal system. Notorious tough guy Marty McSorley, the former bodyguard of Wayne Gretzky, was in the twilight of his career and playing with the Boston Bruins. With more than 3,000 minutes logged in the penalty box, McSorley's body had taken a pounding over the years, but he was still one of the best at what he did—protecting his teammates. Long considered an outstanding defenseman and a highly respected player, McSorley made a costly error in judgment that night, which ultimately cost him his career. Here's what went down.

The Bruins were playing the Vancouver Canucks on the road that evening and two legendary enforcers, McSorley and Donald Brashear, squared off to settle some bad blood on their very first shift. Brashear got the better of McSorley in that one and then played up to the crowd by dusting off his hands to embarrass McSorley. McSorley took it as a sign of disrespect and cross-checked Brashear to provoke him into a rematch. Brashear wasn't interested, though, and McSorley was issued a 10-minute game misconduct penalty as a result. While McSorley was in the penalty box, Brashear parked himself in front of the net and wound up falling into Bruins goalie Byron Dafoe, hurting Dafoe's knee and ending his season. McSorley was irate. He knew that Brashear would never have been in that position had McSorley been out there doing his job. He knew that Brashear was taking liberties with his players while he sat defenseless in the box.

Later in the third period, Brashear skated by the Bruins bench and flexed his muscles, taunting the team in yet another act of disrespect. According to McSorley, at that point Boston coach Pat Burns yelled to his players, "Are we going to take that, or are we going to stand up for ourselves?" With the game winding down, McSorley knew that he needed to right what he felt had been wronged, so he was going to challenge Brashear once again to a rematch. Not only did he want to redeem himself personally, but he also wanted to punish Brashear for the blatant acts of disrespect toward his teammates. That was McSorley's job, but he couldn't perform his job unless Brashear agreed to drop his gloves.

Finally, with under a minute to go in the game and the Bruins trailing 5-2, Brashear hit the ice to make sure nobody roughed up any of his teammates in the one-sided victory. At that very moment, according to McSorley, Bruins assistant coach Jacques Laperriere said to him, "Mac, Mac, you're up. You're going. You're going." Translation: Go fight Brashear. McSorley knew, and he was ready. So he hopped over the boards in hopes of engaging his nemesis before the game ended. He skated up to Brashear and asked him "to go" several times, but to no avail. Brashear, in McSorley's eyes, was being a coward for not standing up to him and accepting responsibility for his acts of disrespect. Then, with just two seconds remaining, McSorley's rage got the better of him, and as a last resort, he tried to whack Brashear on the shoulder, only McSorley's stick came up and hit Brashear squarely on the side of the face. At that moment time stood still. Brashear, a 6'2", 225-pound goliath, went down like a ton of bricks. His helmet flew off, and the back of his head crashed into the ice. He lay there motionless for a few seconds and then suffered a grand mal seizure. Mayhem ensued, and when it was all said and done, Brashear was carried off on a stretcher. He suffered a severe concussion and would ultimately miss the next 20 games due to the injury.

As for McSorley, it was the beginning of the end. The NHL banned him from playing for one year, the longest suspension for an on-ice infraction in league history. (Prior to that the longest suspension had come in 1993 when Washington's Dale Hunter was forced to sit out 21 games after cheap-shotting Islanders' winger Pierre Turgeon during a playoff game.) In addition, McSorley was prosecuted in a provincial court in British

Columbia, where a judge found him guilty of assault with a weapon—a hockey stick. He faced an 18-month jail sentence but ultimately received an 18-month conditional discharge and served no jail time. The only stipulation was that he couldn't play any sport where Brashear was on the opposing team. It was historic in that it was the first on-ice incident to be tried in court since 1988, when Minnesota North Stars winger Dino Ciccarelli spent a day in jail after smacking Toronto's Luke Richardson upside the head with his stick.

As for McSorley, he maintains that he never meant to hit Brashear in the head. He was swinging for his shoulder, to hack him and force him to turn around and face him, so that they could fight like men. Instant replay of the incident reveals his stick grazing over Brashear's shoulder before continuing on to the side of his head. His stick came up as he was swinging it, however, and that is when the situation went from bad to horrible.

The 17-year NHL veteran and two-time Stanley Cup champion sat out that next year and eventually could see the writing on the wall: his career was sadly over. It was a tragic ending to an otherwise tremendous career. The genesis of the incident was like countless others during his many years in the league, but this one just got away from him.

Marty had his own take on the events that happened that night:

> First of all, I take full responsibility for what happened. I felt bad that Donald got hurt. But when somebody says that I intentionally struck him in the head with my stick, I have an issue with that, because that goes to the core of who I am and the player I've been over the years.
>
> Everything just went wrong in that one final moment. Like in the Bertuzzi incident, there were a lot of things that led up to that moment and people need to understand that. A lot of people don't remember Donald standing in front of our bench, challenging and taunting us by flexing his muscles. You don't do that kind of Mickey Mouse garbage without backing it up in this league. Not to mention the fact that he took out our goaltender, Byron Dafoe, for the rest of the year on a cheap play in front of the net as well. Those are very serious things, very serious. He had to be held accountable.

As for blame, according to McSorley there is plenty to go around:

> Hey, my coaches put me on the ice with 28 seconds left in the game to go after him. They even scrambled to pull one of our guys off the ice from a position I didn't even play just to get me out there. I mean, you don't have to be a rocket scientist to figure out what they wanted

me to do. If you don't do what your coaches want you to do, then you are not going to have a job for very long in this league. That is how this game works.

Look, Donald didn't feel that he had to fight for his actions, and our team obviously disagreed. We felt that he had severely disrespected us, on several occasions, and needed to be held accountable. That is how the code works. So, for him not to turn and fight me was cowardly. Where was his honor in that situation?

When I actually hit him there were only a couple of seconds left on the clock. I had been trying to get him to fight me for nearly the entire game, but he wouldn't go. In that last half minute I practically begged him, but he wouldn't acknowledge me. I mean, if you fight after the buzzer it is an automatic 10-game suspension, so I needed him to turn and face me. That's how the rules of engagement work.

I finally tried to hit his shoulder to get him to drop his gloves and face me, but my stick flew up and hit him in the head. That was my fault and I take full responsibility for that. I didn't mean to hit him in the head with my stick, no way. I am sorry for that, but I am not sorry for trying to get him to fight me. He needed to answer for his actions and he didn't. The situation obviously went from bad to worse from there, and that was unfortunate.

I certainly paid a high price for my actions and I accept that. That is something I will have to live with. As for now, I have put the entire situation behind me and have long moved on with my life. Donald obviously has too, and that was good to see. Nobody wants to see anybody seriously hurt or unable to play the game; that is not what hockey is about. I am just sad that it happened the way it did and that it caused such a black eye for our sport. That was never my intention.

It seems McSorley has kept it all in perspective. "I was pretty strong with my own convictions," he said. "I went out on top as far as I was concerned. I went out and challenged guys and fought them with respect. I played like a true professional my entire career, and that one incident will not define who I am as a player, no way. Did I do some things over my career that I regret? Sure. Was I a choirboy? Absolutely not. But I played the game the right way for the most part, and the people who matter, my teammates, they know that."

## The Bertuzzi Incident

While the McSorley altercation certainly made headlines back in 2000, and deservedly so, it paled in comparison to yet another bizarre episode

## Marty McSorley on the Bertuzzi Incident

"What happened to Steve Moore was awful. But nobody can tell me that Todd Bertuzzi intended for that to happen, no way. What transpired was something that happens quite often in hockey and it just turned out very, very bad that night. So, in my eyes you don't throw Todd Bertuzzi under the bus and get up on your soap box and say, 'Now we're going to clean the game up.' There were a lot of incidents that led up to that event, and unfortunately in the heat of the moment things went very badly. Unfortunately, Steve got seriously hurt and that is the real tragedy in the story. I would also add this to that entire situation, though: Was the coach partially liable? Hey, let's put the blame where it belongs. Has Todd Bertuzzi stood up and said he was wrong and that he was sorry? Yes he has. But if we are going to throw the book at Todd, we are throwing the book at just one of the guys who is at fault in my eyes. He was not on the ice at that point of the game to score a goal, so why was he out there? There is a lot more blame to go around if people really want to press the issue; Todd's not alone in that one. Sure, he was wrong in how he went about his business, and trust me, I have been there, but it goes much deeper than most people think."

that happened on that same sheet of ice in Vancouver four years later. In fact, perhaps no event in professional hockey history has had the impact of what is now commonly referred to simply as the "Bertuzzi incident." The hockey honor code is all about accountability and responsibility, and this tragic event now serves as the poster child for what can go horribly wrong with the game's self-policing system.

Vancouver Canucks star forward Todd Bertuzzi broke the code all right, and he paid a hefty price for it, to the tune of millions of dollars and permanent damage to an otherwise solid reputation. Colorado Avalanche forward Steve Moore, meanwhile, who was on the receiving end of Bertuzzi's code violation, paid an even bigger price—suffering a career-ending neck injury. Here is a blow-by-blow account of what led up to the event, what happened that day, and what followed.

During an otherwise routine NHL game on February 16, 2004, between the Colorado Avalanche and Vancouver Canucks at the Pepsi Center in Denver, the first of what would be a cataclysmic series of events took place when Avalanche rookie forward Steve Moore, a Harvard graduate not known as a big hitter, knocked Canucks captain Markus Naslund unconscious with an open-ice shoulder/elbow hit to the head. It was a questionable hit that left Naslund with several cuts and a hyperextended elbow, but no penalty was called. It was a ballsy move, to be sure, by a young Avs winger trying to make a name for himself by taking out an extremely respected team captain, who was also leading the league in scoring at the time. It is important to note that no action was taken by Vancouver to exact any revenge for the hit during the game. Afterward, however, Canucks forward Todd Bertuzzi called the officiating "a joke," and his teammate, Brad May, allegedly indicated that a bounty had been placed on Moore's head.

With both teams on high alert, they met again just 16 days later in Denver. Moore, who was expecting retaliation, per the rules of the code, received none. He was probably spared because the game was tight, with the teams skating to a 5–5 tie—certainly not the ideal environment for Vancouver to be a man short on a power play with their playoff position on the line. Adding to the drama was the fact that NHL commissioner Gary Bettman and executive vice president Colin Campbell were in attendance, perhaps keeping an eye on the situation to make sure that it didn't get out of hand. The lone incident in the game was a scrap between Colorado's Peter Worrell and Vancouver's Wade Brookbank.

The teams met yet again on March 8, in Vancouver, in a battle for first place in the Northwest Division. The game got under way with Colorado jumping out to a quick lead. The Vancouver players then decided that they needed to right the wrong that had been exacted on their team captain a few weeks earlier. So the wheels of the code were put into motion just six minutes and 36 seconds into the game when Steve Moore was challenged by Vancouver's enforcer, Matt Cooke. The two dropped the gloves and Cooke clearly got the better of him. Moore, who had never fought before in the NHL, stood up for himself. It wasn't pretty, but he "showed up." He followed the unwritten rules of the code by answering the chain of accountability and with that, it should have been over. Justice served. That's the way it's supposed to work anyway. While Cooke wasn't able to pummel Moore perhaps the way he would've liked, he got his opportunity. He defended his captain's honor and did so on his home ice. Case closed, right? Wrong.

The Avs went up 5–0 late in the first period and with that, the gloves continued to come off. Vancouver's Jarkko Ruutu and Colorado's Rob Blake went at it at 17:42, while the Canucks' Brad May and the Avalanche's Peter

Worrell squared off for the second time less than 20 seconds later. May tallied two quick goals in the second period, however, to get Vancouver back in it, 5–2. It was all Colorado from there, though, as they went on to add three unanswered goals in the second and third periods. May, who had already received a 10-minute misconduct penalty for taunting Colorado goalie David Aebischer, made his fourth trip to the box midway through the third for a roughing penalty. This lopsided game was getting out of control.

Things finally came to a climax at 8:41 of the third, with the Avs leading 8–2. With the game completely out of reach, Bertuzzi hit the ice and challenged Moore to drop the gloves. Moore, who felt that he had already answered for his questionable hit on Naslund, did not respond. He felt that any more fighting could better be accomplished by his team's enforcers. Bertuzzi did not see it that way. His captain and good friend had missed three games because of the concussion Moore had given him, and in Bertuzzi's eyes Moore had not paid enough.

By now Bertuzzi, an All-Star winger who is 6'3" and 250 pounds, was chasing Moore around the ice, demanding that he turn and face him like a man. When Moore refused yet again, Bertuzzi took matters into his own hands by grabbing the back of Moore's jersey and delivering a roundhouse sucker punch to the side of his head, knocking him unconscious. Then Bertuzzi tackled him and drove him face-first into the ice, severely injuring Moore's neck. When Moore's teammates saw what was happening, they came to his aid and tried to get Bertuzzi off. Andrei Nikolishin was first on

### Darren Pang on the Bertuzzi Incident

"One of the things about the Bertuzzi incident that made it so scrutinized was the fact that there was a vengeance about it. I mean, there were known, public quoted threats that had been talked about openly by some Vancouver players leading up to that game. They basically said stuff like, 'We will retaliate,' 'We will get him no matter the cost,' 'We will have his head.' And then to go out and actually do it in the manner that Bertuzzi did it was a clear violation of the code in my eyes. You just can't do that. I am pretty sure Steve Moore felt that he had answered the bell in the first period when he fought Matt Cooke, but Bertuzzi obviously felt differently. There was a lot of emotion there, and things just got out of hand."

## Tony Twist on the Bertuzzi Incident

"The thing with the Bertuzzi incident that really bugged me was that he hit him from behind. I mean, if you want to sucker punch a guy, great, go for it, but do it to his face so he can see you. You just don't hit a guy from behind, because that is when guys get really hurt. That to me is where he broke the code, right there. You need to look a guy square in the eyes before you start whaling away. If he would have turned him around and then popped him, we wouldn't be having this conversation because it never would have turned out the way it did. But—and this is a big *but*—Moore was also at fault for running around and not turning to face him. He had it coming and he needed to take his medicine for the hit he dished out to Naslund. His fight with Cooke earlier on didn't really do much. He needed to answer the bell. The punishment didn't fit the crime, so to speak. That was just a bad deal all the way around, though, for everybody."

the scene and jumped on his back. The result was a pile-on of players that caused even further injury to Moore's badly fractured vertebrae.

The fans at General Motors Place, who initially reacted with scattered cheers, quickly went silent when it became apparent that Moore was seriously injured. After a 10-minute delay, the officials were able to restore order. Bertuzzi was given a match penalty for attempting to injure and was thrown out of the game, and May and Kurt Sauer were both issued fighting majors as well as game misconducts. Meanwhile, Colorado coach Tony Granato was screaming at Vancouver coach Marc Crawford and had to be restrained at the bench. It was utter pandemonium.

Throughout the commotion, Moore lay motionless in a pool of blood at center ice. Team doctors rushed to his aid and quickly realized that he had a serious spinal cord injury. Finally, he was strapped to a stretcher and taken to a Vancouver hospital, where he would remain for several weeks. Incidentally, the game resumed after the ice was cleared, only to see more carnage as Worrell and Brookbank each got tossed for fighting. Worrell was then pelted with debris as he left the ice. Milan Hejduk's hat-trick goal was the final nail in the coffin as Colorado went on to win the game, 9–2. Emotions were running so high that fights even broke out in the crowd after the final buzzer. It was, without a doubt, one of hockey's ugliest moments.

The aftermath was drama unlike anything the sports world had ever seen. Commissioner Bettman's reaction was swift and severe. The NHL suspended Bertuzzi for the final 13 games of the regular season as well as what turned out to be seven playoff games. The suspension cost Bertuzzi nearly $502,000 of his $6.8 million salary. In addition, the Canucks were fined $250,000. It was a strong message that management was also going to be held responsible for Bertuzzi's actions.

Two nights later Bertuzzi issued a tearful apology. "Steve, I just want to apologize for what happened out there. I had no intention of hurting you. I feel awful for what transpired."

"I don't play the game that way," he added. "I'm not a mean-spirited person. I'm sorry for what happened."

Almost lost in the aftermath was Moore, who suffered three fractured vertebrae, a fractured jaw, nerve damage, facial cuts, post-concussion symptoms, and amnesia and had to spend several weeks in the hospital for rehab. As of this writing, his doctors do not know when, or if, he will ever play again. Because of his uncertain future, Moore was not re-signed by the Avalanche the following season when his contract was up.

"The attack has been bad for our game," Moore said to the CBC. "I don't want to be the cause for any more negativity to the NHL. My biggest hope is that there's a serious evaluation of preventing this from happening again. There's been so much damage to the game. When you talk to people who don't know the game, the only thing you hear about hockey is that it's so violent."

### Paul Stewart on the Bertuzzi Incident

"Fans have no idea just how important having a feared enforcer on your team really is. With one, teams won't try to play dirty against you because they know that enforcer will reign down on them. Without one, you get what happened with the Bertuzzi incident. Maybe if Vancouver had a really tough, feared guy, like a Tie Domi, on their roster, then no-name guys like Steve Moore wouldn't be running over All-Stars like Markus Naslund. Personally, I tell you what I would have done in that situation if it was me playing for Vancouver at the time of the hit on Naslund. I would have skated over to his bench and pointed right at him in front of his 19 teammates and said, 'When I get you out on the ice I am going to kick your ass, and just beat you for what you did.' That sends a very powerful message and that kid would learn never to play that way again after a good ass whipping."

## Trent Klatt on the Bertuzzi Incident

"I am very good friends with Todd. We were teammates together for a lot of years up in Vancouver. If you want my opinion on that entire ordeal I think it is the NHL's fault for creating the instigator penalty, which has just ruined the game as far as I am concerned. Let's just pretend that there was no instigator penalty. Here is what would have happened that night when Moore took out Naslund in Denver. Vancouver's tough guy Brad May would have grabbed Steve Moore right after he hit Naslund and taught him his lesson. Then, both players would have gone to the penalty box for five minutes. As soon as they got out, Colorado's tough guy Peter Worrell would have skated up to Brad May and told him never to do anything like that to Steve Moore again. Boom, then those two would have fought. They too would have gone to the penalty box for five minutes each for fighting. After that, it would have been over. End of story. You never would have heard of it again. But, because of the instigator, guys don't have to be held accountable. They can go out and cheap-shot guys like that and then hide behind the rule. It is ridiculous. It is the fault of the NHL for not understanding that, and they are just setting themselves up for more of this in the future by allowing the rule to stay in place. The players can't police themselves properly with it because if and when they do, then they get fines and suspensions, which ultimately hurt their teams. It's a joke."

Later in 2004, after a lengthy investigation and the specter of an 18-month prison sentence for assault, a British Columbia court gave Bertuzzi a conditional discharge, one year of probation, and 80 hours of community service after he pleaded guilty to assault causing bodily harm. He would be spared a criminal record.

Moore later filed multiple lawsuits in Ontario and British Columbia seeking approximately $15 million in lost wages and damages. Named as defendants in the suit along with Bertuzzi were Canucks forward Brad May, Canucks coach Marc Crawford, and former Vancouver general manager Brian Burke, as well as the Canucks organization and the partnership that owns the team, Orca Bay. Moore contended that he sustained serious physical and psychological injuries and continues to suffer from the injuries two years later. The suit claimed that Bertuzzi "inflicted significant permanent and debilitating injuries" on Moore after Bertuzzi made "violent, physical contact." In addition, Moore's parents were also seeking damages related to shock and distress after watching the incident on live TV.

When the dust finally settled, nearly everybody had an opinion on the incident. While many felt that Moore had it coming—an eye for an eye, if you will—most felt that Bertuzzi clearly broke the code. Hitting Moore from behind in the head, and not giving him an opportunity to defend himself, crossed the line into criminal territory. Was it premeditated, or was it an emotional outburst in the heat of the moment? Only Bertuzzi knows for sure. Still, others blame the coaches for having those players out on the ice during garbage time of an 8–2 blowout. "I'm glad the NHL has finally stepped in and put him [Bertuzzi] back in the game and reinstated him," said Wayne Gretzky, who served as the executive director of Canada's 2006 Olympic team. "Nobody condones what Todd did. I'm sure he'd be the first one to tell you it was a mistake. But you know it's time to move forward. We will invite him to our training camp. He's an elite player and I expect him to have a great year and be part of Team Canada come February in Italy."

Not everybody was as forgiving as No. 99, however. Here are what a few hockey aficionados had to say. "You've got only one brain," Calgary enforcer Krzysztof Oliwa told MSNBC. "You fight and you may get hurt, but at least you have a fair chance. This kid never had a chance."

Of Bertuzzi, ESPN's Jim Kelley said:

> The fact is, it's very much a part of who he is and how he plays the game, and it's been that way almost from the day he first laced up his skates. It's a part of the dirty side of hockey that has existed seemingly since it became an organized sport. The NHL, which embraces and sometimes even sells violence as a part of the game, deserves some of the blame. Bertuzzi, unquestionably, deserves more than he will ever be able to admit. But in a larger sense, so does every coach who has ever led a kid to believe that retribution is part of the game and every parent who has never told a child otherwise. It extends to every member of every front office—from the grass-roots level, to major junior and to the pros—who has subscribed to Conn Smythe's adage "If you can't beat them in the alley, you can't beat them on the ice" and assembled their team to do both. The blame even extends to a great many broadcasters and writers, on both sides of the border, who feed the beast. … It's all a part of the culture of the game, one that rewards the bully and humiliates the victim.

This one incident has become the mother of all code violations, and deservedly so. However, it is not as simple as it may seem. One can only

## Barry Melrose on the Bertuzzi Incident

"In my opinion, yes, Todd Bertuzzi broke the code that night. Steve Moore was held accountable that night when he dropped the gloves and fought earlier in that game. It's not like he ran scared or anything; he showed up. He may not have gotten the beating that Bertuzzi or his teammates felt was appropriate for what he did, but he showed up and answered the bell. It should have been over at that point. When Bertuzzi hit him from behind, that was it for me. You just don't do that in hockey for precisely the reason of what happened: people can get seriously hurt. I don't think Todd is a dirty player or anything else, I just think his emotions got the better of him that night and he paid the price for it when the league came down on him."

imagine if back in the day there were dozens of cameras from all angles focusing in on each and every vicious hit and dirty play. Couple that with the fact that there are so many sports media outlets and talk shows that cover events like this in a *Bonfire of the Vanities* fashion. The media devoured this story and showed only that final blow over and over and over and over again on the highlight reels. That's okay, but they should have mentioned some of the events that led up to that to give people the entire story.

Again, I am not condoning the attack for a minute. It was wrong. Period. I am only suggesting that the media could have better explained the events that unfolded over the course of those three weeks so that viewers could understand the entire situation. Certainly most people would agree that, yes, Bertuzzi broke the code. But they could have at least understood his rationale of seeking retribution for the hit on Naslund. Bertuzzi, an emotional player, wanted to get Moore's attention in order to get him to drop the gloves. I am sure Bertuzzi did not know that his punch was going to knock Moore unconscious and that his momentum would cause him to fall on top of him and fracture his vertebrae.

Many players would argue that while Bertuzzi wanted to hurt Moore, he did not want to injure him. There is a big difference. Players can play hurt. They can't play injured. Many others contend that the instigator rule, which gives the instigator of a fight an extra two minutes in the penalty box, is to blame as well. With that extra penalty, the enforcers are not free to challenge a player immediately after an act of disrespect without creating a major disadvantage for their team. Some players feel that if their enforcers were allowed to police the game as they saw fit, without risking the extra two-minute penalty, then these types of incidents wouldn't occur in the first place.

As for the legal ramifications, yes, Bertuzzi should have been punished by the league, and he was, dearly. In my opinion, he should not have been punished criminally, however, because if that were the case the courts would be full of football, baseball, basketball, and hockey players who assault people every day when they go to work. Professional sports are not a part of the real world and should not be treated as such. The league differed from my opinion, however. Although hockey remains the only major team sport to condone fighting, the league was quick to point out that the Bertuzzi incident in their eyes wasn't a fight; it was an assault. And to them, there is a big difference.

In hockey the game governs itself. That's what is so unique about it versus others sports. In fact, the only other sport that can even remotely compare is baseball, specifically the National League where pitchers have to hit in the lineup. It's the ancient Code of Hammurabi, which says that if you bean my guy then we're going to bean yours. As a result, that threat of a 90 mph fastball striking the side of their heads tends to clean up the game.

### Darby Hendrickson on the Bertuzzi Incident

"I played on Steve Moore's line that game and was on the ice when the incident happened. It was really scary. I couldn't believe it when I saw it. You know, it was a tough situation for me personally because I was also friends with Todd from when we were teammates together. I think the media had built up that entire situation so much up in Vancouver, and that was all a part of it going into the game. I know that Steve felt bad about the hit on Naslund earlier on in the events that led up to that night, but he was just playing hard. Markus went through a bad concussion, too, which I am sure was extremely difficult for him as well. Steve played him extremely aggressively and when you play that hard, things can happen. The whole thing was just a big revenge/retaliation situation that went bad. The tragic part about the whole thing is that Steve hasn't been able to play hockey since then, and I am sure that has got to just be devastating for him. Ironically, I was with Vancouver when the McSorley incident happened, and then I was with Colorado when the Bertuzzi incident went down. So I had a unique perspective on both events. They certainly brought the code into the spotlight, that's for sure."

That's the code, for better or for worse. The players know that every time they lace 'em up and step onto the ice, their careers could be ended in an instant, and those risks are accepted. This incident somehow fell through the cracks, though: Moore's actions weren't policed the way they should have been, and things went terribly wrong. It's like notorious enforcer Dave "Tiger" Williams once said: "You consent to assault when you lace up your skates. It's what hockey is all about."

Luckily, Steve Moore wasn't paralyzed. He may never play the game again, but at least he can walk. Certainly, hockey fans everywhere wish him well in his recovery. If he had gotten up from that hit that night and just skated away, we might not be having this national discussion about the code. As long as the league continues to judge dirty play by the amount of physical damage done to the opposing player, with officials overlooking dirty plays that cause little or no injury, it's never going to get any better. Change can be a good thing, and some of the frontier justice mentality that is out there these days may need to come in line with the 21st century sooner than later.

## Some Perspective

Although the McSorley and Bertuzzi incidents had their unique points, they were very similar in scope. The common denominator was that the intended victims refused to fight. They were provoked in manners deemed acceptable, but when the players did not respond, the provocation crossed the line. That is where the matters left the realm of hockey's code of justice and entered the court system. There is obviously a very fine line between what is part of the code and what is outside of it. Precisely where that line lies has yet to be defined.

Notably, on April 30, 2004, just a few months after the Bertuzzi incident, yet another heinous act occurred in pro hockey. This time it wasn't in the NHL; it was in the American Hockey League, where winger Alexander Perezhogin of the Hamilton, Ontario, Bulldogs became the first player in league history to get suspended for the remainder of his current season, as well as all of next one. It was the longest suspension on record in the AHL's 68-year history. Perezhogin, a native of Kazakhstan, was charged with assault causing bodily harm over a stick-swinging incident that left his opponent, Cleveland Barons defenseman Garrett Stafford, convulsing on the ice. Tensions had been brewing between the two and finally came to a boiling point when Stafford swung his stick at Perezhogin, hitting him on the back of his helmet. Perezhogin then retaliated with a two-handed, baseball-like swing to Stafford's face, rendering him unconscious and bleeding profusely. Stafford was rushed to the hospital where he needed 20 stitches to repair the gash on his face and treatment for his head injuries. In addition to Perezhogin's historic suspension, Stafford was also suspended for six games.

With such an egregious offense occurring just months after the highly publicized Bertuzzi incident, one may be led to believe that it will indeed take a tragic death for the sport to change. In fact, in the last decade alone there have been several high-profile injury cases of junior hockey players being paralyzed due to hits from behind and vicious cross-checks. Broken necks, crushed vertebrae, and severed spinal cords are all the result of reckless and dirty play, and that has to stop. No one disputes that. Shattered dreams and devastated families are what are left in the aftermath of these terrible acts. As if there weren't reason enough to clean up the violence, not even millions of dollars in lawsuits have proven to be enough of a deterrent. Many wonder if hockey's culture of violence will ever change. One can only hope so.

This is the "chicken or egg" scenario that the pro-fighting and anti-fighting camps always come to. While both agree that cheap shots and dirty play are the root of destruction in hockey, they continue to debate which side has more success in preventing it. The pro-fight faction contends that fighting cleans up the dirty stuff by virtue of intimidation and accountability for those players who may commit those offenses. The abolitionists, meanwhile, contend that fighting promotes violence and breeds a culture ripe for tragedy. Who's right and who's wrong will be debated for years to come. That much is for sure.

With regards to the legal aspects of hockey's ugliest incidents, that is a slippery slope. When professional athletes step onto the playing field, they accept an inherent risk that they could be injured. They also understand that the normal laws and rules of society may not apply. Yes, it is a different world for professional athletes, and it has always been that way, for better or for worse. Should athletes be able to do illegal or immoral acts while on the field, court, or ice without legal ramifications? If they attack someone in a game, is that different from a normal person attacking a fellow employee at work? As a society we have to ask ourselves that question and decide what boundaries are acceptable.

According to Ontario criminal defense lawyer Patrick Ducharme, law enforcement should stay out of professional sports unless they're committed to staffing every game and charging every player who violates the law. "They should stay out forever or they should get in every day," said Ducharme. "They've dealt with the symptoms of violence, sometimes criminal, with suspensions, without looking at the root causes. And the root causes are that they've not only tolerated but rewarded violence outside the rules. And also condoned a system of vigilantism."

Athletes assume that whatever violations may occur on the playing field will be handled justly by the game's officials as well as their respective sport's governing body. They are the ones who discipline and punish. When players who are used to playing by those sets of rules suddenly find themselves in a court of law defending their actions on the playing field, however, things go from black and white to extremely gray. It is within the realm of gray where the aforementioned incidents fall.

# SECTION II

# Defining the Code

BERTUZZI
BELONGS
BEHIND
BARS

"The code isn't just about fighting. If a player is being aggressive with a guy who is uncomfortable playing physically, then that guy's teammate will stand up for him. Sure, the ultimate accountability for that incident is the fight, but 99 percent of altercations are cleaned up by players before they ever get that far. That comes down to respect. And it is important to note too that respect goes both ways. Players who take advantage of other players in a disrespectful way, those guys don't always get the respect that matters most: from their own teammates in the dressing room.

"Hockey in my eyes is about competing and battling and scoring and skating and winning games together as a team. The code just reinforces those things and keeps everybody honest and on the same playing field. You have to look at what the purpose of fighting in hockey really is. It is certainly not about entertainment. It is just one small part of this game, but an important one. It is there to allow everybody to enjoy the game. Most fans don't know the rules of the code because they are unspoken by the people who live and play by them. It is truly a fascinating component of this game, and I am glad to see it come to light in this book so that more fans will be able to understand it better and therefore enjoy the game even more on another level."

—DOUG RISEBROUGH
Minnesota Wild general manager

# 2

# Why Is There Fighting in Pro Hockey?

In further analyzing the code, we need to understand why there is fighting in hockey in the first place. Many casual fans and anti-fighting lobbyists don't understand why it exists, so hopefully this will shed some more light on it. The National Hockey League is unique in that it is the only major professional sports league to allow fighting, or fisticuffs, to occur "within reason." (Lacrosse is the only other professional sport in North America to not eject its players for fighting.) There are generally two types of hockey fights: spontaneous and premeditated. While the league doesn't openly condone premeditated fights, spontaneous fights are considered to be a relatively safe release of emotions for players who might otherwise settle their differences with dangerous stick work. The league feels that allowing players to release their pent-up emotions right there on the spot, in front of the officials, followed by a trip to the penalty box to blow off some more steam, is ultimately safer than letting those aggressions fester.

Hockey, unlike professional wrestling or roller derby, is the real deal. There are no scripts or story lines in hockey, and when guys get hurt, the blood and carnage is authentic. Fighting in other sports usually consists of two guys pushing and shoving each other until an official breaks it up. Occasionally, a guy might connect with a punch after a hard foul in basketball or following some chin music in baseball between a pitcher and a batter, but for the most part the suspensions, fines, and threat of injury are simply too great for players in those sports to risk. In hockey it is different. The fighting is not sporadic or even for entertainment purposes; it is there for a reason, and there is a definite method to its madness.

There is a reason hockey players don't wear face masks. It is so that everyone, big or small, fast or slow, can be held accountable for their actions. Take football for instance. Sure, these guys are huge, they are strong as oxen, and they hit unbelievably hard. But the trusty face mask each player wears will almost always prevent any real damage from fists when a battle ensues. An occasional finger might sneak through in the heat of the moment, but that is nothing compared to a full roundhouse haymaker that hits you square in the mouth. When was the last time you saw a football player lose some teeth or get a black eye from a fight? This is not to suggest that football players aren't tough. It is just to offer some insight into how justice is meted out differently between the two sports.

A football player can hit a guy in retaliation for cheap play, but he has to wait until that perfect moment during the game, which may or may not ever come. In hockey, meanwhile, a guy can whack another guy anytime or anywhere he pleases. He may or may not get away with it, but he can certainly hurt him nonetheless by punching him in the face. That constant threat of pain and suffering is what separates hockey players from other athletes. Hockey players play in a constant state of controlled fear; how much fear varies from man to man, but it's there. It has to be, or they would never worry about skating through the slot or going into a corner to retrieve a loose puck.

It is important to note, too, that while fighting is an accepted part of pro hockey, the threat of fighting is by far the bigger factor. Again, this is the theory that having a great offense is predicated on having a great defense. In the past teams would often load up on tough guys to deter other teams from taking liberties with their star players. As a result, opposing teams would have to also load up to stay competitive. With the salary cap put into effect in 2005, however, teams can no longer afford to employ that strategy. In the new NHL, all players must be able to skate and handle a puck; the goons, or pure fighters, are nearly extinct.

## Creating Space for the Offense

For the most part, fighters are there to keep the peace and protect their skill players. For teams to have success, they have to put the puck in the net, and that requires talented players who are usually smaller and faster than the other guys. In order for the skill players to do their jobs effectively, they must be allowed the freedom to skate, pass, and shoot without the fear of being run over by a bigger player who is out to intimidate them. Intimidation plays a major role in hockey, and if players are scared of being smacked around or hurt, then they will play more conservatively. They may think twice about skating to the net or going through the crease to attack a rebound, and that will hurt their chances of winning.

This is where enforcers come in. Enforcers keep a watchful eye on their star players and make sure that the opposition thinks twice before taking any liberties with them. Take the Anaheim Mighty Ducks, for instance. In 1997–98 they had to play without their two best players, Paul Kariya and Teemu Selanne, for much of the year due mostly to rough injuries. In fact, after missing the first part of the season over a contract dispute, Kariya returned only to suffer a major concussion from a vicious cross-check to the face by Gary Suter following a goal. Without them the team suffered greatly and missed the playoffs. So that off-season the team brought in tough guy Stu Grimson to protect them. The mere presence of the "Grim Reaper" on the bench that year sent a clear message to the opposition: stay away from Kariya and Selanne, or else. Teams couldn't employ dirty tactics to slow the stars down, and it gave the players more space on the ice to do what they did best: score goals. And do you know what? It worked. That next season Kariya and Selanne ranked number two and number three in the league scoring race, respectively, and the team made the playoffs. Coincidence? No way.

Enforcers create space not only for their teammates but also for themselves. You see, respect is earned the hard way in the NHL, and tough guys make room for themselves by building their reputations. Space is a precious commodity on the ice because when you have it, you can skate, pass, and shoot without the fear of being run over. In his appropriately titled autobiography, *Looking Out for Number One*, Edmonton Oilers enforcer Dave Semenko remembered his days in junior hockey when his reputation as a badass garnered him plenty of room to maneuver. "It was just like public skating," he joked.

# 3

# What Prompts Dropping the Gloves?

Following are the top 10 reasons gloves are dropped in professional hockey.

### Retaliation and Retribution

The first and main reason for fighting is for the retaliation of cheap shots and dirty play. It may occur in the heat of the moment for something that happened right then, or it may be a premeditated retaliation to right a wrong that took place earlier that game or even earlier that season. The fight can be between a victim and an assailant, an enforcer and an assailant, or even one enforcer and the assailant's enforcer. Whichever way, justice will be served and a message sent.

"Someone in my shoes has to know when to get involved," explained longtime enforcer Donald Brashear. "Vancouver has a skilled player like Pavel Bure. If somebody runs Pavel, I have to jump right on his ass. If it happens to be a tough guy that runs Pavel, I'll just take him and we'll fight. Otherwise, I'll say, 'Hey, leave No. 10 alone, or you and I are going to go.' Or, 'I'll cross-check you in the face. Or take your legs out.'"

Revenge is serious business in pro hockey, and players don't forget about cheap shots or dirty play. They have a long memory for things like that and will often wait as long as it takes to achieve what they believe to be justice.

A funny story to illustrate justice mentality comes from Lawrence Scanlan's 2002 book *Grace Under Fire: The State of Our Sweet and Savage Game*. In it, Scanlan describes a scene back in the late 1960s where the

St. Louis Blues' team doctor, J. G. Probstein, recalled defenseman Noel Picard coming into the locker room with a nasty cut over his eye that would ultimately require 11 stitches to close up. Anxious to get back onto the ice, Picard declined any local anesthetic.

"Doc," he asked as he was about to leave, "how long you gonna be down here?"

"Till the end of the game," he said.

"Good," said Picard, "because the guy that did this to me will be down to see you in 10 minutes."

With the instigator rule, tough guys don't usually just go out and whack a player, because that would put the opposing team on a power play. Instead, they have to pick their spots. The best spots, of course, come when your team has a comfortable lead. That is when an enforcer can go out and take care of business without having to worry about taking a selfish penalty.

Of retribution, longtime ESPN TV analyst Darren Pang said:

> You know there is a big difference between public vengeance, like what happened in the Bertuzzi incident, and getting retribution. If a guy like Gordie Howe ever got disrespected out on the ice, he took that guy's number down and saved it for later. He didn't tell anybody about it, he just locked it into his memory. Stan Mikita told me a story about that one time. He said that he went into the corner with Gordie one time and gave him an elbow to the chops. When he got back to his bench his teammates all told him that he had better keep his head up, because No. 9 was going to be coming to get him. So, he said he was prepared for it and kept his head on a swivel for the rest of that game, but nothing happened. The next game came and went with no incident, and then the next with the same outcome.
>
> Finally he made a comment to one of his teammates, saying that Gordie must have let him slide because he hadn't done anything. Well, sure enough, a few shifts later Gordie came up to him behind the play and gave him a perfectly timed elbow right in the mouth, knocking him to the ice. He had waited for that one perfect moment when he could exact revenge without taking a penalty or stirring it up. I am not saying it was a clean hit by any means, but it was in retaliation for what Mikita had done to him earlier, so it was all a part of the code of retribution. There was no fight or anything else afterward. It was over. The message was clear though, if you messed with Gordie he was going to remember it. Stan learned his lesson that night and never disrespected Gordie again.

## Swinging the Momentum

The second reason for fighting is to provide a spark or catalyst to wake up your team. Fighters will challenge opponents when their team is down for the sole purpose of winning the fight and thus swinging the momentum of the game. If a player battles like a warrior and wins, the crowd gets pumped up and the players get a shot of adrenaline to inspire them to work harder. It is all about gaining a mental edge or psychological advantage in hockey, and a good scrap can achieve that in a heartbeat.

Sometimes the tough guy's job is to fire up his team by whatever means necessary. The "dance partner" he chooses may not always be an enforcer either. It could be an agitator or someone who has been playing particularly physical that night. The main goal for this type of fight is to win convincingly, no matter what, because as inspiring as it is to win a fight, it is equally uninspiring to lose one. A loss can be detrimental, especially if it comes when you are down by a couple of goals or in front of your home fans.

The bottom line here is that the fans need to get out of their seats and get fired up every now and then, particularly in a low-scoring game. The players feed on that energy boost big time. A flamboyant fighter can also entertain the crowd by showboating around a little bit or hamming it up. Arenas nowadays will even play theme music, such as "Hit Me with Your Best Shot" or "Hell's Bells" when a particular brawler is about to square up with an opponent. If the players are having fun, then the crowd will follow suit. Again, it is all about momentum. When the players are up, they are loose and playful—they've got "jump." That jump is what it is all about in this game, and it's all in the head.

And don't kid yourselves: fans love hockey fights. Just Google the term "hockey fight" and you will get more than 18 million hits. For many, that is the sole reason they come to the games. There are fanatics who follow fight logs religiously, post results on their websites, collect and trade fight videos, and run fan clubs. There are even groupie wannabes who wait around after games in hopes of getting autographs from their favorite tough guys. It should come as no surprise that fighters are oftentimes teams' most popular players.

On the topic of momentum, Marty McSorley said:

> If you are not hated on the road, then you are not doing your job.
> If their fans got nervous when I was on the ice, and screamed and

## Rob Ray on Swinging the Momentum

"It was especially tough to fight a guy on the road, because no fighter ever wants to lose at home. No way. When you have 20,000 fans cheering for you and pulling for you, you just don't want to let them down. So, guys are even more jacked up in front of their own crowds, and that made it even tougher. When you are at home you just know that you have to dig a little deeper and put on a good show. When you lose a fight and get your ass kicked at home, it can actually hurt your team more than if your star player got hurt and couldn't play. Momentum is an amazing thing, and when your team has it, you are unstoppable. It is like a drug. It is just a big boost of confidence. But, when you lose it or are trying to keep up with a team that has it, that can be demoralizing. So, winning a fight really lifts your team and gives them that high that they need. Your teammates are like a sponge when there is a fight. When you win, they absorb that confidence and emotion; and when you lose, they just sink down a notch or two. As a fighter that just adds even more pressure to the equation. Most fans have no idea about stuff like that."

hollered at me, then I took that as a compliment. They watched for me to make sure I didn't take advantage of their favorite players. That's their job as fans. That stuff was fun, and you had to embrace it. It wasn't personal, but being a villain on the road meant that you were well respected and even feared, which could oftentimes be a huge psychological advantage for you and your team. Now, conversely, that also meant that you were a hero at home, in front of your own fans. So, it went both ways and it certainly made life interesting. ...

Sometimes I would do little things to get the opposing crowd riled up, though, just for fun. I remember playing at the old Chicago Stadium, against the Blackhawks. Just before the end of the national anthem, Denny Savard would start skating around his own end to get the crowd pumped up. They went crazy when he did it and it was pretty neat to watch. Well, one time we were in town to play them for a big game and right before Denny started skating around to get his fans going, I did the same thing on my end. Oh my God, did their fans ever go crazy. It was hilarious. Total mind game. My teammates were all trying not to laugh, because they knew what was going on. So sure, sometimes you do little things to get under your opponents' skin and to get them off their games a little bit. If they are thinking about you, then they are not thinking about playing hockey. ... Playing the villain sometimes could be fun, especially when the fans were totally into it.

The code can be completely different for guys when they are playing on a bad team. When you are an enforcer on a bad team it is your job to go out and try and turn the game around. A tough guy knows that he can swing the momentum 180 degrees from a dull, boring game to one the fans are totally into, and the players respond to that. That guy knows when he has to use his shift to try and stir it up out there in order to get his teammates and his fans back into it. That is a tough job, I have been there. It is particularly tough when you are playing on the road on an opposing team's home ice. It goes against who you are as a person and as a player to go out and start something when nothing is going on. But hey, that is the nature of the beast with this role.

I would also add that when that situation arises, it means even more to be able to do it with respect and honesty. What I mean by that is if it was my responsibility to go out and stir something up, then I would go up to their tough guy and bring it up with him directly. … I would talk to him directly and put him in a position to address me out on the ice, with respect.

Now, that tough guy knows the code and knows that he needs to match you, because that is your job. … Even if he is tired or sore, he knows that he needs to face you and give you your shot to turn your team's momentum around that night. It is a battle, one on one, and we both know our roles. A victory will spark your team's emotions and force them to play harder, while a loss can do just the opposite. It is a tough job, but a true fighter relishes that moment out there and fights for his teammates.

That momentum works both ways, though, and McSorley didn't relish being too far up in a game at any point because he knew that his opponent would be coming for him to swing the pendulum his way. He continued:

You know, as a fighter you could just tell when the other team was going to come after you in hopes of swinging the momentum the other way. I mean, sometimes it could be tough because maybe you had beaten up on a team pretty good in the first period of a game and had built a nice lead. The guys are loose in the locker room and they are happy about scoring goals and playing good. Well, for me, I knew that when I got back out onto the ice, the tough guy on the other bench just got screamed at by his coaches for allowing his team to be in that situation. So he was going to be coming for me to make a statement and to get his guys fired up. I knew this and I had to be ready for this. It was hard to stay on an even keel in situations like that. On one hand I wanted to let my hair down a little bit and

## Derek Boogaard on Swinging the Momentum

"Swinging the momentum can be an amazing thing, and a fight can do that. It is a great feeling to win a fight because you really do spark your teammates. You can see it in their eyes after that, and in their step; they just have a lot more enthusiasm. When they see you out there sacrificing for them, then that rallies everybody to try harder. Then, to get the crowd going too—that is awesome. To tell you the truth, though, I don't even hear them when I am fighting a guy because my adrenaline is pumping so hard. Momentum swings both ways, though, and when your team is up, you can expect your opposition to come looking for you to get it going back their way. That is when you have to be ready for guys to come at you. Occasionally your coach will tell you not to waste your hands on fights like that, though. They would rather you stay healthy for the fights that really matter."

enjoy the moment with my teammates. But on the other hand I felt the stress of what was inevitably going to happen out on the ice 20 minutes from that moment. That was the just the nature of the beast of what I did for a living.

Veteran enforcer Mike Peluso had his own interesting take on momentum:

Momentum is an amazing thing, it really is. As a fighter it was way better fighting at home, because your home fans gave you even that much more adrenaline. A good crowd, like at the Chicago Stadium, was a huge advantage for you. The fear you had going into it wasn't so much about getting hurt, but rather about losing and disappointing them. You just did not want to lose at home; that was tough to swallow. When you were on the road it was a different mind-set. You would be happy to just hang on and get a draw most of the time. In fact, if you won on the road, it just meant that there was going to be a rematch because nobody likes to lose badly at home. So, that was something to consider too.

You know, I fought Tony Twist a lot over my career and I didn't beat him very often, but I did knock him down one time during a game in the minors. We were in Peoria, and it was the first game of a five-game playoff series. We made eye contact before the opening puck was even dropped and we waved each other over to center ice to get it on. I tell you what, winning that fight gave us so much momentum, it was amazing. He had a big black eye for the whole series and it was like that was a big beacon for us to rally behind. We took it to their biggest baddest dude and wound up on top. It was unreal. We went on to sweep them in three straight games. Playoff hockey is so emotional and if you could win a fight in the opener, it was like it set the tone for the entire series. So, you had to be real careful as a fighter not to lose that first one, or it could really swing the momentum the other way.

In fact, sometimes your teammates would tell you not to fight a guy if the momentum was on your side, just in case you lost. I remember Chris Chelios telling me that a couple of times. He knew it was a risk for me to fight a guy who had a good chance of beating me because it would swing the tide away from us. That was hard to do as a fighter, to turn down another guy's request to drop the gloves. It just went against everything you believed in, but you had to be smart and sometimes you had to pick your spots. The team had to come first. That is the difference between a team fight and an individual fight. So, you swallow your pride and tell that other guy that you just can't go, and he'll have to wait for a rematch. Hopefully he would respect that; otherwise, he might start hacking your guys just to goad you into it. You never knew.

You also had to be careful not to get into a fight where you get out of control and wind up ejected with a game misconduct penalty. One time in St. Louis Tony Twist and Kelly Chase wound up beating up on Jeremy Roenick and Steve Larmer, and both Twister and Chaser got game misconducts. You could just see the fear in the eyes of every Blues player on the bench when the P.A. guy announced that each guy had gotten ejected. I was sitting on the bench with Stu Grimson at the time and we were just licking our chops. It was hilarious: for the rest of the game their guys wouldn't even go near the puck. They were terrified with no protection out there. We even wound up getting into a line fight and I wound up pairing off with Brett Hull of all people. I had him strung out and was going to pop him, but I let him off the hook. I just wanted to see him squirm a little bit, to show them that if they were going to take liberties with our stars, then we were going to do the same with theirs. Then, the next night, everything was back to normal; it was all good. Twister appreciated me not doing anything with Hull because he felt pretty helpless not being able to protect him. He owed me one after that.

## Intimidation

Number three on the list is good old-fashioned intimidation. It is a serious motivating factor and it changes the way players go about their business. Fear is also a strategic tactic in pro hockey, and together the two can be a lethal one-two punch. Whether it is from verbal threats or by an enforcer's

## Tony Twist on Intimidation

"I used to have fun fighting, I really did. Sometimes I would even tell my line mates that they could go out and do whatever the hell they wanted to out on the ice and I would have their backs. I remember telling Tyson Nash that one time. I said, 'Nasher, you're on my line today and I am feeling generous. I am giving you a free pass to go out and do whatever you want, anywhere to anyone. You can hack, slash, clip, hit someone in the head. I don't care because as soon as they come for you I will be there to step in. Just go for it.' I would tell those guys that right in the faceoff circle too, so the guys on the other team could hear me. It would just scare the hell out of them, and my guys could skate end to end untouched. It was awesome. Intimidation gave you power, it really did."

mere presence on the ice, players can and will be intimidated into playing their game differently if they are afraid of what may be coming.

As for verbal abuse, fans have no idea just how much trash talking actually goes on out on the ice between the players. Agitators are constantly trying to intimidate their foes and throw them off their game. They want to threaten them, taunt them, heckle them, humiliate them, and mock them like a schoolyard bully would. Their goal is to fill their opposition's heads with images of carnage. "This is what is going to happen to you," they are saying, "if you think you can skate near my crease with the puck." Sometimes players will say stuff out loud right in the faceoff circle for everyone to hear, challenging a player's manhood by announcing that he is going to beat the crap out of him as soon as the puck is dropped. It is all a mind game. The tricky part of it, however, is figuring out which guys are all talk and which ones are actually crazy enough to follow through on their threats.

Enforcers are there to protect their star players. If the scorers don't get the space that they need to be effective, then it is the enforcers' job to create that space for them. Intimidation by force will accomplish that goal most of the time. Hacks, jabs, pokes, and shoves are all methods to get guys to give you more room out there. It's funny how the threat of being punched in the face repeatedly can change someone's thought process.

"You might change three guys' minds about what they're going to do," said Carolina Hurricanes enforcer Doug Weight of intimidation. "You might get [an agitator] thinking, 'I don't want to fight and I don't want to

## Paul Stewart on Intimidation

"I remember one time back in 1976 during an exhibition game when I skated over to the Philadelphia Flyers' bench and challenged every guy there. I wanted to intimidate them. I did it for a reason, not because I was cuckoo. I did it because I was trying to establish something that we all know about when we are kids and we first walk onto that schoolyard. I needed to establish myself as a tough guy and I needed to back it up. I needed to make my own reputation because that is what it is all about in this business. Once a guy like me, who wasn't a great skill player, did that, then I had a spot on the roster. I became invaluable. That was my role and I embraced it."

get hurt, so I'll just chill tonight. I'll take it easy.' That frees your skilled players to play."

Here's another great example of how intimidation works. One of the toughest hombres ever to lace 'em up was a kid by the name of Gordie Howe, who came along back in the mid-1940s. Howe played for the Detroit Red Wings and made quite a name for himself as a solid two-way player. As a young player in the NHL he took a lot of abuse by the veterans and as a result, he didn't get a lot of space for himself out on the ice. Howe quickly learned the value of toughness, though, and before long he was leading his Wings to four Stanley Cups in the early 1950s.

Howe made a huge statement on February 1, 1959, when he fought New York Rangers policeman Lou Fontinato at Madison Square Garden. Despite suffering a busted finger and a gash above his eye, Howe was able to smash Fontinato's nose good during their brawl. And so Howe established himself as the league's new "toughest man." Word soon spread to stay away from Howe, who was notorious both for his use of his elbows and for his ability to carve up his opponents with his stick. Howe had now earned the respect of his peers and instilled a sense of fear and intimidation in all of them. As a result, he got space to score lots of goals.

Other guys also developed the tricks of the trade to intimidate their opponents. For longtime New York Rangers enforcer Nick Fotiu, it was all about presence and intimidation:

> To me it was about protecting my teammates so that they were allowed to play the game. You had to have a presence to keep them [your opponents] honest. You didn't want them taking liberties with your star players, and if they did, well then they were going to have to be

held accountable. You know, if you look at my career penalty minutes, I only have around 1,300 or so over my 14 years in the league, which isn't all that many for a tough guy. That number means so much to me, though, because it signifies the fact that my presence alone out there negated most fights from ever even happening. I mean, if you could get to a point where your presence alone could serve as a deterrent for your opposition from playing dirty and running your top guys, then you won half the battle before you even stepped onto the ice.

You also had to be able to intimidate the other team if you were going to win. I used to love intimidating the opposition; it was a lot of fun. I remember when the Flyers would come to Madison Square Garden in New York to play us. I knew exactly what time they were going to arrive and what door they were coming in. So I would do like 200 push-ups right before they got there and would tape my wrists and get my arms all pumped up. Then I would put on a tank top and position myself right by the door where they came in. I would stand there looking just sweaty and pissed while I was sawing my sticks for that night's game. Well, when they walked in and started heading to their locker room, I know that they would look over at me and see me all pumped up with my muscles all bulging out.

That had a psychological effect on their tough guys for sure. They would come in tired from a long trip and then start thinking, "Oh man, look at this freaking guy!" Then, when they were getting dressed, I would go run a lap around the concourse and dump water all over me to make it look like I was sweating like crazy. I would then go down by their locker room while they were getting dressed and talk to the trainers. They would say real loud, "Oh, you're not playing tonight, Nick?" and I would say "No, I just felt like running three miles before the game to really get warmed up." I know that their guys could hear it, and I wanted to plant that seed. Then, and here is the kicker, I would buzz around like crazy during warm-ups, real fast. Finally, when the game started and I got my first shift, I would come out like a bat out of hell, just banging guys and scaring the crap out of them. You just knew that they were over on their bench thinking, "Man, this freaking guy is nuts. He just ran three miles. Look at him!"

Maybe they would think twice about starting something out on the ice with one of my guys because of that, because they didn't want to have to fight me afterward. Intimidation could be a very, very powerful tool. Every sport has it, too, because it is so effective. You know, I never ever watched the other team warm up because I didn't want to get intimidated. I didn't want to see how fast they were skating or how hard they were shooting or the expressions of determination on their faces. I knew the power of intimidation and didn't want the

## Dave Schultz on the Broad Street Bullies

"Our attitude was that nobody was going to intimidate us. Period. We were proud of guys coming down with the 'Philly Flu,' because that meant they were intimidated before they even stepped foot in our building. My old coach, Freddy Shero, paid me a great compliment one time when he said, 'Dave Schultz gives the Flyers courage on the road.' I took great pride in that because having courage on the road, that confidence that you could play against any team, anywhere, was a huge factor. We weren't going to be intimidated at home, and damn it all if we were going to be intimidated on the road either. I used to hear stories from opposing players about when they would have to come into Philly to play us at the Spectrum. They would all be laughing and joking on the bus from the airport until they came to the Walt Whitman Bridge; then the entire bus would go silent. The big joke was that they would pull up to the arena and turn off the engine, only the bus would keep shaking.

"Intimidation went both ways, though. Shit, when I played in junior and had to go up to Moose Jaw to play those freaking animals, yeah, I was intimidated. Even going into Boston to play the Big Bad Bruins was tough. I will never forget sitting in the penalty box and having Bobby Orr and Phil Esposito skate by and say, 'Hey, asshole, the boys are going to get you tonight.' You don't think that was intimidating? There were times I had the 'Boston Flu,' too, trust me. Those guys were plenty tough and we had some tremendous battles with them over the years, no question. I had a lot of respect for them, though. We kept each other honest."

same thing to happen to me that I was always trying to impose on them. I never wanted anybody to know what I was thinking, ever, and that is what gave me my mental edge all the time.

Beyond that, hey, I grew up in Staten Island and was the heavyweight boxing champion of New York City when I was 19. So people knew that about me, and they knew that I could take care of myself. When people know that you are tough they leave you alone, and believe me, that was fine with me.

## Intimidation 101: The Broad Street Bullies

While individual intimidators play a huge role in the game of hockey today, a few decades ago one team intimidated like no other: the Philadelphia Flyers. Known as the Broad Street Bullies, they terrorized teams throughout the 1970s, winning a pair of Stanley Cups along the way. So mean and nasty were they that many opposing players were absolutely terrified to play them. They were the first team to use fear as a tactic, and it worked.

## Paul Stewart on the Broad Street Bullies

"I will never forget watching Dave Schultz just take apart Dale Rolfe at the Spectrum one night. It always sickened me that (a) none of his teammates went in and helped him, and (b) the Flyers had elevated fighting to a tactic. I respected Schultz because he would take on anybody and he would do it from the front, with respect."

Sometimes players would coincidentally get "sick" the night before they had to play them, clearly faking it to avoid having to suit up. There was even a term for the faux illness, the "Philly Flu."

Led by their fearless captain, Bobby Clarke, the team featured real-life characters who had mean nicknames to boot: Dave "the Hammer" Schultz, Bob "Mad Dog" Kelly, and Andre "Moose" Dupont. They beat the hell out of their opponents and scared them into playing a style of hockey that they otherwise wouldn't play. The Bullies would come at their opponents in droves and pound them into submission. Visiting teams coming to Philadelphia used to compare walking through the front door of the Spectrum with walking through the gates of hell.

"It wasn't just two or three guys you had to worry about," explained former Toronto Maple Leaf Borje Salming to Ron Spence of Hockeyenforcers.com, about the anxiety of having to play against the Broad Street Bullies. "It was 20 guys. You would see their sticks come flying at you. If they hit you, you'd be dead. ... They really tried to kill you. They really tried to force you out of the game. If they did some of those things today, they would be suspended for life."

They were the ultimate band of brothers and they were led by their fiery coach, Freddy Shero, who wasn't apologetic about his team's philosophy on winning.

"If we can, we'll intimidate our rivals. We try to soften them up, then pounce on them. There are lots of ways to play this game. Our way works."

McSorley added:

> The Broad Street Bullies were equal opportunity punishers. They would collectively beat the hell out of you. That was their strategy. They didn't care who you were. They would whack the finesse players just the same as they would the heavyweights. That is how they built their reputation. The thing that was unique about Philly during those days was that you never just fought one of them, you fought all of

## Glen Sonmor on the Broad Street Bullies

"Freddy Shero was one of the smartest hockey minds this game has ever seen. We used to be teammates together and were good friends. He was the first coach to use fighting and bench-clearing brawls as a tactic. His Broad Street Bullies were all about intimidation, and nobody did it better. He knew that his guys were collectively tougher than any other team in the league, so he knew that when the dust settled after a big fight, more of his guys were going to come out on top. So, if his team was down, he could send 'em all out there to stir it up and really swing the momentum to the way he wanted it to go. It was a designed tactic to change the tempo of the game and it absolutely worked. In fact, he was the reason the league put in all of the rule changes about guys coming off the bench and the 'third man in' rule. Man, those guys were tough, though. They used to love to beat the hell out of their opponents. The 'Philly Flu' was a real thing, boy, and guys did not want to play them. They won with fear, and opposing players were truly scared of them. Shit, once you can achieve that, the game is already half won."

them. If a guy would start beating one of them, they would all jump in. At the end of the day they felt that their 20 guys were tougher than the other team's 20 guys. As soon as there was a fight, they all paired up and went at it. So, if you were a goal scorer, you might have to square up with Bobby Clarke, who was tough as hell. It made a lot of guys nervous to go in there, no question. They were really good at playing that way and a lot of teams were simply afraid of them. And once your opponents are afraid in this business, the game is over before it even begins.

## Sending a Message

The fourth reason for fighting is to send a message. This message can be from an individual or in the form of a team skirmish. As for the individual message, if a team is getting beaten soundly, the losing team then employs the tactic of getting into a fight at the end of the game. That sends a message of future anxiety for certain key players who were now "put on high alert." It stops short of being a bounty, but players know they are going to be targeted when they meet again.

The team skirmish, meanwhile, is all about building team unity and male bonding. When a team gets beaten soundly, they may go out and stir it up collectively after the game—a whole team's stand. Afterward the players all go back to the locker room and celebrate like warriors. It is a tremendous show of solidarity when guys know that they can count on each other in battle. This sends the other team a distinct message that not only should they never come into the home team's house and beat them, but they should also be very worried about the next time the teams face each other, because they may very well decide to beat them up and humiliate them, too. When teams have to worry about rough play, then they are not totally focused on playing their game, and that is precisely the kind of distraction that fighting can have on a weaker opponent.

This tactic often occurs right before the playoffs, when one team knows that they will be facing that opponent again in a few weeks. It gives the opponents something to think about. It also occurs when one team has dominated another team for a long time. The underdog needs to show them convincingly that they will not be intimidated any more. Period. Years of routs and embarrassment on the scoreboard can cause a team to go ballistic, and sometimes that is what it takes to get that monkey off their backs.

Sometimes, in order to send a message to an entire team, enforcers have to make a statement and then take their medicine. Such was the case for Marty McSorley one time during his playing days with the Oilers. He explained:

> I remember when I was with Edmonton and playing against Doug Evans from Winnipeg one time. He used to use his stick on Gretzky a lot and it was hurting our team's chances of winning. He was a dirty little guy, and he wouldn't stop his annoying tactics, so I finally drilled him. I got a four-game suspension for it, but it was worth it. And the team didn't pay my fine or reimburse me for my lost wages either. I just felt that it was the right thing to do. My job was to look out for the welfare of my teammates, and if anybody took liberties with them, then I was there to stand up for them. That is what I did. Needless to say, he left Wayne alone after that, and the game was much cleaner afterward as a result. So, when people piss and moan about violence in hockey, they don't understand what things like that can accomplish. It was part and parcel to making sure his dirty tactics didn't injure anybody, and that cleans up the game for everybody. Overall, I wanted to keep my opponents honest and make them pay when they did things that were disrespectful toward my teammates.

For many enforcers in years past, the vast majority of their ice time would come in the waning moments of a blowout game, when both coaches would empty the benches in order to make a statement. Longtime enforcer Jack Carlson, who played 11 years of pro hockey, recalled one such instance:

> I remember one time when I was with Minnesota and we were playing Philadelphia at home. We were up like 7–0 and there was about 20 seconds left in the game. I lined up out there opposite Paul Holmgren and Battleship Kelly; they had all of their tough guys out there ready to go. Paul, who was a buddy of mine and former teammate with the old Fighting Saints, looks at me and says, "Jack, we've got a bench full of guys over there who want to just wrap this thing up and get home. Let's not start anything." I said, "Sounds great to me, no problem." So the puck is dropped and I skate back to get it and when I turn around there is one of their guys cross-checking me in the back of the head. Well, about 45 minutes later the final buzzer sounded and Paul got to head home! Both benches cleared and it got pretty ugly. I just winked at Paul as we were heading to the dressing room after that one.

## Trying to Draw a Reaction Penalty

The fifth reason for fighting occurs when a less-skilled player attempts to draw a higher-skilled player into a fight in order to get him off the ice, thus giving his team an advantage. This act of toughness is used to goad the opposing team's player into what's known as a "reaction penalty." However, with the instigator rule, which penalizes the instigator of a fight by giving him an extra two minutes in the box, this tactic is tougher to pull off than it looks. The "willing" participant would have to be suckered into taking an undisciplined penalty, which may be hard to achieve. When it is achieved, however, a team will get a four-on-four situation; and with the other team's top player potentially in the box and out of the lineup, this can be an effective tactic as well.

## Deterrence

Yet another reason for fighting in pro hockey is deterrence. Fighting serves as a deterrent for players on opposing teams from playing dirty. Players know that if they play dirty then they will have to be held accountable by having to fight in front of thousands of fans and risk being beaten up or humiliated by the other team's enforcer. Teams even stockpile tough guys in order to send messages to their opponents that they are not going to be intimidated. Not only do tough guys provide the elite players with room to breathe out on the ice, but they also protect them from injuries. The elite players are the ones who the fans pay big bucks to see score goals, which makes their bodyguards good for the business' bottom line.

Teams will go to extreme measures to protect their players. Take for instance the 1997–98 Stanley Cup champion Detroit Red Wings, who had a tough guy on every line taking a regular shift and were ready and willing to wage war at the drop of a hat: Darren McCarty, Brendan Shanahan, Joey Kocur, and Martin Lapointe. Considered to be one of the hardest punchers of all time, Kocur was the most feared by far. Nobody was going to mess with their top guys, Steve Yzerman, Sergei Fedorov, Igor Larionov, and Nicklas Lidstrom, no way. That strategy kept their opposition on edge and allowed their elite players to move about freely in the offensive zone.

McSorley weighed in on the strategy:

> Fighting is all about deterrence. Hopefully my presence out on the ice would deter dirty play and disrespect toward my teammates. I tell you what, fights settle the game down and clean them up. I've seen it happen a million times. And most of the time it didn't even come to that; things were settled with words or by us just being visible on the end of the bench.
>
> I will never forget when I was with Edmonton and a game would get chippy. Dave Semenko, one of the toughest guys around, would skate over and just look at the agitator who had been stirring it up or pissing off one of our finesse guys like Gretzky or Mark Messier. He just had this way of looking at him and then he would very calmly say, "Okay, somebody is going to get hurt out here." And that was the end of whatever was going on, guaranteed. Nobody wanted to mess with that guy. He cleaned up the game way more than people will ever know. Nobody wanted to piss him off, nobody.
>
> The mere presence of a tough guy, in many games, will in itself deter any scrums, cheap shots, unnecessary obstruction, or little intimidation tactics, and keeps the game flowing freely. That veiled threat of knowing a fight could happen at any moment really cleans up the game. You have to remember this about tough guys. The real tough guys, the respected ones, go after the guys who need to be addressed. If not, your better players are going to get hurt and the fans are never going to see their abilities out on the ice because they would be on the shelf.

## Job Security

The seventh reason for fighting in pro hockey may sound like an odd one: job security. That's right, often young players who understand that their role on a team is that of an enforcer, may need to get their PIMs, or penalties in minutes, up. While many teams have grizzled veteran policemen, such as Tie Domi or Donald Brashear, other teams may have an enforcer-by-committee approach, which includes a few young bucks or even an old dog, all trying to get more ice time. The best way to get ice time in pro hockey is to get out there and show the coach what you can do. If fighting is what you do, then you need to make the most of your time out there, regardless of how little it is, and mix it up with another willing dance partner. If the circumstances are right in the game and things are not out of control, then coaches will often give this type of behavior a green light and reward the fans with something to cheer about. A player who has been out due to injury or was even listed as a healthy scratch will often fight as soon as he is back in the lineup, just to showcase his desire and heart to his coach and teammates.

### Jack Carlson on Job Security

"I think that the code is about playing with respect. My job was to protect my teammates at all costs and to make sure nobody took any liberties with them. That is what the code is all about: standing up for your guys and making sure that they are dealt with respectfully. You know, I don't know how many fights I won or how many I lost, but I showed up for every one of them. The biggest thing about fighting is how your teammates react to it. When your teammates know that you will be there for them no matter what, then that is all that matters in this business.

"You had to play injured, too. That was a big part of it. It was tough, though, because your fingers were always busted up and you were never really healthy. You just sucked it up and marched ahead because there were always a bunch of kids in the minor leagues who were ready to step in and take your job as soon as you couldn't do it. Management would hold that over your head all the time. It was extremely difficult at times. It was tough, and it felt very isolating. In fact, most people have no idea just how lonely of a job it was to be an enforcer.

"You know, with the code you didn't need the tap on the shoulder. You just knew who you were supposed to get and when to do it. That was your job. And when your home crowd was too quiet, you took it upon yourself to get them fired up. I would just look at Dino Ciccarelli and say to him, 'Get it going, Dino. Stir it up.' He would go out there and piss off a few guys and then I would come out and take care of business. As a tough guy, that was what we did."

## Protection

Number eight on the list is protection. Enforcers, or bodyguards, do just what their name implies—they protect key people. Take the amazing Edmonton Oilers of the 1980s, a true dynasty. Well, as we all know the biggest reason for their success was one guy, Wayne Gretzky. The Great One was immensely talented, but at just 6' tall and a mere 180 pounds soaking wet, he was also easy prey for the bigger, stronger thugs who wanted to smack him around and slow him down. So the Oilers brought in McSorley and Semenko to serve as his protectors. Now, if anybody so much as breathed on Gretzky, those guys were going to pummel them. With those two, along with a host of other tough guys on the roster, Gretzky was able to wheel and deal, leading his club to four Stanley Cup championships.

Believe it or not, the league averaged twice as many fights during the late 1980s, Edmonton's glory days, than it did during the early '70s, the era of the Broad Street Bullies. For the Oilers, more fights meant more success on the ice.

In addition to protecting their stars, enforcers also have to protect their other teammates from time to time, even when they don't particularly feel like doing so.

McSorley joked:

> With regards to cleaning up other players' messes, I used to call Tony Granato the Don King of pro hockey because he was the ultimate fight promoter. Tony was a very feisty, chippy player, an agitator, and that is just what he did. The guy used to love to stir it up for no good reason, which would ultimately lead to guys like me having to go out there and take care of his dirty laundry. I remember one time when we were teammates and we were playing in a game and were up like 4–1 late in the third period. The other team's tough guys were out there and were just skating hard and trying to help their team score a goal. I mean nothing was going on in the game that warranted any rough stuff, and it was pretty clean all the way around. Well, Tony jumped out there and, for whatever the reason, started chopping and hacking one of their big guys.
>
> Now the guy was pissed, so I had to race out there to make sure that Tony didn't get killed by this guy. I matched up with this guy, and he backed down because he didn't want to start anything with me. Tony, meanwhile, didn't realize just how close he came to getting completely cleaned up by this guy. That is a big part of pro hockey:

## Rob Ray on Protection

"To me, the code is all about respect. Hockey is a very fast, emotional, temper-filled game, and we look after each other out there to make sure nobody is doing disrespectful things. Everybody in the game has a role. My role was to look after not only the goal scorers but also guys like Matthew Barnaby and Darcy Tucker—guys who were agitators. They used to try to get under people's skin out on the ice; that was their role, to take the other team's star players out of their rhythm and just piss them off. Well, it was my job to protect those guys because those are the guys you win and lose with. They are so valuable to your team, and if they are getting beat up on, then your team can't play well and win. It was funny, sometimes I would just sit at the end of the bench and pray that those guys would just shut up and not stir it up out there. Sometimes you just weren't in the mood to get into a fight for no good reason and have to fight other people's battles. But then on the other hand, I was very grateful for those guys because they were keeping me gainfully employed."

keeping a sense of balance out there. Tony and I are good friends, and I have a lot of respect for the way he played the game. He took a lot of abuse out there, and guys tried to hammer him whenever they could. He was tough, though. He blocked shots, cut off angles, went hard into the corners, drew penalties, went to the net hard, fought for rebounds, and always finished his checks. As an enforcer, you want to protect guys like that because they are working hard and giving it their all for the team.

What used to really bug me was when a teammate would hack a guy after a whistle and do something stupid. That stuff drove me nuts. I would ask him after the fact, "Why did you do that?" Sometimes guys don't think about the repercussions of their actions out there. I mean, it wasn't because I didn't want to fight—I was always up for that—it was just understanding the difference between taking good penalties versus bad penalties. It was also about sending the right message or setting the right tone for a game. Those are all important factors, but to achieve them takes some common sense. Regardless, I had to react and get out there to protect my teammates. That was the bottom line. I needed to do whatever it took to help my hockey team, and that was my role. I understood that and I embraced it. Jumping over the boards to take on another team's tough guy when that situation presented itself has to be first nature for you in this business, or you won't stick around very long. That is just the reality of what we do.

Sometimes players will respectfully decline an invitation to fight based on "not wanting to piss off their coach." If that pass is granted, however, it just means that the fight moves over to one of his teammates, who must then answer the bell for him. Such was the case one time for Kelly Chase, who was protecting his star player, Brett Hull. Chase explained the incident:

> Sometimes you have to make a point out there. I remember one time when I was with St. Louis and we were playing Dallas. Derian Hatcher was just absolutely abusing Brett Hull. So I went up to him and challenged him to go, because that was my job, to protect our skill players from guys like that. Well, Hatcher basically said, "I can't fight you because I am playing a regular shift right now and getting a lot of ice time. I can't risk pissing off my coach, sorry." So if he wasn't willing to be accountable for his actions, I then had to take it a step further and challenge the next guy up the ladder. We then started taking liberties with their star player, Mike Modano. Nothing was really getting resolved, though, so I wound up dropping the gloves with Benoit Hogue, which was a real mismatch, and ended up breaking his jaw and cheekbone. I didn't want to hurt him like that, but I had to make a point. Their team needed to understand that if their guys were going to continue to take liberties with our best player, then they were going to have to be held accountable. …
>
> Hockey is all about responding to situations that happen out on the ice and rectifying them as quickly as possible so that games don't get out of hand and guys don't get hurt. I wasn't going to sit on the bench and be humiliated because I couldn't do my job. Sometimes you had to make a judgment call about how you were going to go about doing your business out there. Needless to say, Hatcher didn't touch Hull anymore that night.

## Prison Justice

Coming in at number nine is the "prison justice" philosophy. This is a tactic used to scare the hell out of anybody and everybody to let them know that there is a new sheriff in town. It is widely understood that new prisoners will try to make a name for themselves when they first arrive in the clink. Many will seek out and challenge the toughest guy in the yard with the assumption that if he wins, then nobody is going to mess with him. Rookie fighters are notorious for trying to goad the veteran enforcers into battle, knowing that if they win they will garner instant respect. The veterans know this too, however, and are selective about who they will dance with, insisting many times that the new guys get in line and wait their turn.

## Mike Peluso on Prison Justice

"I remember first breaking into the league with Chicago back in '89. I was one of 75 undrafted free agents trying to make it. Luckily the coach, Mike Keenan, liked fighters and gave us a lot of opportunities to showcase our talents in practices and in exhibition games. I wasn't just happy to be there, though; I was hungry. I wanted it so badly, and I played like it. Plus, we were making 200 bucks per game, which was great because I was totally broke at the time.

"Well, in my first game we were getting beat 4–1 on our home ice at old Chicago Stadium. So, I just took it upon myself to jump out there and stir it up. I got into my first fight and the crowd got into it, and I kind of got noticed. The next game I did the same thing, and I wound up playing in all eight exhibition games. I did get sent down to the minors, but I made it back up later that season. So it all worked out. What is so amazing is that I wasn't even a fighter prior to that. In fact I had played college hockey up in Alaska that year, but that was my new role and I just embraced it.

"Training camp was always an adventure because they would bring in a truckload of young kids who wanted to make the team and were willing to do anything to do it. Most of them knew that if they didn't, then they were going to be heading back to the minors or, for some, back to the farm or the factory up in Canada. So, these guys were hungry, just like I was when I first came in.

"The exhibition season was always a time for young guys to show their stuff, and that was when you had to be careful. The kids were coming for you because they knew that if they could beat you, then they could make an argument to the coaches that they deserved a spot. You could spot them a mile away, too, because they were wearing what we used to call football numbers, like No. 68 or No. 77, because those were the jersey numbers that nobody used at the time. It was pretty funny. I mean, when you saw No. 79 coming at you, you knew right away what his intentions were. You would get some seriously sore hands during that time of year from all the fighting, that was for sure."

## Bad Blood

The 10th and final reason for fighting in hockey is plain old bad blood. When two players have a personal feud with one another, they are allowed to settle their differences on the ice like men—assuming the conditions are appropriate in the game, such as in a blowout. Reasons for personal feuds vary and can have a long history that goes back for years. Some guys simply don't like each other. Some guys have been playing against each other since they were kids up in Canada and want to settle old scores. These fights can be premeditated or spontaneous; it just depends on the situation that given day.

Bad blood can exist between two teams as well, particularly when one has dominated the other for a long time. Such was the case for the Minnesota North Stars, when they exorcised the demons of Boston back in February 1981 at the Garden. Lou Nanne, who played for 11 seasons with Minnesota in the '60s and '70s and then served as the team's long-time general manager, recalled the incident:

> The biggest statement we ever made as a team was back in 1981 in Boston, when we had it out with the Bruins [just before] the playoffs. That was just something we had to do and we did. There was a lot of bad blood there that had been brewing for a while. We set a record with over 400 penalty minutes that night, and it was a real statement on our part. Our team just seemed to gel after that. We just finally said that we were not going to take it anymore. They had been running our players and intimidating us for so long and we drew a line in the sand and said that's it. Hey, it worked because [even though we lost that night] we went on to sweep them [in the first round of the playoffs], and that momentum carried us all the way to the Stanley Cup Finals.

Fighting and retaliation are synonymous with bad blood, which has been a part of the game since its inception more than a century ago. It fuels the soap opera drama that is at the core of every great rivalry and leaves the fans begging for more. Will Team A finally be able to get past Team B in the playoffs this year, exorcising its demons once and for all? Can they get that proverbial monkey off of their backs? Questions like these are posed every time those two teams hit the ice, and that is what bad blood is all about.

# 4

## What Are the Rules of Engagement after the Gloves Come Off?

While the rules of engagement aren't written in black and white anywhere for quick reference, there definitely exists an unwritten, unspoken code of honor that hockey players have lived by for more than a century. And while the rules of the code are open to interpretation, they are rarely discussed. These rules are learned, for the most part, in Canadian junior hockey and carried forward into the professional ranks. Getting two willing combatants to agree to drop the gloves, however, can present a challenge at times.

With the instigator rule, which tacks on an extra two minutes in the box for the aggressor, players have to mutually agree to fight in order to avoid giving the other team a power-play advantage. Enforcers will pick their spots, knowing that there is a time and place for everything. There are team fights and individual fights. A team fight is for the good of the team and is intended to be a wake-up call for the entire roster. A good team fight is usually worth the ensuing penalty if it inspires the guys on the bench. An individual fight, however, can go either way. If it is for personal reasons, then that fighter has to get the green light from his coach. The last thing he wants to do is to put his team into a bad situation by taking a selfish penalty. A player needs to know the situation at all times because he never wants to hurt his team's chances of winning.

There are also the occasional "spontaneous combustion fights," which happen in the heat of the moment. For instance, maybe a guy takes a run at your goalie; or high sticks you; or elbows you; or runs you from behind and hurts your knee, causing an injury—those are catalysts for spontaneous fights. But for the most part, fights today are more about one party courting the other, in a sort of mating ritual on ice.

With the bench-clearing brawls and *Slap Shot*–type scrums of the 1970s and '80s all but gone, fights today are more about mutual challenges being accepted between two heavyweights who respect one another and understand that each is doing his job. Typically, when a player wants to draw another guy into a fight, for any of the aforementioned reasons, he will issue a verbal challenge of sorts to his would-be dance partner. It may be as simple as muttering the words "Wanna go?" as he skates by. If the other guy is interested, then he's got a date. If not, they won't fight.

(It is interesting to note that "Wanna go?" may also be expanded to the more taunting "Wanna go, pretty boy?" This is in reference to the 1986 cult movie *Youngblood*, which starred Rob Lowe as a lightweight trying to prove himself in the rough-and-tumble world of junior hockey with the fictitious Hamilton Mustangs. Lowe, who is defending the honor of his teammate, a bad mullet–wearing Patrick Swayze, challenges Thunder Bay goon Karl Racki by asking him, "Wanna go, pretty boy?" The ridiculous line, which has become a classic among hockey aficionados, is used when an opposing player really wants to piss a guy off and challenge his manhood.)

"As for the rules of engagement, it could be a look or a glare, or it might require a little more, such as a cross-check to the back to get them to turn and face you," said Marty McSorley. "You didn't want to jump them or do anything dirty, and you didn't want to take an instigator penalty either. From there, you might tell them, 'Okay, we have to go,' or 'Let's do this,' or 'It's time.' If he was a professional then he would engage you and fight you like a man."

The code also says you don't fight a guy who doesn't want to fight. Other challenges are nonverbal and may include grabbing a player's shoulder to turn him around, shoving him from behind, or perhaps slashing his stick. One of the preferred methods for enticing an opponent into a scrum is what's known as a "face wash." It is a gentle shove to the face with an open hand and is one of the most provocative insults in the business. It is a clear sign of disrespect and serves to incite a reaction. A good face wash inevitably results in escalation and retaliation, or both, which is by design.

More subtle methods may work, too, such as a simple wink or a nod. Basically, a would-be fighter wants to get the message across that he wants

## Mike Peluso on the Rules of Engagement

"In all my years in the NHL I never once had a coach tell me to fight. I never got a single wink, tap, or pat on the shoulder. I know other guys who did, but I never needed it. I just knew. Now, I did have some coaches who talked around it in a very politically correct way, however. I played for some pretty tough coaches in my day, too: Mike Keenan, Darryl Sutter, and Rick Bowness, who felt that fighting and intimidation were the secrets to their team's success. They wouldn't tap you, but they would certainly talk around it by saying stuff like, 'What have you done tonight?' or 'What is your role with this team?'

"I remember one time playing for Keenan and we were up in Montreal. There were about two minutes left in the first period and we were down 2–0. We were playing just dead-assed and Keenan wanted to fire us up, so he kicks me in the butt and says, 'What is your role here, Mike?' I turned around and looked at him and said, 'Well, I haven't touched the ice yet tonight, Coach, so how the hell do you expect me to do my role?' He thought that was pretty funny. Keenan would reward you with ice time if you were doing your job, so that was a real incentive. If I went out and got a big hit or beat somebody up and really got the crowd going, then I knew I was going to be going out there every other shift after that.

"As for initiating fights out on the ice, for me, it was mostly about eye contact. That is how I liked to engage my opponents to see if they wanted to go. A lot of other guys liked to stretch by each other during the pregame warm-ups. Sometimes two opposing tough guys will sit on either side of the red line and start talking to each other before the game. They could either be chit-chatting about hunting or fishing, or talking trash about what they are going to do to each other once the game starts, you never know. They sort of feel each other out at that point and get a sense of what is to come.

"I remember doing that one time with a guy, and he just said to me, 'You got me last time so we're going again.' I just said, 'Sure, you got it.' Then, when I went to the locker room before the start of the game I was just pumped. We wound up fighting as soon as they dropped the puck. It was awesome. I beat him again, too, which made it even better.'"

to engage his opponent. He will do whatever it takes to goad him without drawing an instigator penalty. For the most part, hockey enforcers are stand-up guys, and they will usually look their opponents squarely in the eye to make sure they are committed. (Hitting them from behind, or suckering them when they are not looking, is a clear violation of the code. Players know that if they violate the code in that manner, all bets are off; they will have to pay the price.)

If the other party is up for it, then the fight is on. The players will drop their sticks and gloves and square off. The strategies and tactics that players employ from this point vary, but each has one clear goal: to win at all costs. A win can boost a team's morale, while a loss can take the wind out of their sails. Some fighters study other fighters on tape, while others will even hire former professional boxers to learn proper techniques and training methods. They want to know as much as they can about their opponents before they square off. They will study the tiniest irregularities and tendencies, like the way a great center man can win a faceoff by watching when the skin on the linesman's knuckles turn from white to pink as he is just about to drop the puck. Everybody is looking for an honest advantage in this business, because the stakes are just that high.

"It didn't take very long to figure out why you were going into a game," said former enforcer Dave Richter. "I mean, if you had been sitting on the bench for two periods and your team was down 3–zip, and all of a sudden your number gets called? It doesn't take a rocket scientist to realize what your coach wants you to do. You certainly weren't being called upon to score a natural hat trick or anything, that was for sure. You needed to go out and stir it up to try and start something so that your teammates would get fired up. That was how it worked sometimes."

And when you're trying to get that advantage, preparation is key.

"I'm well aware of the enforcers on the other teams," said tough guy Jim McKenzie. "I start thinking about the next game right after the game I'm playing ends. I think about how the other team's enforcers fight, what they do, who would try to draw me into a penalty, who is a right-handed fighter and who is left-handed. It's important to me to know all these things. I even check out their jerseys to determine whether their sleeves are long or short and if any alterations have been done on their jerseys."

McSorley said that he prepared in a different way:

> I used to go to the gym and hit the heavy bag and the speed bag to get into shape. I did some work with some boxing coaches early on too, but for the most part I just went out and trained hard and tried my best. I never watched fight videos either, ever. I mean, I have had people send me videos of myself fighting and I couldn't even watch them. I just didn't want to see it. I would overanalyze things if I watched them and then be too hard on myself for what I should've done. So I just focused on being in great shape and on being mentally and physically prepared instead. It was much harder for me to train to be a good player than it

was for me to be a good fighter. I was a pretty good fighter, so I focused on the fundamentals of skating, shooting, and passing so that I could help my team in other ways as much as I could.

Enforcers in the NHL come in a wide assortment of sizes, shapes, and colors. There are African American tough guys, Native American tough guys, Polish tough guys, Russian tough guys, and even one from Paraguay—former Minnesota North Star Willi Plett. The average size of today's tough guy is about 6'4" and 225 pounds. The biggest is 6'9" Ottawa Senators defenseman Zdeno Chara, and the smallest is 5'10" Toronto Maple Leafs winger Tie Domi. It's true what they say, though: size doesn't matter. Domi, once described as a "bowling ball with teeth," is one of the toughest, most feared fighters in NHL history.

Regardless of all of those varying factors, tough guys all share one thing in common: respect. They have to respect each other because they know that on any given night they can get beat. Whether they say it or not, fear drives all of these men: fear of pain, fear of failure, fear of humiliation, and the fear of losing their jobs and livelihood as a result of any of those aforementioned factors.

## Fighters Fight Other Fighters

With regard to etiquette, many subtle nuances serve as guidelines for the rules of engagement. The first rule is that for the most part, fighters fight other fighters. Sure, if a situation presented itself where a smaller skill player hit a guy with a cheap shot or ran over a goalie, then he would be fair game. It is understood that heavyweights can intimidate lightweights, telling them what might happen to them if they don't clean up their act,

### Rob Ray on Who to Fight

"There is more to the code than anybody outside of hockey could ever possibly understand. By the time we, as heavyweights, actually dropped the gloves in a game, there were several prior events by other guys that led up to that. I would say eight out of ten, or 80 percent, of the fights that go in the National Hockey League aren't even between the actual guys who originally had a problem with each other. Because we couldn't fight with the smaller, finesse players and goal scorers, that left the fighting up to the middleweights and heavyweights. Everybody fights within their weight class at this level, unless somebody does something really stupid to deserve otherwise. That is how the code works."

or what might happen the next time they want to skate through their turf, but they can't fight them unless they obviously deserve it or are willing participants. This falls under the adage of "pick on someone your own size." Enforcers abide by this, or it would be total chaos. Bigger players would be pummeling smaller players every chance they got and the games would be blood fests with no goals being scored.

## Homework and Style Points

According to ESPN's Lindsay Berra, here is the skinny on how many enforcers do their homework in hopes of revealing their opposition's tendencies and weaknesses:

> Fighters talk amongst themselves, with teammates, with coaches, with their buddy from junior in the other conference and find out who's bringing what. They know who is the smartest, who is the most patient, who is the nastiest and who has the most stamina. They know who favors uppercuts, who has the deadliest left, who likes to clutch and grab, who is all bark and no bite. They watch videotape of their own fights and others to pick up on subtleties in another guy's stance, or those who have a tendency to leave an opening for an overhand right. They monitor games, taking note of the score, the physical tempo, who is on the ice when and with whom. They know who will respond to the simple taunt, "Wanna go?" and who requires an extra shove or butt-end.

Each guy has his own style, however, and Berra broke down a few of the scouting reports:

> Domi, he just stands in there and punches. Don't be thrown off by his small stature. He'll swing you around and spin you off balance and try to throw some big lefts, too. Montreal's Darren Langdon is just plain smart. He's hard to hit, he holds on, and he can go forever. Edmonton's Georges Laraque, Philadelphia's Donald Brashear, the Rangers' Chris Simon, they're all just plain big, and they're all lefties. If you're a righty, the toughest thing about fighting a southpaw is you're definitely going to get hit, but you've got just as much of a chance of hitting him as he does of hitting you. Laraque is so strong, he manhandles all of the other heavyweights. Longtime Sabre Rob Ray threw all rights. Blue Jacket Jody Shelley is big and strong and he'll go toe-to-toe with just about anybody. And Vancouver's Brad May, he tries to hurt you with every punch. He never throws a set-up. Every toss is a haymaker from his feet and if it lands, lights-out for that unfortunate son.

## J. P. Parise on Strategy in the Old Days

"You know, back in the old days of the '40s and '50s, fighting was much different. As soon as a player grabbed the other guy for leverage, he lost the fight and it would be broken up. Fighting then was more of a stand-up boxing match, with each guy exchanging punches. In fact, two guys would go at it until they were tired and then just skate away to the penalty box. Nowadays it is all about hanging on with one hand and throwing with the other. So much more balance and leverage is involved now. It is completely different. Many contend that the old way is more honorable and more sporting, but who knows?"

One tactic in particular that gets the fans really pumped up is what is known in fighting circles as "going for it," which means simply putting your head down and whaling away with one hand as fast and hard as humanly possible, like a jackhammer. The downside to this strategy is that it usually involves taking just as many hits to the face as you give out. Because you're on skates, hockey fighting is all about balance and leverage, and it is very different from a street fight. The icy surface changes everything and hockey fighters have to grab onto one another in order to stay up. It is when one fighter falls down that the linesmen will come in to break it up, many times determining the winner, so fighters put a big premium on staying on their feet.

"The important thing is that when you fight you have to be willing to take a punch," said longtime enforcer Darren McCarty to Ron Spence of Hockeyenforcers.com. "You're going to have to. And it's not how many you give, it's how many you can take and how to take a punch properly. As long as he doesn't get you on the button square, then you'll be all right. I was always told that it was better to give than receive. I'd just as soon get a few in early. Get the guy on his heels. But that's a different technique than some other players."

Other guys are old school down to the bone.

"Whenever I got in a fight on the ice, I would grab the sweater of the guy I was fighting around the armpit of his power arm," wrote Gordie Howe in his biography *And...Howe!* "And that would tie him up, immobilize him. Whenever that arm would go, then I would just fend it off and use my other arm. I'd reach in and do that first thing."

Still others had their own methods, such as Bob Probert, long considered the toughest human ever to lace 'em up. Probie seemed to get tougher as his fights went on. Many opponents suspected that he even enjoyed taking a couple of shots early on just to get him going. He liked to see his challenger gain a little confidence in their eyes so that he could rain down on them with his fists as soon as they showed signs of tiring. He used to take his jersey off during fights, too, so that his opponent couldn't grab on to him. He is probably the reason the tie-down fight strap rule, which forbids players from removing their jerseys, was put into place. Once players had even marginal success against Probert, there was going to be a rematch, because he hated to lose. He would fight guys over and over until he won. That is why he was the most feared fighter of his era, bar none.

Perhaps the best perspective on strategy comes from former professional heavyweight boxer Scott LeDoux, who has trained hockey enforcers for nearly 30 years:

> Back in the '80s I used to work with Brad Maxwell and a few of the guys from the Minnesota North Stars. I also worked with the New York Islanders back when they won their four Stanley Cups. I worked with guys like [Bob] Nystrom, [Clark] Gillies, and [Dave] Langevin, and I tried to teach them how to execute a punch properly by turning on it. I really tried to prepare them to fight under those circumstances, with skates on and them holding on to the other guy's jersey. I had a great perspective, too, in that being from Minnesota I had played hockey growing up, so I could relate to how different it was from

### Derek Boogaard on Strategy

"When I am in a fight I want to win, period. I try to look at my opponent as someone who wants to hurt me; therefore, I want to hurt him. I know that sounds bad to say, but it is the truth in that situation. It isn't personal, but you have to make sure you take care of business out there. Otherwise he is going to clean you up and you could get hurt. Each situation is different, too. I mean, if I am out there to just settle things down and get into a scrap, that might be nothing too serious. The linesmen will come in and break it up and that is that. But if I am going after a guy who ran my goalie and hurt him by doing something dirty and broke the code, then I am going to be furious. Then I am coming and I am coming hard to teach him a lesson. That rage has to drive you so that you can do your job sometimes."

## Mike Peluso on Strategy

"My strategy was pretty straightforward: I just started throwing lefts and didn't stop until either one of us went down or the linesmen broke us up. I either won or lost, there wasn't much middle ground for me. I didn't grab on a lot, either. I just threw as fast as I could. I learned my lesson with grabbing on too soon from guys like Basil McRae, who used to cut his sleeves and then Velcro them together, so that when you grabbed them they would just tear away up to the shoulders. When you had nothing to grab on to, you were screwed, so I tried to go as long as I could before grabbing hold of my opponents. I was a lefty, though, and that was an advantage over a lot of guys who weren't expecting it. I was usually able to get off a quick one right off the bat as a result, and sometimes that was enough to give me the edge.

"For me, being 6'4" and 220 pounds, I was a decent fighter, but I was much more intimidating as a forechecker going into the corner with smaller guys. So, I could stir it up out there and then back it up, whereas a lot of pure fighters didn't get as much ice time. I was lucky in that way. I had a couple roles I could fill."

actual boxing. I also had a lot of experience bare-knuckle brawling in my day, and let's just say I never lost a fight. Ever.

Hockey fighting is very different from boxing, where you can set people up with combinations. In hockey things happen so quickly and there is just no time. So, turning their shoulders on their punches so that they punched straight was the big thing, along with leverage and balance. I always felt like the best strategy in a hockey fight was to just give the guy three straight jabs right down the chute as fast as you could before the other guy could grab onto your jersey. Basically, my theory was that if you could stun the guy early on, that was the best approach that I tried to teach. I discouraged them from throwing hooks and uppercuts too, because you lost power when you did that. Uppercuts were only effective when the other guy would put his head down. You cannot be defensive in a hockey fight or you will lose. You have to be on the offensive right out of the gates. I couldn't stress that enough.

Each guy had their own philosophy on how to do it, and I tried to work with them accordingly. I just made sure that they had a plan going into each fight because they only had about 20 seconds to get their business done before the linesmen would break it up. They had heavy bags in their locker rooms, and I would bring them to my gym to spar with them, too. It was a lot of fun. Hey, some people called hockey fighting barbaric; others said it was refined. For me it was a science.

Lately, I have been working with the Minnesota Wild, too. I worked a lot with their enforcer, Derek Boogaard, and, man, is that kid tough. Wow! He is one big kid. He has been knocking everybody out lately. I think that he is going to be very good for a lot of years in this league if he can keep it up. With Boogaard being 6'7" he has just an unbelievable reach, so I was able to get real technical with him and teach him how to really use that to his advantage. He could just hold guys off him with one hand and whale away with the other. Once he got going it was going to be over pretty quickly. He can really turn on guys. He is dangerous.

The funniest story I remember about the old days was when the Stars and Islanders played each other one time and Brad Maxwell wound up squaring off with Garry Howatt, two of my star pupils. Well, Maxie was a lefty and wound up dropping Garry. Afterward Howie came up to me all pissed off and said, "You didn't tell me he was left-handed!" I just looked at him, smiled, and said, "You didn't ask."

You know, when people make comparisons to boxers dying, there is a big difference. Sadly, an average of six boxers have died every year for the past 10 to 15 years in the ring around the world as the result of a traumatic injury. But in hockey, even though they are bare-knuckle brawling, they are only having brief, 20- to 30-second encounters. Boxers fight 10, 12, 15 rounds and take repeated blows to the head day in and day out for years and years. Plus, in hockey, being on skates absorbs some of the blow because their feet aren't really set like they would be while standing on the ground.

## The Free Pass

Another key component of engagement is being injured. If a player challenges another player to a fight, the other player has the right to respectfully decline due to an injury. Enforcers are constantly battling injuries ranging from broken knuckles and fingers due to hitting helmets, to separated shoulders, to facial cuts and lacerations. In order to prevent further injury or serious long-term damage, fighters occasionally have to say no. If this is the case, that player will tell the initiator that he can't go that night, but will explain to him why. Ninety-nine times out of a hundred, that is all that needs to be said. The fans may view this as cowardly, but it couldn't be further from the truth. All fighters battle through injuries from time to time, and they know that the roles could be reversed. That courtesy and respect is appreciated and reciprocated among the heavyweight fraternity.

McSorley told a story about the free pass:

> One tactic I used when I was tired and caught down deep in the other team's end, and the other team would start a quick odd-man rush breakout into our zone, was to just grab a guy and start roughing him up. It was a last resort kind of a move, but it usually worked because the officials would have to blow the whistle and it would kill the other team's momentum by stopping the play. I wouldn't fight him; I would just wrestle with him behind the play so that I wouldn't get an instigator penalty. Then we would each go to the box for two minutes with coincidental roughing minors and our team wouldn't be down a man on a power play.
>
> Well, one time I was playing against Minnesota and I tried that move against North Stars defenseman Doug Zmolek, who was not a big fighter or anything, but I was desperate and just grabbed him. Well, Doug thought I was trying to fight him, so he dropped his gloves and just popped me hard in the mouth and knocked my tooth out. I was stunned. I mean, I wasn't even planning on fighting him, but he nailed me. Well, we wound up going, but it got broken up pretty quickly. Then, later in the game, I ran Doug pretty hard into the boards and knocked him down. I then challenged him to another fight, a rematch. Well, Doug just took his glove off and showed me that his hand was all bandaged up from hitting my tooth. He couldn't go. I sort of started laughing, because my mouth hurt like hell and I am sure his hand got stitched up pretty good from hitting it, so we were kind of even. I gave him a pass on that one because he was hurt and I didn't want to force the issue. You can't engage a guy if he is too hurt to go, and I respected that. Doug was not a dirty player or anything, so we just put it to bed and played hockey.

### Tony Twist on the Free Pass

"Sometimes guys were injured, and as a fighter you had to honor that. We have all been there in this business and we have all had to nurse busted knuckles and fresh stitches, so we all understood that stuff. You never wanted to embarrass a guy by taking advantage of him if he couldn't go. You could get in his face and have words, but if you knew that he was hurt you had to give him a pass that night. Again, even though you want to nail the guy, you had to be disciplined in those types of situations because one thing is for sure in this line of work: what comes around goes around."

Now, sometimes guys will use that free pass to their advantage, and that is when you take offense. I have had guys tell me that they were too injured to fight me, and I have respected that. But, a few times those same guys wound up fighting middleweights on our team instead of me a few shifts later, and that really pissed me off. Those are the guys you make a little note of and you put them in your mental piggy bank for later. That just isn't honorable, and those types of players who do stuff like that typically get what's coming to them down the road.

The role of respect in fighting plays out in many different ways. To begin with, fighters know not to embarrass their opponents because they know that the next time, the roles might be switched. Guys want to win and will do whatever it takes to do so, and if that means hurting a guy by breaking his nose or knocking his teeth out, then so be it. However, they also know when a fight is over. If a guy is hurt or down on the ice, they back off. Nobody wants to injure someone by doing something dirty or cheap. Enforcers know that they have to be able to turn off the adrenaline in a nanosecond should the situation turn sour—regardless of who's winning. Fighters can't take advantage of a guy if he is in a bad situation. If a linesman doesn't jump in to break the fight up right away, it is the responsibility of the fighter who is winning to shut it down. Fighters know that they could be in a bad position during their next scrap and hope to receive the same respect if the roles were reversed. Embarrassment and humiliation cut deep, and are extremely frowned upon. That makes it personal.

Fighters also know that if their opponent is at a disadvantage, such as when his sweater is over his head or he doesn't have his gloves off, then they have to back off. They also know that if the fighter is injured, they should be respectful of that, too. For instance, if a guy has fresh stitches above his eye, then a fighter may choose not to hit him there so as not to risk serious injury. Some fighters abide by this, while others feel that if an opponent agrees to drop the gloves, then everything is fair game. Other guys will simply attack those stitches right out of the gate in hopes of opening them up and drawing blood—which is often considered the deciding criteria for who is declared the winner. Each fighter has his own strategy, and it is true to say that the "Golden Rule" applies big-time in hockey fights. Enforcers know which guys fight dirty and which ones don't. If a guy is labeled as a dirty fighter, or one who will "go after those stitches," then he will get what is coming to him in due time.

"The guys that are really tough and respect each other don't hit them when they're down," explained longtime enforcer Sandy McCarthy to Ron Spence of Hockeyenforcers.com. "I fought Stu [Grimson] a couple of years ago, and he fell down in the beginning, and I let him get back up. It tells you something about a player's personality when he hits a guy when he's down. I've hit guys when they're trying to cover up or something, but I've never hit a guy when he's down."

Longtime Buffalo enforcer Rob Ray, now with Ottawa, feels similarly:

> I have fought guys before and could see that they were really hurt, so I stopped. You never want to embarrass or hurt a guy, and sometimes guys, even though they were hurt, were so proud that they would not give up. So, I was like "Come on, man, you're hurt. Let's call it a draw." You give them that opportunity right then and there, and you hope that if the tables are turned down the road that they do the same for you. Look, I have broken my hands, fingers, knuckles, orbital bones, nose, and jaw, over my career. We have all suffered injuries and been on the shelf, so none of us ever wanted to seriously injure anybody and prevent them from earning a living.

That same attitude sometimes even carried over to giving a free pass to a naïve kid who may not know any better. Such was the case for Rob Ray a few years back; he explained:

> One time there was a kid from my hometown who was up on a tryout for an exhibition game. Well, he was a little guy and by no means a physical player. He wanted to prove himself, though, and was just running around hitting everybody. So, finally my coach, John Muckler, said to me "Razor, kill that little bastard!" I was thinking, "Oh man, what am I going to do?" I didn't want to beat up this guy; he was the nicest kid. Well, I went out there and just before the puck dropped I whispered to him, "Listen and listen good. My coach sent me out here after you to teach you a lesson. Here's the deal, as soon as the puck is dropped I want you to take off as fast as you can and I will just pretend that I can't catch you. Don't worry, I'll look after you, but you gotta fly." Sure enough, the puck dropped and he took off like a bat out of hell. I followed him all over the ice pretending to try and grab him. I made it look pretty good. Finally, I came back to my bench all tired out and Muckler came over and said, "You couldn't

catch the little prick, huh?" I said, "Nah, I'll get him next time." Well, the next thing you know the game was over. I felt so relieved. That kid had no idea just how close to getting cleaned up he really was.

## The Rematch

When a particular fighter has declined an invitation, he may want to offer a rematch, or I.O.U., for a later date. You see, sometimes fights are all about rematches. The fans eat that stuff up, too. It makes for good soap opera drama—especially between rival fighters on rival teams that face each other often. Heavyweights keep score of wins and losses the way wingers keep track of goals and assists, and if they lost a previous bout they will probably want another shot at that guy. A good veteran fighter who is well respected will usually grant that wish. It is his call, though, because many of the young fighters who are on their way up the ladder know that in order to gain respect around the league, they will need to beat just such an established person.

Longtime St. Louis enforcer Tony Twist told a story about rematches:

> I can really only say that I lost one bad fight in my career, and that happened up in Spokane, when I was playing junior. I squared off with Link Gaetz and he absolutely lit me up like a Christmas tree, just cleaned me up. Well, a year or two later we met up again in the NHL and he knew that I wanted a rematch pretty bad, so we dropped the gloves at the opening faceoff. We went toe-to-toe for a while, and then

### Kelly Chase on the Rematch

"There was only one instance over my career where I had to turn down a fight, and that was because my coaches told me not to on account of I had a busted up hand. It was with Kenny Baumgartner and we wound up playing them again two nights later, so I asked if I could start the game. They let me and I dropped the gloves with him two seconds into it because I was so embarrassed that I had skated away from him before. Kenny knew what was up and he gave me my rematch. I respected that. When their coach saw that I was on the opening lineup card, he put Kenny on his. That was a classy move on his part. You know, I never scared anybody out there; I just got in their faces and had at it. If they beat me, well then it was the best of seven because I hated to lose. If I lost it was personal until I got it straight. That was just my personality. I wasn't that big, but I didn't back down from anyone out there and I think that gained me a lot of respect."

I smacked him upside his head and hit him so hard that his helmet
flew off and cracked in half. When the ref broke it up and sent us to
our respective penalty boxes, Link skated over to the wrong one. He
was out of it. We got in the box, and he just looked at me and said
"Okay, we even?" I said sure, my hand was hurting. He was a tough
dude, but I never forgot about that loss and that drove me to make
sure I settled the score with him. I cracked a few helmets in my day,
but that one might be the most memorable.

## You Don't Initiate a Fight at the End of a Guy's Shift

Other rules of engagement include things like not engaging a guy to fight
at the end of his shift. It is considered dirty to challenge a guy when he
is exhausted. If a guy just skated hard for two minutes, the last thing he
wants to do is fight someone on his way to the bench. This is why many
fights occur at the beginning of play following a whistle. Again, some
fighters will ignore those rules, and most fighters are such proud people
that they will always fight, regardless of if they are tired. However, when a
guy fights a tired opponent, word gets around that he's a dirty fighter. Once
that happens, he can expect those same tactics to be used on him.

Such was the case for New Jersey Devils tough guy Troy Crowder back
in 1991 when he squared off against Detroit's Bob Probert. Crowder had
beaten Probie earlier, and there was some bad blood between the two. In
an interview with David Singer of Hockeyfights.com, Crowder said:

> I was coming off the end of one of my shifts and I was pretty tired.
> Bob came off and challenged me, and you know, ego says you can't
> skate away from this even though you're tired, because then the fans
> are going to boo you and think you're scared. I ended up dropping the
> gloves and had a fight with him, and as you know, he's very strong on
> his skates. He hit me a few times, but didn't really knock me down or
> out, but I'd lost my balance on a few of the punches and I fell down.
> So that was kind of the end of that, nothing really hurt or anything.
> I went to the box and when I came back to my bench, my coach was
> quite pissed off. He said, "That's bullshit! You got hit at the end of your
> shift." He said, "I'm going to wait until the end of his shift and I'm
> sending you out there after him." So, later on, when Bob was on a shift,
> my coach came by me on the bench and called off one of our players
> to send me out there. I went after him and [afterward] everyone says,
> "He didn't want to fight you; you jumped him." I said, "Look, this is
> kind of the same scenario of what had just happened with me on the
> shift before." I challenged him and we fought and, you know, they were

70

pretty even fights. Some will say I got the best of one and he got the best of the other, but in general, they were pretty even.

Even though the two were bitter rivals that night, the next season Crowder got traded to Detroit to be teammates with Probert.

"We met at a golf course and kind of laughed about being on the same team. Later, we bumped each other a few times on the ice and kind of chuckled about how before that would have caused a fight," joked Crowder. "But he ended up being a great teammate. He even invited me over to his house for dinner just to take the edge off right away."

Another instance with Probert came up with Donald Brashear. Brashear told the story:

> That happened to me once against Bob Probert. He got me at the end of a shift, and I said, "Why did you get me then?" He came right back and said, "Remember that last fight we had in Montreal? That's why I did it. You did it to me one time, and now I'm doing it to you." It's all about respect, but there's also a lot of smarts involved. I consider myself a smart fighter. Sometimes I won't go right away. I'd rather wait for the next shift and get the job done well. When I'm tired, I just go out there and hold on to the other guy. In a situation like that, I can't afford to make a mistake because that mistake can cost me.

## Showing Up

Fighting is all about honor and respect. When it comes to honor, the cardinal rule is "show up." What this means is that if you are a smaller player who breaks the code by getting a guy with a cheap shot or playing dirty, then you better be ready for a fight. Take your medicine like a man and drop the gloves when somebody from the other team challenges you. The code isn't strictly "an eye for an eye," but it certainly says you need to step up and be accountable for your actions. The other team may even send out a smaller guy, rather than sending a heavyweight, in a gesture of fairness. If a player is in that situation, then he simply needs to give it his best shot. If he "turtles," or goes into the fetal position, he will then lose the respect of not only the fans but also his teammates. If a player is going to talk the talk, then he had better be able to walk the walk. Anything short of that is considered cowardly.

Darren Pang, former NHL goaltender and longtime ESPN TV analyst, told the following story about showing up:

Say, for instance, you are playing against a guy who never drops his gloves but was someone who played dirty, was always running guys, and was just always getting under everybody's skin. Well, let's just say you wind up out on the ice with a guy like that and for whatever the reason in the heat of the moment you get into a scuffle with him. Well, if you have that golden opportunity to square off with that guy, and you have the total green light to do so, with no threat of an instigator penalty or anything, and you don't—it could be devastating to your hockey career.

I have seen it time and time again. It is the fall of a hockey player inside your locker room. Without a doubt. His teammates will say, "He doesn't get it, he just doesn't get it." They figure that if he had that opportunity and didn't take it, well, if he really cared about his team and teammates, he would have drilled that guy. So, for as many times as getting into a fight can help boost a player's stock among his teammates, it can also work the other way, too. If you don't show up in a situation like that, then you could be ostracized.

## Gordie Roberts on Showing Up and Accountability

"The code to me was about doing my job. My job was to try to stop the opposing team's skill players. I had to do whatever it took to slow them down, get in their way, and get under their skin. Sometimes that meant having to be held accountable, which was just part of the job. It was never fun, though, to try to slow down Gretzky, knowing full well a guy like Dave Semenko was going to come over and try to bash your head in. I was a middleweight, so I didn't have to take on heavyweights like that too often, but they could certainly make an impression on how you played the game on any given night, that was for sure. The nice thing about the heavyweights is that they usually just fought each other. Most of the fights I got into over my career were the kind that just sort of happened during the course of the game, not the premeditated stuff the heavies deal with.

"Usually you would have to fight more in your first few years in the league to establish yourself as a player and to earn respect. You needed to build a reputation as a player who would stick up for yourself; otherwise, you wouldn't last very long in this league. If you got challenged then you needed to answer the bell. You didn't have to win, but you needed to show up. That was the key. Your teammates and your opponents would see that and you would earn their respect. You also needed to be there for your line mates when they needed you, too. It was very important for them to know that you would be there for them no matter what. All of that is a part of the code in my eyes."

## Fighting Fair

Players also understand the importance of fighting clean. There are some definite dos and don'ts when it comes to dropping the gloves, and they are all part of the code. Tactics such as head-butting, biting, hair pulling, and eye-gouging are strictly frowned upon. So is ducking your helmet down over your face to protect yourself. This is deemed not only cowardly but also cheap in that it almost guarantees your opponent will cut up his knuckles when he hits you.

Pulling a jersey over a guy's head is also looked down upon, especially since the fight strap was put into place several years ago. (The strap, which is located in the back of the jersey, must be fastened to the breezers to prevent the jersey from being pulled up over the shoulders.) Beyond that, basic rules of fisticuffs are fair game. And, while the image of the Hanson Brothers "puttin' on the foil coach..." from the classic movie *Slap Shot*, is funny, it would be a major code violation if a player put anything on his knuckles to gain an advantage over his opponent in a game today.

Being respectful of the referees and linesmen is also very important. Players can never, ever hit or manhandle an official, or there will be hell to pay. Those men are there to protect players from getting beaten up too badly. They watch the action closely and jump in when the situation dictates. They usually stand aside attentively and let the combatants go at each other until one clearly gets the better of the other, or when one goes down. At that point, the players are separated and led to their respective penalty boxes or dressing rooms, depending on the severity of the infractions.

Fights typically go until the linesmen step in and break them up, and it is safe to say that they will usually let the heavyweights go longer than the middleweights or lightweights. They handle each situation as it presents itself, because it is their job to make sure one player isn't seriously hurting another player, such as when both players fall to the ice. Fights are over when the linesmen say they're over, period. Officials have a very dangerous job—flailing skate blades can sever fingers or slice throats—and they take great pride in helping the game police itself. They understand the code as well as the players do and follow the drama that goes on during games in order to assess each altercation as it happens. They know if there is bad blood between two players, and they will monitor them closely to make sure things don't get out of hand.

## Paul Stewart on Fighting Fair

"I stood up for guys that didn't have the capability to stand up for themselves. That is what the code is all about in my book. Nowadays there are just too many players who don't play by the code. I remember one time refereeing a game in Chicago when Basil McRae was fighting Bob Probert. Well, Basil wound up falling awkwardly and might have even broken his leg, but as soon as Probert saw that he was hurt he stopped in mid-punch and backed off. I always respected him for that. That was a very honorable thing to do. A lot of guys these days wouldn't do that because they don't know the code. Look at the whole Bertuzzi mess. He broke the code by sucker punching Steve Moore from behind, and that, to me, as a former tough guy and as a referee, speaks volumes. You don't hit a guy from behind; you do it from the front. Hell, I used to see guys still throwing punches when the other guy was down on the ice. Again, that is so disrespectful. I truly think that a lot of the kids now just don't know the rules of the code."

Another unwritten rule deals with visors or face masks. Players should not wear them when they fight because the opposing fighter will invariably tear open his knuckles when he punches it. Despite the obvious added safety, enforcers refuse to wear visors unless they are nursing an injury. Players wearing visors are stigmatized as being soft. Stitches, broken noses, and missing teeth are deemed honorable battle scars for NHL tough guys, and the last thing they want is to be thought of as a pussy for wearing facial protection. If a lightweight with a visor gets "brave" by running opposing players and playing dirty, he will still have to be held accountable—even if that means having his helmet ripped off by his opponent. If he has any dignity, he will simply take off his helmet before the fight begins.

Said McSorley:

When you agree to fight a guy, I don't care who he is, you want to win. And you will do whatever is necessary, within the confines of the rules, to do so. If you break a guy's nose or knock out his teeth, or break his jaw, that is just part of the deal. Those things can happen to all of us who sign up to do what we do. Getting hit in the face is not fun. It hurts. It hurts a lot. So, you do what you have to do to survive out there and to win. If you see a guy coming at you with a big overhand right, and you have to put your head down to prevent it from hitting you in the nose, you do so, even though you know he may break his hand on your helmet. That is how it goes down sometimes. You don't intentionally try to use your helmet as a shield, but sometimes it may be your only defense against getting knocked out. Maybe that guy won't come at you with a big overhand right next time if he knows the consequences; you have to think about that, too.

Some tough guys even wore certain kinds of helmets, like the old Win-Wells or Coopers, which came down low almost to their eyes, so that they could justify having more protection from certain punches. I hated fighting guys like that because it just killed your hands and they knew it. The honest guys wouldn't wear those types of helmets; they knew better. Other players were simply not great technical fighters and would swing away wildly, which made them more prone to hitting helmets and breaking knuckles. So, you never knew what you were going to get when you dropped the gloves with a guy.

I tell you what, though: when you did go with someone you respected as a fighter, someone who fought you straight up with respect, guys like Bob Probert, Clark Gillies, Wendel Clark, Larry Playfair, and Paul Holmgren, you really appreciated it. It was an honor to fight those guys because they did it the right way.

As for the actual fights themselves, they went as long as the officials said so. Every instance was unique. The linesmen would step in at their discretion, sometimes too soon and sometimes too late, it just depended on the situation. They knew to break it up when one guy had a distinct advantage, or if one guy was in trouble, or if one guy went down. But if a guy went down and then popped right back up, they might continue to let them go, so you never knew. It really varied from instance to instance. Then, when the linesmen grabbed you and started escorting you to the box, you may have words with the other fighter. It just depended on the situation. You might try to provoke him into a rematch by insulting him or telling him that he is going to get it even worse if he continues to harass your finesse players; or you may not say a word at all because you respect the guy. Each situation was completely different.

## The Aftermath: Win, Lose, or Draw

Perhaps the most important element of fighting is being a respectful, gracious winner, or a respectful, humbled loser. Win, lose, or draw, a player's teammates will applaud his courage for showing up. They know it takes guts to fight another man in front of 20,000 screaming fans, and that is how respect is earned. There is a fine line these days between being a gracious winner and a cocky show-off. And that isn't always bad either. Remember, one of the biggest reasons for fighting is to get your teammates as well as your fans pumped up. Nothing brings the fans to their feet faster than a knock-out punch, and fighters know this. It is the grand slam or touchdown bomb of their trade, and they are always looking for it.

Sometimes a fighter can get really emotional and make a spectacle of himself, however, doing antics he normally wouldn't do in the heat of the moment. While it is not condoned, it is understood behavior every once in a while. After all, who knows what kind of adrenaline it takes to battle another human in that type of environment? Most of us would never willingly drop the gloves with a 6'6" 250-pound behemoth whose sole purpose in life is to pummel people. Right? So, when a guy showboats a little bit and entertains the crowd, it has to be taken with a grain of salt. The bottom line is that it is all about respect. If a player disrespects another player, he will get it back even worse, guaranteed. That is the retaliatory atmosphere that pro hockey players live in.

The final component to a hockey fight is the pomp and circumstance of the aftermath. When the fight is over and the players are being escorted to the penalty box, it is customary for players to cheer for their teammate and pound their sticks on the boards as a way of saluting a valiant effort. Even if a fighter got his face rearranged, he can always expect a gratuitous "way to go, killer," "attaboy," or "you own that guy" from the fellas. No matter how bad it looks, you always tell him that he won and that he is still the champ, always.

Sometimes a fight can have potentially deadly consequences, even if the events that led up to it were absolutely hilarious. Just ask Dave Hanson, an enforcer who played 11 years of professional hockey and who will always be remembered for his role as one of the infamous Hanson Brothers in the 1977 cult classic, *Slap Shot*. He had the following to say:

> The most memorable fight I ever got into over my career would have to be the one with Bobby Hull, probably the biggest star in the game at the time. I was with Birmingham and we were playing Winnipeg. I was trying to establish myself as a player in the league and make an impact, so I was playing pretty physical. Well, I am out there skating around and I run into Bobby, which was like running into a brick shithouse. He just bowled me over. So, when the next opportunity came later on in the game, I gave it back to him pretty good. Bobby took offense and dropped his gloves, so I followed suit. We were just going at it with lefts and rights, and then all of a sudden he just stopped. You could have heard a pin drop in there at that moment. I looked up at the crowd and it was like everybody was just frozen. I

looked back at Bobby and I am thinking to myself, "Something doesn't quite look right here." Sure enough, I looked down at my hand and I'll be damned if his wig wasn't caught in my knuckles. I had somehow caught it and ripped it right off his head [helmets were optional at the time]. It was unbelievable.

At that moment I just said "Holy shit!" I didn't know what to do so I just sort of threw it right down on the ice and skated away. They tossed me in the box and threw the book at me: I got two minutes for elbowing, five minutes for fighting, and ten minutes for pulling hair. Well, Bobby skated off and came back out with a helmet after that. Later on I wound up in the faceoff circle with him and said, "Mr. Hull, I am really sorry." Bobby just looked at me, smiled, and said in his deep, raspy voice, "Ah, don't worry about it, kid. I needed a new one anyhow." I was so relieved that he was able to laugh it off because I thought I was going to have to pay dearly for that episode.

Then, after the game, a whole bunch of their fans tried to jump me and kill me as we were getting onto our team bus. It was crazy. My teammates all came to my rescue and we barely made it out of there. The next day the paper ran a picture of a player pointing at the rug out on the ice with the title "Is Nothing Sacred?" I had death threats after that and everything. It was surreal. That was just a moment I will never forget as long as I live. Bobby and I later became good friends, but to this day we have never spoken of that night.

# 5

## How Does the Code Work?

Here is an example of how the wheels of the code are set into motion. During an otherwise random game between St. Louis and Buffalo back in 2004, Blues winger Dallas Drake rode Buffalo's All-Star defenseman Alexei Zhitnik into the boards, causing him to leave the game with a bruised shoulder. Drake was called for charging on the play and was sent to the box to serve a two-minute penalty. Along the way he took a few whacks and received some verbal abuse about what he had coming from several Buffalo players. While Drake sat in the box, he thought about how he was going to have to alter his game plan for the rest of that evening. He knew that he was going to have to keep his head on a swivel for the rest of that game, and maybe even a few more. You see, while the hit wasn't a particularly dirty or malicious one, it was, however, meted out against a respected player—an untouchable, if you will.

You don't just get to tee off on a player of Zhitnik's stature in the NHL without facing the consequences. Drake knew that and knew that he was going to have to be held accountable. He didn't know when, or where, or against whom, but he knew somebody wearing a Sabres jersey was going to be coming for him sometime soon to right what they felt had been wronged. That is all part of the code, and Drake knew the consequences when he hit Zhitnik. Drake wasn't going to back down, though. He knew that to earn respect in this league he had to stand up for himself.

Sure enough, just over 10 minutes later, Buffalo's Adam Mair skated up to Drake during a faceoff. He poked him with his stick, giving him

## Paul Holmgren on the Code

"The code to me was mostly about sticking up for your teammates more than anything else. You were there to play for them and you would do anything for them in the process. That is what makes great teams, when players sacrifice for, and make commitments to, each other. You know, being an American from Minnesota I grew up playing high school hockey and then played in college, versus playing junior up in Canada. So, I had to learn about the code as I went along. I considered myself to be a physical player coming into pro hockey, but I was pretty wet behind the ears. I mean, I liked to hit and I liked body contact, but as far as fighting went, that was something I didn't really know much about. My toughest fight up until that point was with my big brother in my basement. So coming to Philadelphia right away really helped me because there were plenty of players on that team who were certainly used to playing that style of hockey. To learn the ropes from guys like Bobby Clarke, the Watson brothers, and Moose Dupont really helped make the transition much easier for me. Those guys were tough. The old saying that there is strength in numbers was certainly apropos to the Flyers. Plus, they had just come off of winning back-to-back Stanley Cups, so to come into that winning environment was great, too."

the signal. No words were needed to understand what was happening. It was payback time, and Drake needed to answer the bell. Drake is a tough, respected player in his own right, so he stood up and fought Mair like a man right then and there. Both players dropped the gloves and went at it until the linesmen felt that they had gone long enough. Justice was served. Mair had restored Zhitnik's honor by seeking retribution for his hit, and Drake stood up and took his medicine. Sound barbaric? No way. That is the code in its simplest form. It wasn't personal; it was business. Mair was just doing his job, and Drake knew that.

"When you do something to a skilled player, something like I did by hitting [Zhitnik], you usually have to step up and defend yourself," said Drake. "I've hit guys before, hit guys from behind, even hit guys in the right way, and you have to be accountable. That's part of the game. That's part of playing that way. You step up and defend what you did. It's been like that for 100 years."

Now, hypothetically, had Drake not stepped up and faced Mair, then someone else would have had to step up for him. If that were the case, then things would have escalated to the next level. It would have put all

## J. P. Parise on the Code

"I think a big part of the code is having respect for older players who paved the way. I will never forget when I was playing in Boston one time and I was well into my thirties, just about at the end of the line. Well, I was skating up the ice and my defenseman passed me the puck and it got deflected and was coming at me very slowly. Meanwhile, Terry O'Reilly, who was just a 21-year-old kid at the time, had lined me up in his sights and was coming at me full speed. Just as the puck got there, I saw O'Reilly out of the corner of my eye and figured I was dead. My head was down and I was completely in a vulnerable position. Just then, he grabbed me and said to me, 'Hey, you better be careful out here.' He totally let me off the hook, I couldn't believe it. I mean, he could have killed me, no question. I was just a small, old guy on his last legs and he knew that. I have never forgotten that to this day and that still means a lot to me that he respected me that way. I consider him to be an extremely honorable person for doing that."

of the Blues' star players on notice that they were now fair game, just like Zhitnik. Pretty soon Sabres tough guys would be checking St. Louis' skill players and taking liberties with them. Maybe a slash here or a face wash there, forcing them to play more conservatively. The Blues would then have to retaliate, because their star players would have no space to operate, so they would then send out their tough guys. Before long it would look like World War III. That is how things get out of control in pro hockey if players don't abide by the code. When the players police themselves, justice is served accordingly.

Longtime St. Louis Blues enforcer Tony Twist further explained how the code works:

The code is something that has always been around in hockey. As players we have always had the opportunity to police ourselves in order to give ourselves and our teams the best opportunities to succeed. The code is not always about fighting either. It is about intimidation through respect.

Here is how it works. Let's say my St. Louis Blues were playing the Detroit Red Wings. We have Chris Pronger on our team and they have Steve Yzerman on theirs, both of whom are very well respected finesse players. Maybe Red Wings agitator Martin LaPointe decides to make a run at Pronger. Well, the first thing I am going to do when I get on the ice is go right up to Yzerman and whack him across the ankles. He is then going to look at me and go, "What the hell was that for?" and I am going to tell him it is in retaliation for his boy LaPointe running my boy Pronger. I will tell him that if he leaves my guy alone then I will leave him alone.

So, what does Yzerman do? He is going to go straight to his bench and tell his boys not to touch Pronger, otherwise he is going to continue to take some serious abuse. Now, if it continues, then things will escalate. Detroit's tough guy Joey Kocur will have to come onto the ice, and he and I will have words. He will then go back to his bench and tell his guys to clean it up, otherwise he knows that he will have to fight me. Now his players are going to have to answer to him. Ultimately, that show of intimidation cleans up the game. That is how it works.

If Joey decides that they aren't going to clean it up, then he and I will fight each other. As heavyweights, we understand our role in the game, and that is what we would do in order for the game to settle down. If things continued to escalate, then other people would get involved, too, which would make it very dangerous for everybody out there. The bottom line, though, is that the finesse players would have no space to operate and would be in constant fear of being whacked. The game would slow down and it would turn into a giant mess. That is how a small incident can grow into a really big one. That is how the code works; it keeps everybody in line and prevents guys from getting out of control.

Part of the code also says that you fight within your weight class, unless you do something really stupid, in which case all bets are off. But for the most part heavyweights fight heavyweights, middleweights fight

### Dale Hunter on the Code

"The code is about protecting your skill players. You had to make them feel comfortable out on the ice so that they could do what they did best, score goals. If they felt threatened or intimidated, then they couldn't do their jobs. You just couldn't let the stronger players take liberties with them, and that is why we stood up for them. The code was also about everybody doing their role, whatever that was. Mine was to keep people on their toes by making big hits. A big hit could change the momentum of a game just as a good fight could, so that was always what I was looking for out there. I took a lot of penalties along the way, but I played pretty aggressively and wasn't afraid to mix it up out there. I wasn't a heavyweight or anything, but as an agitator I knew that I had to be accountable for my actions. We all had roles, and if each of us did them to the best of our abilities, then our team would have success. That is what the code was about for me."

## Jeff Odgers on the Code

"The code to me was all about playing hard and sticking up for your teammates. I was the guy who was there for them when liberties were taken and when things got out of control. If anybody tried to take advantage of our star players, then I had to step in and make sure that person was held accountable for his actions. You know, nobody dreams of being a fourth-line winger in the NHL; that is a tough job. As kids we all had visions of being the guy who was on the power play and who scored that big goal in overtime. That is what we all strived for. But as you get older and wiser, you realize some of your limitations, where your skill level was, and what you could bring to the table. At a certain point you come to the realization that if you want to make it in this league you have to adapt and embrace whatever role the coaches have in mind for you. For me that was being a tough guy. No, it wasn't as sexy as being a goal scorer, but it was my ticket to play and I was able to do so for a pretty long time. I just wanted to be in the NHL more than anything in my life, and that is how I was able to make my dream come true. I didn't love fighting, but I did enjoy being respected and liked by my teammates for protecting them. There is great honor in that. The code gave me that opportunity, so I am grateful for that."

middleweights, and lightweights fight lightweights. Sometimes, however, it is not the enforcers who have to stand up to a bully. It is someone a little lower on the fighting food chain, such as a gritty defenseman who isn't afraid to mix it up every now and then.

Take for example an instance that occurred early in 2006, when Minnesota Wild defenseman Willie Mitchell went after Phoenix Coyote's captain Shane Doan, following a vicious check by Doan that left Wild winger Andrei Zyuzin in a bloody heap. Mitchell felt that even though it was a close game, he had to stand up for his teammate, so he immediately dropped the gloves and went after Doan to seek justice. As a result, Mitchell took an instigator penalty and left his team in a precarious position. With the five-minute fighting major, the two-minute instigator, and the 10-minute misconduct, Mitchell spent a total of 17 minutes in the box. In a situation like that, however, it was worth it. The already well-liked and respected team captain gained even more admiration from his teammates that night, and his selfless actions served to unify the team.

"I don't regret anything I did," said Mitchell. "I would do it 100 times over. I expect my teammates to do the same thing for me, that's all."

There are also times when the tough guys have to let their star players fight their own battles, particularly if they are playing aggressively. That is all part of the code. Take for instance Wild star forward Marian Gaborik. Gabby is considered an "untouchable" and has several bodyguards who protect him out on the ice so that he can have space to score goals. That is his job. Throughout the 2005–06 season, however, Gaborik was getting roughed up pretty good and none of his teammates were standing up for him. Time and time again he would take a hard check after scoring a goal or a face wash following a whistle—disrespectful acts that would usually require retribution from an enforcer. But that is not so all the time. Because Gaborik plays hard and tends to provoke that sort of reaction by occasionally slashing and hacking his opponents, his teammates are forced to let him fend for himself more than they'd care to. If somebody dropped the gloves with Gaborik, three guys would be there to make sure he didn't get punched. But as for the chippy stuff?

### Darren Pang on the Code

"The code in my eyes is a very detailed way of describing how the game polices itself. The code has been around for more than 100 years, yet is not written anywhere and needs never be spoken of. Most kids learn it as they make the transition from midgets to juniors in Canada. If you are a player that reaches that level, you either understand it or you don't. And if you don't, you will sooner or later, guaranteed. Nobody takes you aside and tells you the rules. They are just passed down by example from the older kids who move on to the next levels. It is all about playing the game with respect or paying the price for it if you don't. There are even codes within the code, nuances that go on in our game that are both communicated and uncommunicated, and that is all a part of it as well. It is about accountability and playing the game the right way.

"As a goaltender I was at the heart of a lot of it. The code says you don't take liberties with the opposing goalie or you will have to be held accountable. So if guys came in my crease I had to make them pay. Players know that, too. I knew that if I whacked a guy who tried to run me or trip me or screen me or hit my glove with his stick, then my guys were going to be there to defend me no matter what. It was automatic. You can tell pretty quickly which teams are close teams and which ones are going nowhere fast by the amount of time it takes for them to retaliate against an opposing player disrespecting their goalie."

"Sometimes he's got to, not answer the bell, but understand that when he does that stuff, he's going to get shots back," said Mitchell. "You see him out there. He'll swing a heavy stick."

The important thing here is that the finesse player who plays aggressively knows he is going to have to take a hit now and then. As long as it doesn't go too far, the enforcers are all right with letting him take a hit or two. And when the star needs backing, those enforcers will be right there waiting.

# 6

# The Code and the Special Games

## Great Rivalries Produce Great Fights

Fans love drama, and there is no greater drama for sports fans than a storied rivalry. In hockey, perhaps more so than any other sport, there is an abundance of simply outstanding rivalries. Because professional hockey has roots that go back so far, and because its original franchises were begun in such relatively close proximity, generations of fans have been able to watch those rivalries grow over time. Not only were they able to see great games, great players, and great goals being scored, but they were also able to see the carnage and bloodshed firsthand. Great rivalries are usually synonymous with great fights.

When their teams won, the fans rejoiced. And when their teams lost, their hatred of those arch nemeses just grew and flourished. As the years went by, the politics and the soap opera antics only added fuel to their fires. Yes, to those of us who follow them, great rivalries are actual living, breathing entities. We mark those dates on our calendars as soon as the schedules are released, and we then wait in eager anticipation. We want to be there when history is made; we want to say that we were there; we want to believe that our presence made a difference. Special rivalries are just that intense.

Among the NHL's greatest all-time rivalries are two common denominators. The first is geographical proximity, and the second is being one of the storied "Original Six" franchises: Boston, Chicago, Detroit, Montreal, New York, and Toronto.

When you look at the league's first great rivalries, both factors are prevalent. For starters you have Toronto versus Montreal, a rivalry that goes deep due to their cultural differences: English-speaking Ontario versus French-speaking Quebec. Then you have Chicago versus Detroit, which goes back to the 1930s. More recent geographical rivalries include Wayne Gretzky's Edmonton Oilers versus the Calgary Flames, in what is known as the "Battle of Ontario." Others include the Philadelphia Flyers versus the Pittsburgh Penguins, as well as the New York Rangers versus the New York Islanders. Boston also had great rivalries with both Philly and Toronto back in the 1970s. Many rivalries have come and gone, such as the Chicago Blackhawks versus the Minnesota North Stars, which ended when the North Stars moved to Dallas in 1993, but the memories remain forever ingrained in the minds of the fans who rooted for them.

## Great Fights Swing Momentum in Big Rivalry Games

Enforcers are a huge component of great rivalries and truly make a difference in those games. Physical confrontation and intimidation come to the forefront in rivalry games, and enforcers know that they need to step it up even more on those nights. A big hit or a big punch can swing the momentum, and that might be the catalyst that sparks the home team to victory. It is not just enforcers who have to rise to the occasion in games like that, however. Everybody has to get involved, including the most unlikeliest of heroes, whomever that might be. In the most intense rivalry of the past 20 years, that unlikely hero was Detroit Red Wings goalie Mike Vernon, who duked it out with Colorado Avalanche goalie Patrick Roy on March 26, 1997, en route to leading his team to a pair of Stanley Cups. That single incident has become the emblem for the toughness and guts of the modern-day rivalry.

All great rivalries have a checkered past complete with vengeance, retribution, and violence. They also feature a genesis, and a history chock full of storied chapters. And that history almost always starts with a flashpoint, an incident that set the rivalry wheels in motion. The Colorado-versus-Detroit flashpoint transpired in the opening game of the 1996 conference finals when Detroit's Slava Kozlov shoved Colorado's Adam Foote headfirst into the boards. As a result, Foote suffered a nasty cut to his face that required nearly two dozen stitches to seal up. In an attempt to seek justice for his fallen comrade, Avs agitator Claude Lemieux retaliated by decking Wings winger Kris Draper from behind, forcing him into the boards, a few nights later. The play was widely viewed as a deliberate cheap shot, and Draper suffered severe facial injuries that required plastic surgery. Even though Lemieux was suspended for two games, his Avs went on to win the series and the Stanley Cup.

That next season the teams met three times with no incidents of retribution. Many were upset that Lemieux showed no remorse and offered no apology to Draper, which only fueled the fire. Finally, on their fourth and final meeting of the regular season, in Detroit, all hell broke loose. Wings enforcer Darren McCarty, anxious to seek revenge for his friend and teammate, pummeled Lemieux into a bloody mess. Lemieux, who later claimed that he had been sucker punched, turtled and didn't fight back.

Pretty soon mayhem broke out at Joe Louis Arena and everybody was pairing off, totally old-school. The crowd was going absolutely insane and before you knew it, both goalies, Roy and Vernon, came skating out of their creases like madmen and squared off in a fight at center ice. Roy was bloodied by Vernon, who got the best of him. More fights broke out periodically throughout the rest of the game, with nearly 150 penalty minutes being racked up. At the end of three, the game was tied 5–5 and went into overtime, where McCarty of all people scored the thrilling game winner. It was a game for the ages. It had taken a whole year, but justice had been served.

The teams met again in the Western Conference Finals, with the Wings beating the Avs in six games. The series was full of drama, including questionable hits by Draper on Peter Forsberg and by Mike Keane on Detroit's Igor Larionov—both of which took the respective players out of the game. So pissed was Avs coach Marc Crawford at one point that he scaled the glass separating the two benches to hurl obscenities at Detroit coach Scotty Bowman.

Detroit, meanwhile, went on to win its first Stanley Cup since 1955. The Red Wings would later confess that they were unified and inspired by their huge brawl. It had a profound effect to be sure, as a demoralized Roy would later say that "the Wings won the Cup that night." After the series Lemieux extended his hand out to Draper, but Draper was upset that Lemieux wouldn't make eye contact with him, so he refused to shake it.

The drama continued the next season, when the two teams met again early in Detroit. Lemieux, who was viewed as public enemy number one in Motown, salvaged his pride during the opening faceoff, when he answered the code by dropping the gloves with McCarty. He even switched places with Avs enforcer Jeff Odgers just so he could line up across from McCarty and get it over with right out of the gate.

"That was the perfect match-up," said Lemieux. "If you're going to do it, do it right off the bat. I'm not going to hire a bodyguard. I can take care of myself. I've done it for 13 years and I did it tonight. I had five guys who would have been willing to go and go after him, but that's not the way to go. The guys last year, in that fight when I was down, fought their heart out. That was my payback."

"I respect him for what he did," said McCarty. "He's got to stand up for himself and his team, and you respect him for that as a hockey player. But I still have no respect for him as a person, as a human being."

Detroit went on to win their second straight Cup that season, but the subplots with the Avs kept on coming. There was yet another rare goalie fight, this time between Roy and Detroit goaltender Chris Osgood; Detroit's Kirk Maltby broke Valeri Kamensky's forearm with a slash; and Colorado's Peter Forsberg shoved Brendan Shanahan into the glass in Game 1 of the 1999 playoffs, giving him an extra 40 stitches for good measure. McCarty and Lemieux continued to battle that season, too, with McCarty ultimately refusing to shake Lemieux's hand after Colorado won their playoff series.

All of those little things go into making a great rivalry, and that is why this one will forever be remembered as one of the best. Sadly, with free agency the way it is nowadays, and so many players changing sweaters every season, rivalries aren't like they were back in the day. So when a special one like that one comes along, the fans really appreciate it.

## During Playoff Hockey, the Code Calls for Restraint

Most die-hard hockey fans will tell you that there are in fact two hockey seasons every year, the regular season and the playoffs. Playoff hockey is so much better than the regular season that it almost can't even compare. It's magical. The players are just so into it, it is almost unexplainable. A player's tolerance for pain and suffering skyrockets as soon as the quest to hoist Lord Stanley's Cup is official. Cuts, bruises, and various other battle wounds are all displayed proudly when the postseason starts. Injuries are deemed honorable if they occur during this time because they show players are sacrificing their bodies to keep their team going. It is not spoken of or written down; it is just expected. Yes, playoff hockey has very much to do with the code.

Yet, it is a different part of the code, playoff hockey. Because fighting, believe it or not, is almost completely absent when the postseason starts. No one wants to put his team at a disadvantage with so much at stake. Taking a costly penalty and putting the other team on the power play can be the difference between a win and a loss. So players play extremely hard, but they usually refrain from dropping the gloves. Discipline is the key to success in the postseason.

Players will square off, however, when there is either a serious code infraction that warrants retribution, or it is a blowout game and they want to send a message for the next night. For instance, if the score is 4–1 late in the third period of the first game of a seven-game series, you can bank on there being some intimidation tactics going on. The winning team wants their opponent to know that they should be afraid and that more punishment is coming. Those are the mind games and psychological tactics involved with playoff hockey.

But as the series goes on, the stakes rise exponentially. Players wanting to lash out in frustration or attempting to set a tone for the next game have to remain disciplined. Dumb penalties, especially fighting majors for no good cause, are seen as just plain selfish. Incredibly, many enforcers are left off their playoff rosters, either because teams don't want to risk having them sucked into a brawl in an emotional situation or because they would rather carry another skill player as insurance. Many injuries occur during the playoffs because passion and tension run high; therefore, some teams decide they can't afford to carry a role player who may not be called upon to hit the ice. Instead that player will be listed as a healthy scratch and will have to watch the game from the press box. For the skill players this just means that everybody else will have to step up. Since the enforcers aren't there to fight, the other guys know that they will have to protect each other instead. For the enforcers, on the other hand, playoff hockey can be extremely tough. To protect their teammates and fight in the trenches all season long and then to be left behind so close to the finish line is one of the brutal ironies of the postseason for them.

Particularly in the era of the new rule changes, enforcers have to be more well-rounded if they want to make the postseason roster. For the lucky designated hitters who do make the cut and get to skate in the big dance, their roles are many times shifted to do things such as fourth-line penalty killing. The playoffs usually mean a short bench to begin with, so just to be a part of the action is reward enough for many of them.

As for the games themselves, they are usually full of drama and suspense. The story lines unfold as the series begin, with players often harboring ill will from past rivalries and bad blood over the years. Natural rivalries that meet up in the postseason are rekindled and given new life. It is as if the players themselves somehow obtain Herculean strength during this time, playing through any pain and injuries that would otherwise sideline them. Heroes are created during the playoffs. They are driven to win and advance to the next round, and eventually have a long embrace with Stanley.

Most players will not touch the Stanley Cup unless they have won it. It is one of those magical superstitions that adds to the legend of the Cup. It is out of respect; you don't touch something that special without having earned the right to do so. Amazingly, when the players win it they are granted 24 hours alone with it, to do as they wish. The parties and stories of where Stanley has been over the years are insane.

From the bottom of Mario Lemieux's swimming pool to tubing on a lake in northern Minnesota with Jamie Langenbrunner, the Cup has been around the world and back more times than anyone can remember. Visions like those, of partying with their friends, family, former peewee coaches, and teammates, drive these men to extraordinary depths of sacrifice and courage. They all want to hoist that beautiful goblet and drink champagne from it like a rock star. For the players, that is it, that is what they play for...to hoist the Cup.

When the playoffs start, many players will also stop shaving. The idea is to not shave until they have won the Cup. Silly? Perhaps, but it is yet another reminder of what time it is when you see an entire team of scruffy bearded warriors all battling together. The "playoff beard" is just another wonderful sign of the postseason. Others include black eyes, stitches, and facial cuts, because if you advance long enough into the playoffs, your face will tell the story. If not, you haven't seen much ice time. And that doesn't include all of the unseen welts, bruises, and lacerations that are covered up under layers of protective equipment. Collectively, those wounds are badges of honor to these men, something they wear with great pride.

Players know that they have to step it up in the playoffs and do the dirty work that nobody wants to do. They know that they have to go hard into the corners or in front of the net, which will almost always have severe consequences. That doesn't matter, though, because in the playoffs it is all about the team. It is as if the playoffs have their own code, their own set of rules for what players can and can't do. If you are a hockey fan, the playoffs are truly the best of times.

Everything is different when the playoffs get going. Players do things that they just wouldn't normally do, and that is why the fans love it so much. It is not uncommon to see superstars getting cuts sewn up on the bench so that they won't miss a shift. Players take pucks to the face, high sticks, and crushing body checks with more regularity in the postseason. Superstars will drop the gloves if they have to. They also block shots, laying it all on the line for their team. Guts and passion are synonymous with the postseason. Like the old saying goes, "In the playoffs, will beats skill."

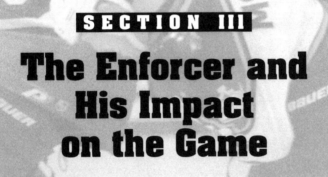

## SECTION III

# The Enforcer and His Impact on the Game

"Everybody had a role on a hockey team. The scorers scored, the agitators stirred it up, and the enforcers fought to keep everybody in line. I embraced my role and made the best of it for a long time. I always remembered Don Cherry's classic quote about enforcers who tried to change their stripes: 'A crusher who becomes a rusher soon becomes an usher.' I never wanted to forget that because if I was going to fight, it was going to be for my team and for my teammates. Fighting wasn't about me; that is selfish. It was always about being there for and protecting my guys. I just tried to play honest and I tried to play with respect. I knew my role out there and tried my best to do it. I never cheated my teammates or the system, and I was proud of that. I honored the code."

—BASIL McRAE
15-year veteran NHL enforcer,
retired in 1996

# 7

# Big Hitters Mean Big Business

Big hitters are not only adored by the fans, they are also coveted by coaches and general managers. A big hitter's impact on a game can be immeasurable. A perfectly timed center ice body check that catches its unsuspecting prey with its head down is worth its weight in gold. Executed properly it is a thing of beauty. It can send a direct message to the opposition and has serious psychological implications. A good hit will make the other team take notice and force them to change their game plans for fear of it happening again. Nobody wants to be on the receiving end of one of those, nobody. If a big hitter establishes his space out on the ice, the opposition will respect it and simply stay away from him, seeking another route down the ice. Big hits can also force turnovers and create odd-man rushes, which will turn a defensive play into an offensive one in a split second. In addition, they can either get the home crowd into the game or, conversely, silence the opposition's fans.

Decking an opponent with a crushing check can swing the momentum in a heartbeat the same way an enforcer can with a knock-out punch. As a tactic, it can completely unglue some teams altogether and really change the complexion of the game. They will either be intimidated, in which case they will play scared, or they will overcompensate out of revenge or retribution and play out of control. The bottom line here is that big hits can and do change the flow of the game. A seasoned veteran can sense just the right time in a game to pull off a big hit, and if he is successful it can have a huge impact.

We, as sports fans, just love big hits. We really do. We love to watch them up close and personal, at the arena, and we love to watch them on our couches in front of the tube sipping on a cold one. And while most of us love the technical grace of a well-executed jab in the boxing ring; a 50-yard touchdown pass on the gridiron; a towering grand slam on the baseball diamond; a monster dunk on the hardwood; or a top-shelf slap shot from the blue line in hockey—nothing compares to big hits. Whether it is a knock-out punch, a bone-crunching sack, a collision at home plate, a hard foul, or a perfectly timed body check, we can't seem to get enough of it.

As a society, we love the "thrill of victory and the agony of defeat." In fact, that is what keeps us coming back for more. The ticket prices at stadiums and arenas across our country keep getting higher and higher, and the television revenues from these events continue to spiral upward. We are all voyeurs, waiting and watching to see that one big hit that will make the opening lead-in on that night's *SportsCenter*. We all want to say we saw it, were a part of it, could see it coming, and could even feel it. That is the child in all of us, living vicariously through sports.

Paul Stewart, a former NHL tough guy turned NHL referee, recalls giving the fans that thrill:

> I used to love to get the crowd going. It was fun. I remember playing in Birmingham one time and taking their guys apart one at a time. I went after the first guy, then the second guy, and on down the line. I was on a mission that night. I just went right down the list in order to establish myself out there so that nobody could touch my guys. I used to walk by the dressing room before our games there and peek into the owner's office. He would be there with his little daughter and I would tease her by saying, "Tell your daddy to bring lots of Kleenex, he's gonna be crying tonight." He would just wink back at me and laugh. Hey, I was good for business. The fans used to love the games I was in because I wasn't afraid to mix it up with anybody. I definitely gave them their money's worth, that was for sure.

Everybody loves the "big guy": the heavyweight champ, the slugger in baseball, the middle linebacker in football, the power forward in basketball, and the enforcer in hockey. Guys like Muhammad Ali, Babe Ruth, Lawrence Taylor, Charles Barkley, and Tie Domi, who are larger than life in more ways than one. And it's not just the fans who love these guys. The general managers, coaches, and team owners love them, too, because

## Dave Hanson on Being an Enforcer and Big Hits

"The code was about one thing to me: respect. And that was absolutely earned as an enforcer. If you fought clean and didn't try to embarrass your guy, you could expect the same treatment in return. But, if you were a guy who ran around and picked his spots, or fought guys when they were injured, or grabbed them at the end of their shifts, you would be dealt with accordingly. We all talked amongst ourselves, and we knew who those guys were. Those guys did not have the respect of their peers. Everybody knew who the legitimate tough guys were out there.

"I just loved to fight. I certainly wasn't a goal scorer, but I just loved dropping the gloves out there. It was such a rush. To know that you beat a guy and to hear the crowd roar, it was instant gratification. And then to go over to your bench and see your guys all cheering for you in appreciation, it didn't get any better than that. As much as I loved to score a rare goal, I also loved connecting on a perfect punch or landing the perfect body check. I had no reservations on who I would fight and I just really enjoyed that sort of primal challenge. I didn't win 'em all, that was for sure, but I won the majority of them. And if I did lose, it certainly didn't deter me from fighting again. In fact, it probably drove me even harder. Standing up for my teammates and just being there for them really motivated me.

"You know, everybody's journey to the National Hockey League is a little bit different. Mine, of course, will forever be linked to the movie. As for the legacy of *Slap Shot*, I don't know if there was any significant social commentary, it was just fun. Hockey fans loved it and could relate. It was a hilarious movie, a real classic. Hey, we have been referred to as the most famous hockey line in history, and that just speaks volumes about how much people have enjoyed the movie over the years. For me personally, it opened a lot of doors. In fact, I signed with the Detroit Red Wings shortly after it came out because of it. I remember their slogan that year was 'Aggressive Hockey is Back in Town,' and I was going to be a part of that. It is pretty amazing how things just work out sometimes."

they sell tickets and attract corporate sponsors. Yes, the big "business" of sports is just that, big business. And the bottom line in this business is winning. Period. When your team is winning then everybody is fat and happy. The fans are filling the seats, the advertisers are buying air time, and the owners are in the black counting their millions. When you have all of those things going on, then the players get paid—and that is what it is all about in pro sports. When you're losing, meanwhile, it's like a cancer eating its way through the clubhouse, locker room, front office, and fan base. Losing is the worst thing that can happen to a franchise, and players want no part of it.

Having said that, it is little wonder why players will sacrifice their bodies in order to help their teams win. Sure, they do it for the love of the game and for the dream of one day hoisting Lord Stanley's Cup. But they also know that if they don't play hurt, or don't score a goal, or don't come up with a big hit, then their days are numbered. There is big pressure on these guys to produce and to play hard every day and every night. Otherwise they will have to get real jobs like the rest of us and worry about how they are going to feed their families. Sure, hockey is a game, and most players will tell you that they would play for free. But that is so cliché at this level. It may very well be true for some, but when players get to the NHL, they want to stay there. Millions of dollars are on the line in a career that averages just a couple of years at best. They need to get a return on that investment.

They want to play against the world's top players and live like rock stars. That is the reward for all of the hard work they put in on the backyard pond, or in junior hockey, or on the bus when traveling throughout the minor leagues. When you make it to the "show," you get paid. And there is just as much pressure to stay there once you arrive as there was in the journey to get there. For every job, or roster spot, there are dozens and dozens of capable young players waiting in the wings. They are waiting for an injury; for a slump; for any sort of opportunity that will allow them to showcase their talents. Everybody wants a piece of that pie.

It is important to note that while big hits are a part of the game, reckless or cheap hits certainly are not. A big part of the code is about being physical, but playing dirty is simply unacceptable. If you take a guy out with a dirty hit, there will be hell to pay. Most players will tell you that they are most worried about the low hits that threaten their knees, which are so vulnerable. Torn ligaments are career-enders, and it can happen in a heartbeat. There is a right way to hit guys in pro hockey, and doing things like sticking your leg out to trip a guy is definitely not it. If players are going to hit a guy, they need to use their whole body and do it cleanly.

Clean hits are respected and feared at this level, while cheap ones are detested and avenged. A cheap hit almost guarantees swift retribution, no matter the player. The game will police itself against things like this, and an instigator penalty is an acceptable price to pay in order to seek justice for something considered so disrespectful. Players today also have a distinct advantage over their brethren of old in that they are able to watch the instant replay on the arena scoreboard. They can see the hit from every angle to help them determine if it was indeed a cheap shot or just a player who got out of position. It adds an entirely new component to mediating justice, and most would agree that it is a good thing.

# 8

## On Playing Hurt

art of the unwritten warrior code is that players must play through pain and hardship. They don't have to, of course, but they all do. It is just understood. Hockey players, perhaps more so than any other athlete, are expected to suck it up and work through their injuries. That is the culture of the sport, to sacrifice your body for your team and to lay it all on the line. Pro hockey is all about the team, and players will do whatever it takes to help their team win. If that means playing with a broken arm, so be it. If that means getting your mouth quickly stitched up between shifts with no anesthetic, then so be it. That is all part of the deal. In fact, it is not rewarded behavior, it is expected behavior. It is a state of mind unseen outside of professional sport.

It is a mentality that has been handed down from generation to generation, starting with guys like former Montreal Canadiens winger John Ferguson, one of the toughest SOBs who ever played. When Ferguson went on to become the general manager of the New York Rangers, he was notorious for insisting that his players suit up at all costs. Any injury, Ferguson used to contend, could be cured with "a little tape and aspirin." The guilt and peer pressure was overwhelming. Players simply did not want to let their teammates down, no matter what, and Ferguson played into that. For instance, if a player came off the ice with a sore leg, Ferguson would say to him just loud enough for his line mates to hear: "Your leg is bad? Gee, that's a long way from your heart."

Speaking of heart, the honor of wearing the captain's "C" is part of the code, too. In fact, it might be the most coveted and respected role in all of hockey. Players such as Steve Yzerman, Cam Neely, and Bobby Clarke epitomized the position because not only were they prolific scorers, they also never shied away from dropping their gloves to protect their teammates. They led by example and that is what made them such enormous fan favorites. For players like these, there is a reason why the "C" is sewn onto their sweaters right over their heart. It takes a lot of courage and responsibility to wear it, and players don't take that lightly. Most captains have missing teeth and stitched up faces, because playing injured is just part of the job when you are the captain. Whether it means dropping the gloves, dishing out a hit, or blocking a shot, they know that they need to do whatever it takes to help their team win.

Most outsiders probably couldn't stomach the pregame locker-room scene. There might be players getting shots of cortisone in their knees or shoulders; broken fingers being taped up; stitches being removed (to prevent an opposing agitator from seeing them and trying to bust them open again); and ice bags strewn about by players who were hoping to "freeze" any lingering muscle pulls or deep bruises before the puck was dropped. The hockey player's threshold for pain is unimaginable.

Like soldiers with an unwavering allegiance to their cause, hockey players at times possess an almost superhuman tolerance for pain and suffering. To them it is all about "we and us," not "I and me." It is all about the responsibility they feel toward one another in an effort to help their team in any way possible. For most, it would take an extraordinary set of circumstances to keep them off the ice. This iron will to play at all costs is heightened come playoff time, when the stakes are at their highest. When you play pro hockey, you belong to one of the toughest fraternities known to man. Being soft is unacceptable. This frat house is for men who feel it is their sworn duty to play regardless of their wounds or shortcomings.

In fact, injuries are celebrated in hockey. That's right. It's even got a name, "playoff makeup." Because in the playoffs, you absolutely, positively have to play, no matter how bad you are hurting. Hockey's version of the color wheel rears its head around that time, with bruises coming in a variety of colors, including black and blue, yellow and purple, or blood red—which looks great when contrasted with the freshly painted bright white ice. These wounds are badges of honor among the soldiers who go to war together in quest of Lord Stanley's Cup.

And there won't be any whining or complaining about those injuries either. No way. That would be dishonorable and intolerable. The players will suck it up and hit the ice like they have done a million times before. In fact, they will usually make it a point not to tell anybody about their injuries, and for good reason. You see, when an injury, such as a sprained wrist, is disclosed in the media, then that body part instantly becomes a target. So the last thing an injured player wants is for the other team to know that he is injured. Otherwise, the agitators on the other team will swarm like killer bees, waiting to feast on that tender forearm. They will take any opportunity to slash it, grab it, or check it—just to take that player off his game. Because if he is thinking about protecting his forearm, then he is not totally focused on playing hockey. This is why most hockey injuries are listed in the paper as something generic, like "groin injury." It is a basic vanilla ailment that every player suffers from time to time, except it is one that is nearly impossible to exploit. Yeah, the code protects guys from getting hit there, too. Whack a guy downstairs, and you will get what is coming to you 10 times over.

"You know a guy has a broken wrist, you hammer him there a few times and you don't have much trouble with him for the rest of the night," wrote Punch Imlach in his memoir, *Hockey Is a Battle*. "It's nothing personal. I'd do it myself."

According to NHL statistics, there were 1,251 injuries during the 2002–03 season. At least, that's how many were reported. Because players are so tough, and because they don't want to risk being exploited out on the ice, they report only a fraction of the injuries that actually occur.

And just why are there so many injuries and so much carnage in hockey? The short answer: physics. Just as Sir Isaac Newton said centuries ago, when you have large masses moving at great speeds and colliding with one another, there is going to be some friction. Hockey has been described as a "nuclear" game, with explosive and unpredictable power. You have 12 grown men skating around at speeds up to 30 miles per hour on a 100-foot-by-85-foot ice surface, wielding carbon composite sticks that can launch a rock-hard vulcanized rubber puck as fast as 100 miles per hour. You do the math. Violent collisions aren't the exception to the rule in this sport, they *are* the rule.

Part of the reason for so many injuries in the sport has to do with its confinement. The enclosed rink lends itself to a more intense atmosphere, conducive to violence. Hockey, unlike football, baseball, basketball, or soccer, is completely closed off, with no escape routes, so to speak. In hockey once you are out in that pit of dasher boards and Plexiglas, you are trapped. Many contend that with no place to duck and hide, the hitting becomes even more ferocious. The basketball court has no physical barriers that define its boundaries, and a scrambling quarterback can usually dive out of bounds in order to elude the clutches of a linebacker out to rip his head off. Not so in hockey. When a guy is bearing down on you in the corner, it doesn't matter how fast you are, you are going to get hit hard. Period. And with the players seemingly getting so much bigger, faster, and stronger every season, the rinks appear to be shrinking.

"I've broken my nose five or six times," said New York Rangers agitator Darius Kasparaitis. "I just stop the bleeding, snap it back, take an Advil to forget about the pain, and keep playing. Sometimes you pay a price for how you play. I'll pay that price. Like when I split my lip one time playing in Russia, they stitched it up right there on the bench, without Novocain. I have been called a dirty player, but I think I just play hard, and if you play hard you get hurt."

Hockey has created a culture that breeds athletes who feel they can overcome almost any injury in order to play. From coaches to teammates to team doctors, nobody is going to tell a player, "Sure, sit this one out tonight. That cut above your eye needs some time to heal." No way. Most believe that if you can walk upright and have a pulse, then you can suit up. Many contend that this play-at-all-costs mentality is a learned behavior that follows the simple adage of "leading by example." The grizzled veterans mentor the young guns, who then become mentors themselves, until it becomes a generational thing—passed down like a treasured heirloom. When the respected team captain laces 'em up no matter what, then his teammates will do the same. That is the ultimate sign of respect, to be there for your comrades in battle. All for one and one for all. It is the essence of the warrior code.

Just as a crushing body check that flattens an opponent can swing the momentum of a game, so too can an act of bravery where a player gives up his body for his team. Coaches will tell their players when they are down that many losses have been miraculously transformed into wins over the

## Marty McSorley on Playing through Pain

"I remember one time playing in Tampa Bay and I took a puck in the mouth right at the start of the game. It cut me open pretty good over my lip. Well, I had our trainer put some flies [butterfly stitches] over it so I could get back out there. I knew that I was going to need at least a dozen stitches after the game, but it could wait. Meanwhile, their coach, Terry Crisp, threw their tough guy out on the ice on my first shift back to fight me. That was low. I didn't back down, though. I fought the guy, and I beat him. The butterflies were torn off, though, and there was blood all over. So I headed to the box and the big screen showed me with blood all over my face and of course the fans were going crazy. They just assumed that their guy won because I was such a mess. Needless to say, none of them probably knew that I took a puck in the mouth 20 minutes earlier. Stuff like that is tough, and that was a crappy thing for that coach to do. He should have given me a little bit of time to get my wits about me, but hey, that is hockey and that is what I got paid to do. My teammates knew better, and I knew that, so it didn't matter to me."

years thanks to the heroic efforts of players who were willing to sacrifice their bodies to break their opponents' spirits. And there are countless legendary stories, almost like folklore, of players displaying incredible courage in leading their teams to victory. Like tall tales or ghost stories, they have been embellished over the years to enhance their dramatic impact.

Players young and old have all heard about how Montreal star winger Maurice Richard was knocked out cold during Game 7 of the 1952 Stanley Cup semifinals. After colliding with Boston defenseman Bill Quackenbush late in the second period, he was carried off on a stretcher. He came to, though, and demanded to return to the ice. He then rejoined his teammates with just under four minutes left on the clock and proceeded to make history. With the score tied, Richard, with a bloody bandage covering six fresh stitches on his face, pulled off one of his signature end-to-end runs, skating around three Bruins defenders before scoring the thrilling series-winning goal. That was the day Maurice became "the Rocket" in the eyes of many fans.

Or how about Detroit's Marcel Pronovost, who showed up to each game of the 1961 Stanley Cup Finals on crutches. The Red Wings defenseman would remove his cast to play each night on a severely broken ankle and then have the cast put back on after the game—only to take it off all over again the next evening. You just can't make that stuff up.

Or take Toronto Maple Leafs defenseman Bobby Baun, who broke his big toe more than 30 times. The story of how he scored the game-winning overtime goal in Game 6 of the 1964 Stanley Cup Final, on a broken leg nonetheless, is epic. And, if that weren't enough, Baun actually hid from team doctors after the game, refusing to have his leg x-rayed for fear of them putting a cast on it. He then showed up just moments before the start of the deciding Game 7 already dressed and snuck onto the bench. How did he do? He wound up playing a regular shift that game, having his leg "frozen" after every shift to numb the pain, en route to leading his Leafs to the Cup title. That is how respect is earned in the National Hockey League.

And it isn't just about heroic games either. Most players just go about their business and keep their mouths shut. Amazingly, the goalies might be the toughest of them all. Take Hall of Fame net minder Glenn Hall, who played more than 500 consecutive complete games without a mask. Or the "Gumper," Gump Worsley, who was on the receiving end of more than 1,000 stitches to his pretty mug. For goalies of that era, getting cut was just part of the job. The late Montreal keeper, Lorne Chabot, who played between the pipes back in the 1920s and '30s, used to shave right before he hit the ice. Said Chabot: "I stitch better when my skin is smooth."

The fast-paced transitions in the game are reason for more injuries. Unlike football, basketball, and baseball, where teams can only make substitutions during a break in action, hockey players change on the fly. Guys will skate hard for a one- or two-minute shift and then head to the bench, where they will catch a breather while the next line goes out and does the same. The action turns on a dime, with players skating forward on the forecheck and then instantly skating backward on the back-check. On the gridiron, only after an interception or a fumble does the shift from penetration to protection come into play. In hockey this happens nonstop, and that is what makes it so exciting.

Lastly, players are bigger, faster, and stronger nowadays. Thirty years ago the average NHL player was 5'11" and about 180 pounds. Today that number has grown by two inches and 20 pounds. And that is just on average. The prototypical players have that rare combination of speed and power. They are guys like Eric Lindros, Mario Lemieux, Derian Hatcher, or

Chris Pronger, who are all at least 6'5" and between 230 and 250 pounds. There are some giants out there, though, such as Minnesota Wild enforcer Derek Boogaard, who comes in at 6'7" and 275 pounds. Or Ottawa Senators defenseman Zdeno Chara, who towers over his competition at 6'9" and 260 pounds. Those guys are scary. It is no wonder people think that the rinks have gotten smaller.

Plus, these athletes are better conditioned on year-round programs with state-of-the-art exercise and weight-training apparatuses. And the players' equipment has gotten more high-tech with newer, lighter, and stronger materials being used to help them achieve great speeds while maintaining a high level of protection. Add all of those factors together and it's not surprising guys get hurt.

Shot blocking might be the most courageous element of hockey because guys know that they may have to take a puck in the face in order to save a potential goal from going in. It is an art form to be sure, based on perfect timing and judgment. Go down too soon and the player can go around you or pass off; go down too late and you either miss the puck or take it right in the face. The code honors shot blockers for their courage, selflessness, and vulnerability in the line of fire.

Those guys, the muckers and the grinders, the fourth liners, the guys with heart—they make the difference in hockey. Sometimes, just sometimes, the best players with all the talent in the world and the fat contracts can't hold a candle to the guys with heart. That is the great equalizer in this game—the heart. Some guys have it, and will play through pain, while others simply don't.

## On Injuries from Fighting

When two willing participants drop the gloves and go, they both under-stand the inherent risks involved with regards to being injured. So many things could go wrong out there, but amazingly, they rarely do. To the outsider it may seem barbaric: two grown men bare-knuckle brawling and trying to hold on to one another for balance, all while on skates and on a slippery sheet of ice. Such is the workplace decor of a professional hockey enforcer.

Injuries are commonplace in hockey and occur on a nightly basis. From hard checks to pulled muscles to stick work to flying pucks, players go down from time to time—that is just the nature of this business. Injuries suffered from fighting, however, are an entirely different animal reserved for those elite few who call themselves enforcers. Sure, they are susceptible to all of the aforementioned injuries, just as everyone else on the ice is, but enforcers are prone to even more severe punishment by virtue of what they do for a living.

Being an enforcer is a high-stress occupation that carries with it a great deal of pressure. Pressure to perform; pressure to protect their teammates; pressure to win their fights; and pressure to not get hurt. When a tough guy gets hurt, he knows that he will be replaced in the lineup by a young gun eager to take his job. And the first thing he will want to do once he is

### Neal Broten on Injuries from Fighting

"I guess you could say that I was protected by the code. While I certainly didn't ask for that protection, it was nice to have out on the ice when guys tried to take advantage of you. As a goal scorer you would get hacked and chopped all the time out there, and that was just part of the game. I really appreciated those tough guys, though—the Jack Carlsons, the Willi Pletts, the Shane Churlas, the Davey Richters, or the Basil McRaes. They were selfless in what they did. They were the ultimate team players because a lot of them didn't get much ice time.

"I couldn't even imagine how tough that would be to have to sit on the bench the entire game and then just wait for that pat on the shoulder from the coach that would send them out to fight somebody. I felt bad for them at times, I really did. They were fighting for their lives many times, both literally and figuratively, because they knew that if they didn't do it that there was a chance that they were going to be sent down to the minors.

"The thing that always surprised me the most about those guys was the fact that they were the nicest, most down-to-earth guys, totally opposite of what you would suspect. They are the most fun to hang around with and unlike their on-ice persona, they are just sweet people. To them it was a job and they were just doing their job. Hey, everybody has a role in this sport and if they didn't do their job then I couldn't do mine, so it was a team effort and we all knew that.

"Those guys were so tough, I don't know how they did it. Just to see how beat up they were with stitches and broken noses and busted-up knuckles, it was amazing how they were able to do it as often as they did. I wouldn't have lasted five minutes as a fighter, no way. It's funny, sometimes people ask me if fights in hockey were really real, or if they were like in wrestling. And I would say, 'Hell yeah they were real; otherwise, I would have been in a lot more of them.'"

there is fight, early and often, to prove to his new bosses that he has the necessary "mean streak" that the team needs to win.

So, just how does an enforcer do his job without getting hurt? Well, injuries are inevitable, it just comes down to how manageable they are. Skill, training, preparation, studying, and plain old luck all factor into it. It is hard to imagine what it would feel like to be on the receiving end of a Marty McSorley uppercut, a Tony Twist jab, or a Tie Domi haymaker. They are bone-on-bone impacts that make your hair stand up just thinking about them. Broken bones, concussions, eye injuries, deep facial cuts, and lost teeth are all probable outcomes of a hockey fight.

Perhaps the biggest obstacle facing fighters, though, is the constant threat of breaking their hands and knuckles. You can pick an enforcer out of a police lineup from 25 feet away every time—he's the one with the hands that look like they've been through a meat grinder. Apparently, hitting a guy square in the nose, jaw, teeth, or forehead is not as gentle as it would appear in the movies. The bigger problem, however, is that when the two start swinging away at each other, most of their punches make contact with the other guy's helmet, as opposed to his face, tearing open fingers and knuckles. Those wounds never really get a chance to heal, either, because the men have to keep fighting every few nights or so.

Sometimes enforcers can't even carry their own bags or tie their own skate laces because their hands hurt them so badly. Detroit tough guy Joey Kocur had a half dozen operations on his hands over his career. Florida enforcer Paul Laus, who tallied nearly 40 fighting majors in the 1996–97 campaign alone, apparently had problems even picking up his kids on off days because his hands were so beat up. Buffalo's Rob Ray, meanwhile, had his orbital bone shattered in 1995 by Tony Twist, nearly costing him his eyesight.

"People see us fight and think nobody gets hurt," said Ray. "But the next day your hands are killing you, your shoulders are aching. Your head is pounding. I've been punched so hard I see stars and white dots. You may skate away from a fight and not be bleeding, but it's everything on the inside that takes the real beating."

Marty McSorley was the ultimate warrior and had the battle scars to prove it. In his never-ending quest to protect and to serve, Marty's allegiance to his teammates often meant sacrificing his body for the greater good. Among the ailments listed on his résumé are no less than eight

## Jeff Odgers on Injuries from Fighting

"I remember fighting Marty McSorley one time when I was with San Jose. We were going toe-to-toe and he just caught me square and really rung my bell. He sat me right on my ass and when I tried to get up, nothing happened. So the linesman came over to help me up and grabbed me by the seat of my pants. He asked me if I was all right and I said, 'Yup, just point me in the direction of my penalty box.' It was my home arena, but I was so out of it at that point that I seriously had no idea where I was going. I was seeing two of everybody. It was pretty scary. Luckily I had a while to gather myself in the box, but situations like that can be frightening. I later went and got checked out. Concussions are serious problems for NHL fighters and you didn't want to mess around with them."

surgeries, including two hernias, a separated shoulder, a bum hip, a bad elbow, a broken thumb, a messed-up abdomen, countless busted knuckles and fingers, and a host of calcium deposits and bone spurs that had to be ferreted out. In addition, McSorley has broken his jaw, torn ligaments in his wrists and hands, taken more stitches than he could ever count, lost several teeth, and was even once in a fight where he severely pinched a nerve in his neck to the point where he could not move his arm. Talk about bad timing. Needless to say, McSorley kept a lot of doctors fat and happy over his career.

The long-term health risks for NHL enforcers are many. It doesn't take a rocket scientist to figure out that taking repeated blows to the head is not good for you or for your brain. In January of 2002, researchers at the University of Pennsylvania conducted a study with mice suggesting that repeated blows to the head accelerated the onset of dementia and even Alzheimer's disease. No worries, that is a risk players are willing to take.

Concussions are probably the biggest concern for fighters. By definition they are a traumatic brain injury, and that cannot be taken lightly. And once players receive one, they are much more susceptible to suffering more of them each time they get hit. The concussions can get worse each time, too, eventually forcing players into early retirement. Otherwise, they face the risk of depression, an inability to focus, and worst of all, permanent brain damage. This is called post-concussion syndrome and among its most recent victims was Colorado Avalanche winger Adam Deadmarsh, a two-time U.S. Olympian who had to hang 'em up for good in 2003 after a storied 10-year pro career.

Deadmarsh sustained his first serious concussion while he was playing for the Los Angeles Kings in November of 2000 during a fight with Vancouver's Ed Jovanovski. The two had been jarring for position in front of the net and emotions finally boiled over when Deadmarsh slashed Jovanovski. The gloves came off, whereupon Jovanovski proceeded to nail Deadmarsh square in the face, knocking him out cold. Deadmarsh wound up on the shelf for over a month. He would go on to suffer two more severe concussions afterward, one from a collision with the glass in Toronto and the other from an accidental knee in the head from teammate Craig Johnson in practice. His doctors told him that he needed to consider the long-term ramifications, and he decided to leave professional hockey.

Said Deadmarsh at the time of his retirement:

> I think it's time that I kind of moved on and made a decision and faced the fact that my brain doesn't want to play hockey anymore. It's one of the most frustrating injuries I think you could possibly have from a sports aspect. Unless you have concussions it's kind of hard to explain to someone what it feels like, but you know it's something that's not supposed to be there. It's been the toughest decision I've had to make in my life, yet the easiest one. I say that because I'm retiring from a game I love to play and played all my life, but I think three years with symptoms from concussions is a good indicator that it would probably be a smart move to call it quits. I have a family to consider as well.

According to statistics from the league's Post-Concussion Syndrome Project, roughly 100 players a year are afflicted with the ailment. For safety, as well as liability reasons, players are now required to undergo a battery of neurological tests at the beginning of each season to make sure that they are healthy.

Toronto winger Nick Kypreos suffered a fate similar to Deadmarsh's in 1997 after his head hit the ice during a fight with New York Rangers tough guy Ryan VandenBussche in an exhibition game. Kypreos never fully recovered from the injury and ultimately retired from the game.

That same year Rangers defenseman Jeff Beukeboom suffered a devastating concussion that came as a result of a sucker punch from Los Angeles Kings enforcer Matt Johnson, who afterward received a

### Mike Peluso on Injuries from Fighting at Road Games

"It was always incentive not to get cut on the road during a fight, because you would get sewn up by the home team's doctor. Man, those guys would give you the shittiest stitch jobs you could ever imagine. You would go down between periods or something and get cleaned up, and they would put a Band-Aid over it. Well, when you got home and had your doctor look at it he would go, 'Who the hell did this?' They would put like three stitches into a cut that needed 15! The best thing about getting stitches on the road, though, was that your road-white uniform showed the blood real well. You looked really tough and your teammates loved that stuff. You wanted to hurry up and get your stitches and get back to the bench so you could show them off. Plus, it was kind of another unwritten rule of the code that you didn't have to fight again after getting fresh stitches. Otherwise, they would come out and you would have to sew them up all over again."

12-game suspension for intent to injure. Beukeboom returned to the ice after a few games off, but his rough style of play put him at high risk for more head injuries. The next season he suffered yet another concussion on a minor collision, which left him with migraine headaches, memory loss, nausea, and "mental fogginess." He was diagnosed with post-concussion syndrome and was forced to retire shortly thereafter. He suffered symptoms from the ailment for almost two years before finally recovering.

Another high-profile post-concussion syndrome case occurred in February 1998, when Chicago Blackhawks henchman Gary Suter brutally cross-checked Mighty Ducks All-Star Paul Kariya upside the head. Suter got just a four-game suspension, while Kariya missed the 1998 Olympics and the rest of the season. He returned eight months later, but some say the former 100-point scorer has not been the same player since the vicious hit.

Other recent NHL retirees with post-concussion syndrome include Geoff Courtnall, Michel Goulet, Stu Grimson, Pat LaFontaine, and Brett Lindros. Lindros' brother, Eric, has also suffered several concussions but has managed to keep it under control and currently plays with the Toronto Maple Leafs.

Legendary Philadelphia Flyers enforcer Dave Schultz responded to the discussion about concussions:

I don't want to be too critical of the National Hockey League, but I will say this. They do nothing to prevent concussions. I bet you one out of every 100 concussions is the result of an accident. If a guy falls or takes a knee to his head in a collision, that is an accident. The other 99, though, are total intent-to-injure hits by players running around. There is so much cheap-shotting and dirty play now I can't believe it. And the players are getting away with it. Back in our day if you ran a guy from behind you were going to get the shit beat out of you. Nowadays a guy will run a player's head into the boards and skate away with a penalty or maybe a fine or suspension. That's it. That is not right in my book. The only way a guy will learn never to do that type of thing is to get taught a lesson right there on the spot like a man in front of the whole world to see.

Someone with a great perspective on hockey injuries was the longtime Minnesota North Stars and USA Hockey team physician, Dr. George Nagobads. His job in the trenches was to get his soldiers back onto the battlefield as quickly as possible, while still providing them with the proper medical treatment. Sometimes that was a tall order, especially in the heat of battle. Nagobads told the following story:

I saw it all over my career, I really did. The thing that impressed me the most over my years was the 1980 U.S. Olympic "Miracle on Ice." I served as the team doctor for the team and don't think I ever saw more black and blue bodies in my life. The Americans were fearless in their desire to block shots, and they paid a price for it, too. I remember seeing Kenny Morrow after the game with the Soviets and I don't think he had a single part of his body that didn't have a bruise on it. That is desire and courage, it really is. I am from Latvia, so I spoke to a lot of the Soviet players after that game and they said that in all their years they had never seen anything like it. That was a big reason they went on to win the gold medal.

When I was with the North Stars I used to stitch guys up all the time; that was mostly what I did. It was mostly high sticks that did the damage. I got pretty quick at it because the guys always wanted to get back out there as soon as they could. In fact, a lot of times the injury would sort of numb itself and you wouldn't even need to use any Novocain on it. I was a former hockey player myself, so I knew how badly the guys wanted to get back out there. I would never let them go back if an injury was too bad, though, especially concussions. That could be very dangerous.

You know, in all of the fights that I saw and in all of the faces that I had to fix up afterward, I never really saw anything too bad, believe it or not. It might have looked bad, but they rarely were. The skates absorb a lot of the blows because their feet aren't planted on the ground like a boxer. They slide back and forth and that helps a lot I think. Sure, I would see a knocked-out tooth or a broken jaw or nose every now and then, but usually it was just stitches. Many times you could put butterflies on them and send them out if they weren't too bad; otherwise, you would just clean them up. It always amazed me just how tough those guys were, especially the fighters who might get stitches one period and then get them again the next.

I also served as the visiting-team doctor for all those years, too, which meant a lot of running around if there was a rough game with bench-clearing brawls. Sometimes it got interesting down in the training rooms in those days, let me tell you. I could tell right away in a game if I was going to be busy or not based on the number of penalties and fights that would go on. I would just head down to the training room and start to get my instruments ready when I saw that. I knew that I was going to be getting some customers pretty quickly.

# 9

## On Respect and Toughness

Certain players in the league are universally so well liked that they simply command respect. While all players covet it, along with the rewards and on-ice perks that come with it, respect is an earned commodity in the NHL and cannot be acquired by any other means. Certain players have "it," while others could never dream of getting "it." They are people such as Steve Yzerman, Cam Neely, Wayne Gretzky, Mark Messier, Mario Lemieux, and Jarome Iginla. Another is Joe Sakic, who exemplifies everything that is good about the game of hockey.

Said Marty McSorley:

> The best example of who I feel is an old-time player is Joe Sakic. Joe Sakic goes out and he plays. Period. He's not going to whack you or give you a cheap cross-check across the neck or ribs when the puck starts going the other way. He's not going to do something to goad you into a penalty either. He's just going to play the game. And he plays the game the right way at a very high level, too. That is why I have so much respect for a player like Joe Sakic. I mean, even as a tough guy, to play against Joe Sakic was a real pleasure. I never wanted to run him or do anything cheap to him because I respected him. Sure, I wanted to hit him and I wanted to hit him hard whenever he had the puck, because that was my job. Sure, I made it hard for him when he was in front of the net, too, but he elevated my game when I was out on the ice with him. The guy just has class. He conducts himself like a real professional and he works very hard. That is why his teammates play so hard for him. He earned their respect by being a great leader.

On the other side of the equation are the players who show no respect. With those players, disrespect is a dish best served cold. Rub an enforcer the wrong way by disrespecting him, and his memory is like that of an elephant. He won't forget. And if the code says he can't fight you, he will patiently wait for his moment to "get you." It might be an open-ice check or a scrum in the corner, but rest assured it will happen sooner than later. In the world of respect and disrespect one thing is for certain: what comes around goes around.

McSorley continued:

> Each guy is different and you have to assess every player and his actions when you are out on the ice. For instance, whenever I played against Peter Forsberg I knew that I was going to get slashed and whacked and chopped. As a result, I was much more inclined to return the favor to a guy like that. I didn't feel bad about that one bit either, because you knew that you were never going to drop the gloves and beat up a guy like Peter Forsberg. That is not an option with a player like that. But you did play guys like that even tighter because you knew what comes around goes around. Having said that, if I ever got my stick up on Joe Sakic during a game, I would literally go over and apologize to him out on the ice. That is just how strongly I felt about playing the game honest with guys who have earned that type of respect out there. I am not saying I would intentionally bring my stick up on Forsberg either, but if I did, I probably wouldn't apologize or feel as bad about it, as opposed to a guy like Joe Sakic.

### Paul Stewart on Toughness

"I remember being at a card show with Terry O'Reilly one time and having a guy come up to have Terry and me sign an old photo of the two of us in a fight together. He asked me who won the fight, and I told him that no real tough guy would ever claim to have beaten another tough guy. There is just too much respect there. And then I pointed at Terry and told that guy that if it weren't for him, I wouldn't even have a reputation. So, amongst the heavyweight elite, of which I think I deserve to consider myself a part because I did it for so long, and at every level, there was a certain honor to the fact that you had the willingness to engage guys like Terry O'Reilly in order to stand up for your teammates."

Toughness is also a state of mind. And like respect, a reputation of toughness is also earned. Tony Twist had something to say about toughness:

> Tough doesn't come in any one shape or size. Tie Domi was 5'10" and 190 pounds. For his size he was pretty damn tough, no question. But there is only so much you can do as a fighter when you are not that big. Tough isn't so much about wins or losses; it is about guys who know what their jobs are and they do them well. Guys who are truly tough go out and do their jobs day in and day out, regardless of how he feels or whether he wants to or not. Regardless of who he was playing or who he was going to have to face as an opponent, tough guys don't change their game plans. Guys who are truly tough don't get fazed by whether or not their adversaries are big, tall, little, or huge. They just go out and play their role. It wasn't about killing people, it was about doing your job the right way each and every game.
>
> I played against some tough guys in my day: guys like Joey Kocur, Larry Playfair, Clark Gillies, Bob Probert, and Dave Brown. But the toughest guy in my book was Kelly Chase. What made Chaser so tough was the fact that he took on all comers. He wasn't big enough to knock anybody out, but pound for pound he might have been the best ever. He went out and fought fearlessly, regardless of how big his opponent was. The guy was just deadly. He didn't win all of his fights, but he won enough to instill a pretty good fear into his opponents. I mean he was a middleweight player who, because he was so feared, could do things on the ice that most guys his size couldn't dream of. Other guys his size feared him and that gave him a lot of space to maneuver out there. He was very respected as a player and as a fighter. Between the two of us, man, we had it covered. He dominated the middleweights and I took care of the heavyweights. We were the most feared tandem around for several years.

Toughness isn't just about fighting, either. It is also about what the players call "getting dirty." Seventeen-year NHL veteran Neal Broten had the following to say about dirty work:

> You know, I don't want to take anything away from Gretzky by any means, because he was the greatest player in the world, but when it came to being protected, he was pretty pampered out on the ice. I mean, take a guy like Dino Ciccarelli, who scored over 600 goals over his career. Not that many of his goals were breakaways, and what I mean by that is he earned them by doing the dirty work out front. That guy took more abuse than any human I have ever seen, but he

would always come back for more. He made his living by the side of the net, and he was constantly being whacked across the arms, chopped behind his legs, cross-checked in the back, punched in the head, and drilled in the stomach. Nobody protected him that way, yet he was able to persevere and find success. You rarely ever saw that stuff happen to Gretzky, though, because if guys did that to him they were going to get killed by McSorley and Semenko. Plus, Wayne had earned a lot of respect in the league, too, where guys knew better than to run him. But as far as Dino went, I have a lot of respect for guys like that who could get dirty and score, but didn't necessarily need all of the protection.

## The Tough Guy Pecking Order

In the hierarchy that governs hockey enforcement, the rule is "to be the man, you've got to beat the man." The old grizzled veterans have earned the respect of their fellow brethren and don't have to fight as much as they did years ago. Players know that when they are out there, though, they need to behave; otherwise the vets will come off the bench and give them an ass whipping. For the young guns, however, it is all about showcasing their talents. They need to take people on and beat them in order to gain credibility in the league. And the only way to garner that credibility as an NHL enforcer is to beat guys higher up the ladder than you.

Fighters have a tremendous amount of respect for one another and take their jobs very seriously. The older, more experienced fighters won't just fight any young punk with an attitude that comes along. No way.

### Mike Peluso on the Top of the Pecking Order

"You know, fighters in hockey are kind of like the alpha males out in the wild. The toughest animals get to rule the roost and everybody else follows along in the pecking order. I will give you an example. One time when I was with Chicago and we were playing the North Stars a bunch of fights broke out on the ice at the same time. I was about to square off with Minnesota's tough guy, Basil McRae, and the ref came in and said to the linesmen, 'Just let these two go,' pointing to us. He knew that by letting the two heavyweights go, everybody else would stop and just watch. And sure enough, it worked. They let us fight and every other guy who was paired up just sat back, and then everything was fine. The order was restored and the game settled down. It cleaned the game up, too, with no more cheap stuff. That is how the code works, sort of like the law of the jungle."

## Reed Larson on the Pecking Order

"There is definitely a pecking order in professional hockey, and that is what the code is all about in my opinion. The guys at the top of the food chain were the fighters, and they kept the peace. They left the star players alone and went about their business, which really cleaned up the dirty stuff. They knew that those guys were the bread-and-butter players and that they needed to protect them in order to give their teams a chance of winning. Now, I wasn't a big fighter by any stretch. I was a middleweight who could hold his own, but I left the dirty work to guys like Joey Kocur and Bob Probert—guys who defined toughness in my book. I have never seen two guys more eager to fight than those two. They used to look at the opposing team's lineup like a menu that they could feast from. So I liked the fact that the game policed itself and that guys played tough and played with honor. Fighting was definitely an asset for some teams and certainly a big part of the game. Fighting kept everybody in line, just like when we were kids back in the neighborhood. Somebody had to confront the bully who was picking on the little guys and stick up for them, or it would be chaos. I just never wanted to see it get out of hand to the point where it destroyed the beauty of the game. The code sort of keeps it all in perspective, I think."

In fact, it is a privilege to be able to drop the gloves with a prize fighter like Marty McSorley, for instance. He probably won't just grant you that wish either. There is almost a job interview quality to the whole process, a wooing period, so to speak, where he will either agree to give that kid an opportunity or not. There is seemingly always debate about who among them deserves a title shot—especially during training camp. If someone like McSorley agrees to fight, then that can be a huge feather in the cap for that lucky kid.

It can be somewhat comical to watch the kids approach the veterans in those situations, like bashful awkward teenagers asking a hot girl out on a date. Some will ask very politely if they can please square off with them, while others may ask one of that enforcer's teammates, perhaps a friend of theirs on the opposing team, if he could help arrange for the blind date of sorts. If his wish is granted, he may thank him with a gracious smile or handshake. Afterward, he may even come out of his dressing room to request an autograph for the kids. Who knows, maybe he had that guy's poster up on his wall growing up. It's like meeting a rock star for many of them.

Each of those young guys had to battle his way through the junior ranks and then the minor leagues just to get there, and they want to make the most of their situation. As a fighter you are vying for perhaps one or maybe two job openings on a team, which is slim pickings. You know that if you don't make it you will be sent back down and will have to fight the same old slugs over and over again, until hopefully you get another chance that next training camp. After a few training camps, the young players know that their days are numbered, so they get desperate. Desperate players will do whatever it takes to win. That is when the adrenaline flows like ice water through their veins; and that is when they are most dangerous. They know very well that if they lose, all that awaits them is a bus back to Medicine Hat or Moose Jaw, or wherever it was they came from.

If a young gun makes it past training camp and gets a roster spot, he will be looking to mark his territory quickly. If he gets a chance to fight an established fighter, and holds his own against a guy such as McSorley, even earning a draw, then he will earn instant respect around the league. He is now legit, someone to be taken seriously. If he somehow beats McSorley, then his life will change overnight. First off, McSorley would demand a rematch, ensuring a lot of publicity and attention. The drama and story line would be followed by players and fans alike. Second, that young kid would be challenged by all other young kids on their way up the ladder. They figure that if that guy could beat McSorley, and they beat him, then their stock will have risen meteorically, too. It becomes a chain reaction. Such is the psychology of an NHL tough guy trying to earn his keep in the "show."

For a fighter like McSorley, it is a risky proposition to agree to fight the new kid on the block. If it comes during a game where there has to be retribution for a dirty play, then he would most likely fight anybody on the spot. But if it is more of an instance where the kid is just trying to make a name for himself, that can be tricky. A situation like that has the potential to backfire. If McSorley wins, well, he was supposed to beat the kid—no big deal. But if he loses to a kid who views that fight as a once-in-a-lifetime opportunity, he will now have to offer him a rematch and risk losing credibility by players around the league who may wonder if he is going soft or getting old. It is a situation prime for an upset, because it's a win-win for the kid, but a lose-lose for McSorley. He is supposed to win and won't get anything for doing so. But if he loses, he will have to reestablish himself.

### Tony Twist on Rookies Challenging the Pecking Order

"One of the biggest compliments that I got as an enforcer came from one of my adversaries, Edmonton tough guy Georges Laraque. It was his rookie season and we were playing them one night, and I knew that he would be coming at me in order to prove himself. Sure enough, we were out on the ice and he asked me in French if I wanted to fight. I knew that he was a young kid and that he needed an opportunity to show what he could do, so I said, 'Sure, when the puck drops I will fight you.' Well, we went at it and I got the best of him. We then got to talking in the penalty box and I asked him if he wanted to go again. He just looked at me and said, 'Probably not tonight, but thanks for giving me a shot.' I went and spoke to him after the game and found him to be a very nice guy, a real good kid.

"Anyway, a few days later he did an interview with our paper and talked about how I gave him a chance to showcase his talents, where most other enforcers wouldn't. They felt that they were above that for some reason, and he knew that his job was on the line. So, he said that he had a lot of respect for my code of ethics and that he wished more guys in our line of work were as decent as I was. That meant a lot to me. I gave him a shot, knowing that if a rookie beat me that it could hurt my reputation. But that was the right thing to do because I have been there in that position myself. When I was playing I had an open invitation to anybody, anywhere, anytime. My door was wide-open during training camp or during the regular season; I welcomed everybody. That is something that I am proud of because most guys weren't like that."

The cold hard reality of being an NHL enforcer is that someone younger, tougher, bigger, and faster is always gunning for you. The freshmen want to showcase their mettle for the scouts and establish a reputation in a hurry, and they will beg for the opportunity to do so. If it works out and they win, then there's a new sheriff in town. And along with all of the new-found respect that new sheriff will undoubtedly get, he may also get a fat new contract down the line. A player knows that he needs to get paid while he can, because as soon as he emerges as the new heavyweight champ, then there will be a dozen kids looking to knock him off. Every fighter will tell you that anybody can beat anybody on any given night in this league; it only takes one punch.

Longtime Buffalo enforcer Rob Ray concurred:

There are young guys gunning for you nonstop in this business, especially if you are a respected fighter, because then they all want a

New York Rangers defenseman and enforcer Marty McSorley (No. 55) delivers a message to Edmonton's David Oliver during a game in 2000. *Photo courtesy of Getty Images.*

Quebec's Tony Twist squares off against Montreal's Mario Roberge (No. 32) in a fight from which—like most—Twist came away the victor. *Photo courtesy of Getty Images.*

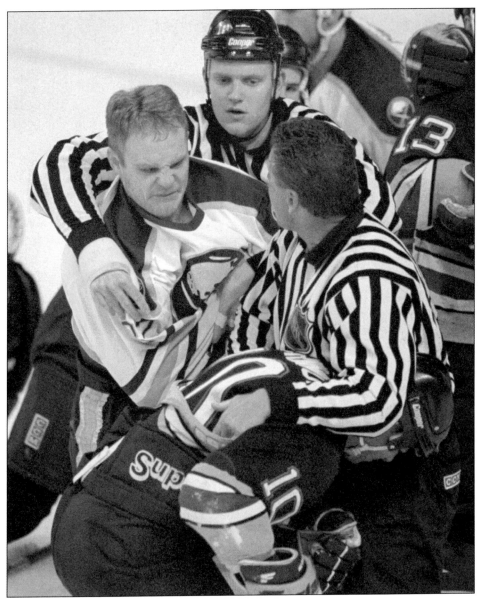

Two linesmen separate Buffalo's Rob Ray (left) and Hartford's Brad McCrimmon during a scrape on April 14, 1996, in Buffalo.

Detroit superstar Brett Hull, shown celebrating the 732$^{nd}$ goal of his career in 2003, is the prototypical superstar that the code is designed to protect.

Kelly Chase (right) of the Blues tussles with San Jose's Ronnie Stern in the third period of a 1999 game at the Kiel Center.

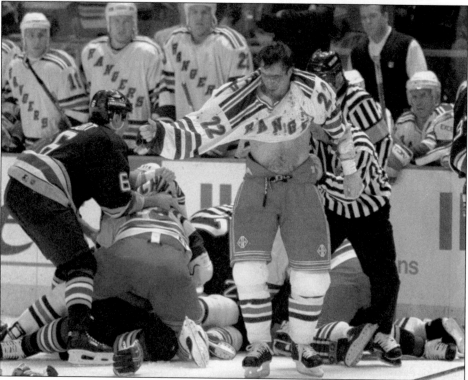

Basil McRae (above, left) and Shane Churla (below, right) were two of the more prominent enforcers of their era.

Andrei Nikolishin (top) comes to the aid of his Colorado Avalanche teammate Steve Moore (bottom) after Moore was hit from behind by Vancouver's Todd Bertuzzi (No. 44), who later delivered a tearful apology (inset) for the incident.

Tie Domi of the Maple Leafs looks determined to retaliate after suffering a bloody hit from Ottawa's Ricard Persson during a 2002 game.

shot. They know that if they beat you, then they will get respect and hopefully a better contract. During training camp it wasn't so bad, because the coaches laid down the rules and wanted to see how guys could play. The exhibition games, those were the worst. That is where the coaches let everybody go and it could be brutal. Guys are hungry at that point because they know that they are going to be sent back to the minors if they don't perform well, so they are very motivated to beat you.

Veteran fighters, for the most part, know that they are going to be tested by the young bucks each and every preseason. That is just the nature of the beast for the select few who make it to the pinnacle of their profession, earning the role of team enforcer. Those who have been there long enough understand and deal with it accordingly.

# 10

## Fear

Fear is arguably the most powerful emotion there is, and it can make grown men do things they never thought that they were capable of doing. It is just an unbelievable stimulus. The three biggest "fear factors" in hockey are the fear of getting hurt, the fear of being humiliated, and the fear of losing. As for the fear of getting hurt, there is a primal instinct of self-preservation in all of us that allows us to protect ourselves from pain. Fear pumps our adrenaline, and that helps us to survive, even giving us superhuman strength. The point is, nobody likes taking a beating, or getting a black eye, or breaking a nose, or losing a tooth. Yet those are all plausible daily occurrences for a hockey player. So how do they manage that fear? One word: *guts*.

Chutzpah is the Yiddish equivalent and it embodies ballsiness, brazen nerves, daringness, and plain old guts. It's all about mind over matter. Guys with chutzpah can take their fear and magically turn it into excitement and passion. They can fight someone bigger than them, even though they don't want to or may be terrified. They do it for any number of reasons, including helping their team win, impressing their coach, saving their job, or just saying to their bully "Enough is enough. I am not going to take it anymore!" Being afraid is a natural feeling that we can all relate to, starting from the time we were tiny babies. It's real and it's in everybody, regardless of how big and tough you are.

"I was afraid every time I did it," said legendary enforcer Stu Grimson of fighting. "I was afraid of being hit, but I was more afraid of being humiliated than anything. That was my greatest fear, and it was a very motivating factor. You're in a building with 18,000 people and everything stops, and the focus turns to you and your combatant. If you don't accomplish what you set out to do, it can be a huge blow to your ego and a letdown for your team."

One player's story of personal justice was particularly interesting, that of Eric Nesterenko, a Chicago Blackhawks center man who played pro hockey for 20 seasons during the 1950s and '60s. Nesterenko, whose story was chronicled in Lawrence Scanlan's 2002 book *Grace Under Fire: The State of Our Sweet and Savage Game*, described how the bullying and badgering he received early on in his career ultimately forced him to address his fear head-on and take a stand.

Hockey in that era was tough, and intimidation tactics were almost barbaric—especially for the new kids on the block. Nesterenko described one time being viciously speared by veteran Montreal winger Bert Olmstead. As he was down on his knees writhing in pain, Olmstead skated by and said with a smile, "Welcome to the league, kid." Another incident spoke of the time famed Detroit tough guy Ted Lindsay smacked Nesterenko in the mouth with his stick and knocked out several of his teeth. "Terrible Ted, too, found Nester's anguish amusing," said Scanlan.

Nesterenko went on to talk about how he knew that he would have to overcome his fear and retaliate or he'd keep getting his ass whipped and never get any respect from the older players. Scanlan wrote:

> Word of the beating got around the league, and next season every thug on every team ran him. A "Shark mentality," as Nesterenko called it. "One guy'd taken a bite outta me, they all wanted a bite." He had to re-establish what he called "his space," the respect for personal territory that all hockey players know about. It's why skating through the crease is seen as so offensive, so disrespectful. Nesterenko regained his space by issuing a threat to every young kid on opposing teams who eyed that space. "I know you're coming after me," Nester would tell them on the ice during stoppages in play, "and if you do, I'm going to hit you over the head as hard as I can with my stick."

Needless to say, Nesterenko finally got his space.

Nobody likes to be bullied, and that is one of the benefits of playing hockey. You stand up for yourself when you can, and when you can't, there's always somebody there for you who can. That's the code.

"It's like the playground," said former NHL enforcer–turned–NHL referee Paul Stewart of fear and fighting, to ESPN's John Buccigross. "There is something about bullies, something about people who try to intimidate. When I played, I was the guy who made sure my teammates were not feeling intimidated and they could go about their business. Fighting was my ticket to get to the NHL. There are players on a 20-man roster that don't feel necessarily courageous. They'll never admit that they are afraid, but when I played, it was like the parting of the Red Sea on the bench. There I was, and I was expected to go out and help those who were afraid play the game, to let no one take their lunch money."

Being afraid is a natural emotion we can all relate to. Having to worry about fighting the likes of Bob Probert and Joey Kocur, meanwhile, is something most humans could not even comprehend. According to Basil McRae, however, for him it was just business as usual:

> The time I hated the most during my career was the time between waking up from your 4:00 afternoon nap on game day, until you played your first shift that night. The nerves started in and you would want to just throw up. Knowing that you were probably going to have to fight a guy like Bob Probert or somebody like that in a few hours really weighed on you. You knew that if it was a playoff game, then that factored in; or if it was a meaningless game, then that factored in, too. You pretty much knew before the game even started what it was going to be like based on the situation going in.
>
> I remember one time when I was with Minnesota and Detroit came to town. During the pregame Joey Kocur, who was one of the toughest guys in the league, came up to me and said, "Hey, I am in the doghouse with my coach. I have to fight you tonight." I was like, no way, this guy could kill me. Well, lo and behold, I was put into a situation where I had to fight him. So we dropped the gloves and I ended up getting in a lucky punch that cut him and even gave him a black eye. At first I was all proud and happy, but then I looked at him and thought to myself, "Oh God, what have I done? Now he is really pissed!"
>
> Sure enough, we had to play them again two nights later in Detroit, where Joey was going to be waiting for me to get his revenge. I can honestly say I did not sleep one single second in those 48 hours. I was so nervous. I saw him smile at me in warm-ups and I knew that I was dead meat, like the bully on the schoolyard taunting you. I remember telling the other two left wingers on my team that as soon as they were out on the ice with Kocur, to please come off as quickly

## Kelly Chase on Fear

"I think that being a hockey enforcer is the toughest job in all of sports. It is an uncomfortable feeling to have to do it, but that is what separated us from the other guys. Guys might say that they didn't mind it or that they didn't get nervous or scared, but they were lying. Just think back to that one time when you were a little kid and the school bully wanted to beat you up in front of everybody. Remember how terrible that felt: the fear of getting punched in the face, the fear of being considered a pussy in front of all of your friends, and the fear of not knowing if and when the conflict was going to ever stop and go away. Were you somebody who was going to give that kid your lunch money every day and just take it? Or were you somebody who was going to suck it up and fight back? Scared? Welcome to our world."

as they could so I could get out there and just get it over with. It was awful. I finally got out there and just hung on for dear life. It felt good to finally get some sleep that night, that was for sure.

I was a decent fighter, but certainly didn't win 'em all. I won more than I lost, and I always put on a good show. I wasn't the biggest guy either, so sometimes I was at a disadvantage being a heavyweight. At 210 pounds I was more of a light-heavyweight, but I never backed down from anybody. I wasn't in the same league as the Proberts and Kocurs and Twists—those guys were just animals. I didn't have the body for it nor the mentality.

Later, I wound up playing in Detroit when they had Probert and Kocur. People just figured that I loved it there because I didn't ever have to fight with those two around. In actuality, it was the worst situation in the world for me because whenever something got stirred up, all of the opposing enforcers would just race to me instead of having to square off with those two animals.

Probert was the heavyweight champ back in those days, and everybody was scared of him. He was so intimidating, not only to his opposition but even to his teammates. I remember once before a game with Chicago he came up to me and told me that he didn't want me to fight Al Secord that night. He said that he had a score to settle with him and under no circumstances did he want me to mess it up. I looked at him and just told him I would try not to, but that if he started something with me that I was going to have to answer the bell. Probert just looked at me and said, "If you fight Secord tonight, you are fighting me tomorrow in practice," and he just walked away. I was like, holy shit, this guy is seriously crazy.

I eventually got traded away and later had to fight Probert. I was scared as hell, so I asked my teammate Kelly Chase how I should handle him. Chaser had fought him with pretty good success and thought that he had it all figured out. He said, "Just keep punching until he comes out of his equipment." Probie had this tear-away jersey and tiny little elbow and shoulder pads, and he would just basically take them off while you were fighting so that you couldn't grab on to him. It was a great advantage because with nothing to grab on to, he would kill people. Anyway, that was his strategy, to keep punching and then skate away as soon as he comes out of his stuff.

### Mike Peluso on Fear

"I couldn't sleep the night before big games where I knew that I was going to be getting into a fight. It could be really stressful. The most anxiety I had was always going into Detroit, where I knew I would have to deal with Joey Kocur and Bob Probert. Those guys were so tough. Every team in the Norris Division had tough guys when I was with Chicago. Minnesota had Basil McRae and Shane Churla, and St. Louis had Tony Twist and Kelly Chase. So you knew who you were going to be dropping the gloves with before you even got there, and that could weigh on you.

"Even though Probert and Kocur were tough, nobody was tougher than Tony Twist. We fought each other in the minors, too. He was just so powerful. We became good friends, though, and really respected each other. It was bizarre, having to fight each other all the time, but we knew it was just business. He knocked me out cold one time up in Quebec when he was playing with the Nordiques.

"We were up 3–0 and he had to try to do something to swing the momentum, so he asked me if I wanted to go. He was an honest guy and always asked first, so I respected that a lot about him. We were on a faceoff and I said sure, so we dropped the gloves. I got off to a pretty good start, and he just caught me with one that turned the lights out. I remember afterward showering and putting my suit on in the locker room, and then taking it off and showering again. I guess I did that three or four times. I mean I was really out of it. I remember just as they were about to take me to the hospital I asked one of my teammates, Bernie Nicholls, how the game turned out. He said, 'We won. You got the tying goal, and I got the game winner. Congrats, buddy!' Well, I wound up staying overnight at the hospital and remember waking up that next morning looking at the paper. The headlines read 'Nordiques Beat Devils, 7–4.' I just started laughing. I thought to myself, 'I am going to kick Bernie's ass when I get back to Jersey!' Needless to say, I finally got a good night's sleep for once during the season."

So that is exactly what I did, and as soon as he got his jersey off I started skating backward and got the hell out of there. Well, he was so pissed that I backed off that he started threatening to really beat my ass. I am now thinking, "Great, now I am going to have Bob Probert stalking me, I am never going to sleep again." I remember one of my assistant coaches asking me jokingly right afterward if I could switch over to play defense, because he had never seen anybody skate backward so fast! Anyway, I went back to Chaser and said, "That's great you gave me Plan A. Now what am I going to do? He is really pissed. What's Plan B?" Chaser just looked at me and laughed.

It's safe to say that even the toughest guys in professional hockey get a little scared from time to time, especially when they know they are going to have to drop the gloves with a guy like Bob Probert. There just isn't a strategy that will work on a guy like that, and the players know it. That is why he and others like him are so feared.

# 11

# Friendly Fire

One of the most bizarre aspects of the code is the fact that in hockey you may have to fight anybody, anywhere, anytime. This can even mean throwing down with your best friend, or having to drop your gloves with an old childhood pal, or an old line mate who was traded away. With free agency, players move from team to team these days with great frequency, which means that good friends often become adversaries.

Situations like these may seem barbaric, but such is the life of a pro hockey player who abides by the rules of the code. It's not personal, either; it never is. It is all business, and the players know that. Both have a job to do and that is the bottom line. And when it's over, it's over. Heck, sometimes fighters who are buddies will be joking around with each other while they are swinging away. It's pretty surreal, but that is how life is sometimes when you are an NHL enforcer.

"I remember one time spending about a half hour before a game talking to my friend Kelly Chase about bow hunting," said 12-year NHL enforcer Jeff Odgers. "Then, later that night our teams played and we wound up having to fight each other. It wasn't personal, we were just doing our jobs. Well, after the game we got together again and just picked up our conversation right where we left off about bow hunting for deer up in Canada. It was like nothing had even happened. People can't fathom how we were able to do that, but that was just how it was sometimes."

## Marty McSorley on Fighting Friends

"I knew most of the guys I was fighting, but for me it was never hard to face them. That was my job. Again, it was all about honesty and respect. I remember having to square off against Kenny Baumgartner, who was a former teammate and friend. He got traded, and we had to go one time. We both had a job to do, and we did our jobs; that is hockey. We both made a good living doing what we did, and it wasn't personal. We each wanted to win and spark our team. That was the bottom line. Whatever happened out there, happened. As long as we fought with honesty and respect for one another, then it was all right. I mean, boxers go out and try their hardest to win and beat their opponents, but they understand that they each have a job to do. They want their opponents to fight fairly and treat them with the same respect in the ring as well. Other guys like Probie and Larry Playfair, they did it the right way, too. I had a lot of respect for those guys. I consider them to be friends of mine, and we enjoy the challenge of battling each other like warriors. It wasn't personal. Heck, I enjoyed seeing them out on the ice. It was a pleasure to play against guys like that. They played the game the right way, with respect."

Fighters each have their own methods of trying to make those awkward situations a little easier to deal with.

"It's always an interesting situation," said 6'6" Atlanta enforcer Andy Sutton to ESPN. "I've had a couple of fights with friends that I've played with on other teams. You look over in the penalty box and the guy gives you a little wink because he knows you've done your job. Any friend who's a real good friend would probably understand at the end of the game when you're out for a beer, or a pop."

Tony Twist looks at fighting friends in much the same way:

It was never personal. That is the truth. In fact, several of my greatest fights of all time came against some of my best friends in the game, including my partner in crime, Kelly Chase. We fought when he was playing in Hartford one time and that was a lot of fun. We are the best of friends, but that is just how it goes down in this business.

Hey, I even fought Kerry Clark, who was the best man at my wedding, five different times. How's that for not personal? The first two came when we were roommates in junior hockey. The first few were more wrestling matches than anything else, but by the fourth they got heated. I remember the fourth one, in Peoria, and I just beat the shit out of him. I wound up on top of him, and he said, "Loser buys pizza!" and I said, "Looks like you're buying then," to which he

## Rob Ray on Fighting Friends

"My best friend in hockey, Matthew Barnaby, I fought him three different times. We even went into business after I retired, and we own a construction company together up here in Buffalo. Once I knocked four of his teeth out. I will never forget it. He had been traded away to Pittsburgh, and during a game one time he was just running his mouth and wouldn't stop yapping at our coach, Lindy Ruff. I was just praying in the back of my mind that he would shut up before anything happened, but he didn't. So, sure enough, Lindy had finally had enough and he sent me out there after him. Hey, you can't disobey your coach in those situations, so I had to go out and fight him. I was actually really pissed at Barney because he knew that if he kept running his mouth the way he was that something was eventually going to have to happen. He just laughed about it afterward, but I thought his wife was going to kill the both of us."

responded, "Yeah, but winner buys beer, asshole!" We laughed about that one for a long time.

Another buddy of mine was Jimmy McKenzie. Jimmy Mac and I fought at least a half dozen times and I just loved that guy. We would chase each other around the ice and then try to beat the hell out of each other. Then we would go to the penalty box and look at each other and just smile.

Then there was the time I fought Rob Ray. "Razor" came out and looked at me on the ice and said, "You don't want to really go with me, do you?" And I said, "You're kidding me, right?" So we dropped the gloves and went at it pretty good. Well, I wound up landing a punch that just shattered his orbital bone on his face. So we go to the penalty box and he looks at me, and he is just a mess, and he says, "So does this mean I can't ride in your celebrity motorcycle event?" And I said, "F*ck no, of course you can ride with me!" He just smiled and said, "It doesn't look good, does it?" And I tried not to laugh and said back, "No buddy, I think you're going to need to get to the hospital pretty quick for that one." He just smiled and that was that. It wasn't personal, just business.

There was one fight with a friend that I felt bad about, though. It was when I was with Quebec and we were playing New Jersey one time, and I got into a pretty good fight with Mike Peluso. Well, I wound up knocking him out cold and went to visit him in the locker room afterward. I said to him, "Mikey, man I am so sorry." He said, "Tony, no problem, every gunslinger has their day." I found that to be pretty profound. That just shows you how guys in our line of work see things. It wasn't personal, it was a job. Mike was a great guy and I felt bad about catching him like that, but that is how it goes. He was trying to knock me out, too, and I just got the better of him that night. You just never knew in this business what was going to happen. It was truly an adventure.

Sometimes it works the other way around—you fight a guy and then you become friends, which is what Mike Peluso told a story about:

Randy McKay and I had fought each other over a dozen times in the NHL before becoming line mates together in the mid-'90s with New Jersey. We wound up becoming great friends. He and I along with Bobby Holik made up the "Crash Line," which is considered by many to be one of the best fourth lines that ever played. We scored a bunch of points, were way up on the plus/minus, and we racked up a ton of penalty minutes, too. That was a great time playing with those guys.

Another situation similar to that happened with Montreal enforcer Lyle Odelein, who I was arch rivals with when I was with Ottawa. I just absolutely hated the guy. Well, he got traded to New Jersey when I was there, and I was just pissed. I remember being down in the equipment room early in the morning one day in training camp, and I saw him there. I didn't say anything to him and just went about my business. Then, our coach came in and looked at both of us and said, "I know you two don't need an introduction..." So I shook his hand and we started talking. Wouldn't you know it but we became best friends and roommates. It was weird. He eventually got traded

### Shane Churla on Fighting Friends

"The hardest situation like that I ever had to deal with was with Basil McRae. He and I were great friends and partners in crime for a lot of years up in Minnesota. I knew down the line, and you always know in this business, that those are your hardest friendships. You just knew that one day down the line you might be looking at each other nose to nose. Sure enough, Baz got traded to St. Louis and his new coach, Mike Keenan, played off our friendship, which was a really shitty thing to do. He sent him out there to confront me after some other players had gotten chippy, and we had to drop the gloves. It sucked, but it wasn't personal, just business. We both knew that and understood that the day we both feared had come true. You just roll with it and move on. That is all you can do. We have still never really talked about it, believe it or not. But we remain the best of friends, and it never hurt our friendship in the least. Our families are close even to this day, too."

away, and I remember talking to him when he was moving out, and he just said, "Peloos, I will never fight you again, man." I agreed, and we never did. We played against each other after that, too, but we just paired up with other people. We were just too close after that. We still finished our checks and hit each other, but nothing serious. We are still great friends even to this day.

Even Claude Lemieux, who most guys detested and thought of as one of the worst shit-disturbing assholes in hockey, wound up being traded to New Jersey when I was there, and we all just fell in love with him. What a great guy. I hated playing against him, but he was the best teammate ever. We became pals, too. Sometimes that is how it goes in hockey. You just never know.

No one is immune from the code of honor, not even brothers. Some legendary brother combinations have played in the NHL over the years: names like Hull, Sutter, Patrick, Richard, Esposito, Niedermayer, Hunter, and Stastny, to name a few. But when push comes to shove, anybody is fair game in pro hockey. That's right, there have even been a few high-profile sibling rivalries over the years in the NHL. Lionel and Charlie Conacher fought each other during a game back in the 1930s. Bill and Bob Plager hold the distinction of recording the first-ever fight in Minnesota North Stars history when they fought during a game with the St. Louis Blues in 1967. Bob also got into a scrap later with their other brother, Barclay, when they were both playing for the Blues back in the 1960s.

The most notorious brother bash of all time, however, was probably between the Primeau boys in 1997. Keith was with Hartford and Wayne was with Buffalo when it happened, and, boy, was mom pissed. Keith wound up getting into a scrum with Hartford's goaltender in the crease. This, of course, is a no-no, and Wayne stepped in to escort him out of there. One shove led to another and before they knew it, they had dropped the gloves. After a few punches, the fight was broken up. While both felt awful about it, they each had to show that they were committed to their teammates, no matter what.

And one can only imagine how many scraps the Sutter brothers got into over the years. It is amazing to think that all six made it to the NHL. Talk about sibling rivalry—oh, brother!

# 12

## Life Off the Ice

The amazing thing about hockey fighters is the fact that they are without question the nicest, friendliest guys off the ice, completely blowing the public perception that they are wild, untamed beasts walking among us. In fact, when young players first get into the league they are typically surprised as to just how sweet most of these guys really are. They are often their team's biggest practical jokers and pranksters, too. Gags such as taping a guy's skate blades before he hits the ice, switching guys' dentures around, cutting the skate laces of guys who always arrive late to practice, clipping rookies' ties with scissors, and nailing rookies' shoes to the floor by their lockers are always good fodder for these fellas. One would imagine that comedy probably helps ease their stress and anxiety.

"I think fighters in hockey are the nicest guys because we weren't the guys who were spoiled all the way up through the ranks," said longtime Buffalo enforcer Rob Ray. "We were the ones that had to work for everything we got. Things weren't handed to us. We had to go out every night and prove ourselves."

It is no wonder why enforcers are typically among the most popular players on their teams. The sacrifices they make don't go unnoticed by the fans. What many don't know about these people is that for the most part, they are also extremely caring and giving people outside of hockey. Many are extremely philanthropic and lead completely different lives both personally as well as professionally off the ice. In fact, did you know that in his spare time, Flyers tough guy Donald Brashear plays the piano and

## Rob Ray on Stress

"The stress of the job was unbelievable. I mean, every time we played Toronto, for instance, I knew that Tie Domi and I were going to have to get into a fight. Every time, no matter what. I think we fought 23 times over our careers. That is just insane. Do you have any idea what that is like, to carry that stress into every game, knowing that you have to get into a fight with a guy like that? It was awful. I mean to sit there on the end of the bench for maybe two full periods without getting a single shift and then finally getting thrown out there cold, it was tough. Just thinking about it was torture. My stomach would just roll and my mind would go in a thousand different directions. How do you even focus on the game in that situation? It was almost surreal. It really sucked. You just wanted to get out there and get it over with. No words were said or anything; you just went out and did your job.

"Tie and I had a mutual level of respect for each other. We both came from similar backgrounds and came up through the ranks together. I see him around now and we will have a beer and shoot the shit like nothing ever happened. We would tell war stories and just laugh. It is funny how stuff like that goes in this line of work. It was never personal. You know, I was always a little bit jealous of him, though, in that he got himself into a great situation in Toronto. He was one of the few lucky ones in our line of work. They gave him the opportunity to play there, and he has the best of both worlds. To see a guy like that take a regular shift while you were sitting on the bench all game was tough, it really was."

visits children's orphanages? Or that Kenny "the Bomber" Baumgartner attended the Harvard School of Business after he retired from hockey? Or that Stu Grimson, a born-again Christian, went on to law school at the University of Memphis? So did former enforcer Jim Korn, who is now a patent attorney in Minneapolis. While certainly not every enforcer is a teddy bear outside of the rink, many embrace their on-ice roles as just that—roles.

It takes a pretty special person to be able to put his own body on the line, night after night, for his teammates. And that is exactly what enforcers do. That is why they are so valuable to teams and why they are usually so beloved by their teammates. It must be difficult to live that "Jekyll and Hyde" lifestyle, in which your occupation is so drastically different from your real-life persona, though. It can be tough on them after a while, and many feel overwhelming guilt because of the emotional strain it puts on not only them but also their families. Sure, they make a lot of money doing what they do, but to be able to muster up all of that rage in the heat of the moment, for so long, certainly takes its toll. Many eventually suffer from burnout, as well as anxiety and sleep disorders from the stress of it all.

It can be difficult for enforcers to turn their feelings on and off. The anxiety of knowing they may have to fight a guy on any given evening can lead to some sleepless nights. That stress and worrying can spill over into their personal lives, infecting their marriages and family time. The sleepless nights spent before games are the worst and can best be described like this: It's 2:00 in the afternoon and they know that at 3:00, when the bell rings, they are going to have to fight the school bully in front of the entire student body. If they don't show up or if they get beaten badly, they will be humiliated. How's that for stress? It can be all-consuming and even toxic. Many throw up before every game, as a sort of sick ritual to deal with their anxiety.

Marty McSorley said the following about being able to turn it on and off:

> It could be hard at times, no question. Sometimes I would go out with the guys after our games and have a couple of drinks to settle down a little bit. It was hard to go from being that pumped up to being relaxed and ready to go to bed, though. That can be a rough transition. Playing on back-to-back nights was hardest because you could never really get a good night's sleep. There were many nights that I couldn't fall asleep and wound up watching TV all night or picking up a book at 3:00 in the morning. The game was still going on in your mind, especially if you had a tough fight that you didn't do well in. Or you might be thinking about the next game and who you were probably going to have to fight that night. It was a lot of stress to deal with, absolutely.
>
> And it wasn't just worrying about not doing well in a fight, either. That is just one small facet of my game. I took it just as hard if I was on the ice for a bad goal and had a bad plus/minus for the game, too.

### Paul Holmgren on Bringing the Game Home

"I would like to believe that I never brought the game home with me, but in hindsight it was probably very difficult not to. I mean, if your team was not playing well, everybody knew. Even your kids hear about it in school from the other kids who all wanted to know, 'What's wrong with the Flyers?' So, it was inevitable, I suppose."

## Tony Twist on His Off-Ice Personality

"My off-ice persona was totally different from my on-ice one. I never wanted to [be] thought of as an animal, so I made sure not to present myself that way when I wasn't in my uniform. On the ice I was a killer, but off the ice I was 'charitable Tony Twist.' I was never an aggressive person outside of hockey, which was hard for people to believe sometimes. They think that because you beat people up for a living on the ice that you did the same off of it, but it couldn't be further from the truth. In fact, I was so tired on my off days that the last thing I ever wanted to do was get into a scrap with somebody.

"It was never hard for me to come home and just turn it off. Never. I left everything on the ice. My family time was precious and I never wanted to [infringe] on that. But, if I didn't do very well in a fight and maybe didn't destroy someone the way I thought I should have, then I would be pissed about it. And if we were going to play that team again down the line, you couldn't even talk to me before that game. I was so focused on beating the hell out of whoever it was that I knew I was going to have to fight that night, that I was just in my own little world."

You are constantly thinking, "What if?" and replaying plays in your head over and over, wondering what you could have done better. I am a competitor and I hated to lose in anything I did, and that negativity can stay with you. It is hard to just turn it on and turn it off; it doesn't work that way. For me, as opposed to a lot of other guys, not being married for my entire career really helped a lot. I never had to worry about my wife or my kids and all of those family issues. I didn't have any distractions in that regard, and that really helped me to focus on doing my job.

For most fighters, their home is their sanctuary. It is time they can enjoy with their kids and time not spent having to worry about which enforcer was coming to town the next night. They can ice their hands, get a good meal, and relax. Rest is a huge component of success for enforcers. They need to be able to shut down and recharge their batteries in order to be effective. While most of the veterans have learned to manage their stress, others struggle with it on a daily basis. Drugs, alcohol, and pain killers, for all of their injuries, can often compound their problems and lead them to spiral out of control if not dealt with appropriately.

Another issue enforcers constantly have to face is how their kids feel about what they do for a living. It can be very upsetting and confusing to them. This varies for each player, based on how old his kids are. Obviously, it gets trickier and trickier as the kids get older and wiser. It gets tougher to explain why their daddy beats up other daddies, why other daddies want to beat up their daddy, why he comes home with big cuts on his face, or why his wrist is broken. Kids watch games on TV and then ask lots of questions. It can be a lot to deal with, that is for sure.

Many of the players find that the best way to deal with those issues is to face them head-on and explain to their children that this is what Dad does for a living. It then becomes a case of "do as dad says, not as dad does," because pretty soon little boys want to be just like dear old dad. The men explain to their kids that the blood and broken bones are all real from the games they play, but that violence should never be a part of their games as kids. It is about setting limits and explaining what is acceptable, both in youth sports as well as in life. It is a slippery slope to be sure.

Longtime enforcer Jack Carlson weighed in on explaining the violence in hockey to kids:

> For the past several years I have been taking my young daughter to Minnesota Wild games. I would get stopped a lot at the arena by old North Stars fans who would come up to me and tell me how much they enjoyed watching me hammer this guy or break that other guy's nose. Meanwhile, my daughter would just look at me like I was some sort of monster. She finally asked me, "Dad, did you really do those things?" I mean, how do you explain that to your little girl? That was tough, really tough. I just tried to tell her that what I did out on the ice was to protect my teammates who couldn't protect themselves, and that it was my job. Stuff like that was definitely rough to deal with sometimes.

## Shane Churla on Turning It Off

"You know, I was a totally different person when I left the rink. My mind-set was to completely shut it off as best I could when I went home. It is funny how people perceive you, though, in this business, because of what you do on the ice for a living. I am sure they all thought I went home and beat my wife, locked my kids in the closet, and kicked my dog. As for my kids, it was tough sometimes to come home and turn it off completely, especially if you had a bad game or if you were stressed out about an upcoming game where you know that you were going to have to get into a fight. I am sure they got scared every now and then when I would come home with a black eye or with stitches, but you just tried to explain it to them as best you could."

## Kelly Chase on Turning It Off

"I was an emotional player and could easily be persuaded to drop the gloves. I was sometimes too emotional for my own good. I never left it at the rink. I took it home with me every night. If I played great, then it was a happy atmosphere; if it was a bad one, then I was miserable. My wife will tell you that there were many long, quiet nights at our house when we lost or if I lost a fight. In order for me to be able to do what I did for a living, I had to think hockey 24/7, and if I didn't I almost couldn't function. It was all I did; it was my life. I dove in and immersed myself into it. I couldn't just do it part way. It was full throttle all the time. That was my personality."

Mike Peluso said that he found advantages to being single during his playing days:

> I was lucky, I was never married while I was playing. I don't know how guys with kids could do this, though. It would be really tough to beat people up and then have to come home and put your kids to bed. I give those guys a lot of credit. Each guy has his own way of dealing with what we did for a living. In fact, I think a lot of GMs back in the day saw it as an advantage for a tough guy to be single. They wanted guys who didn't have to worry about other things like a wife and kids. They wanted you to focus on what you had to do and that was it. That was your career and they wanted you thinking about it 24/7. I remember one time I went up to Stu Grimson, who is a born-again Christian, and I asked him how he could go out and beat the shit out of people for a living. He just looked at me and smiled and said, "The Lord knows that this is just my job." I got a real kick out of that one.

Amazingly, enforcers would often get challenged at bars by drunk idiots who wanted to "see how tough they really were." Needless to say, most players were quick to defuse those situations by either walking away or buying the guy a beer. They didn't need the headache or the pending lawsuit. But some of the fans just had to find out the hard way that these guys weren't professional wrestlers. They were the real deal.

Peluso explained what happens when people meet enforcers:

> People are always fascinated to learn that NHL tough guys are the nicest, sweetest people around. They think we are all monsters until they meet us, and then they are just floored. It's true, out on the ice we were different people, but off of it we just wanted to chill. I think it is because we are selfless people who stick up for others;

that is our makeup. When people find out you were an enforcer, though, they always want to ask you a million questions. Sometimes it can be fun, but other times it drives you crazy. I am a pretty avid golfer now that I am retired, and I go out a lot as a single, where I am paired up with three other guys to make a foursome. Well, sometimes I just don't want to tell stories about beating people up. I just want to relax and golf. So I lie and tell them that I am a sexual marriage relationship counselor. Once they hear that they just shut up and play golf. It's hilarious!

## For Many, Fighting Is Just a Job

For many enforcers, fighting is just a job. And like any job, sometimes you just don't want to be there. We can certainly all relate to that. But could you imagine doing what these guys do day in and day out? It's no wonder that every now and then some of them feel like taking a breather. Well, for some tough guys, taking a night off might be worse than getting a pink slip reprimand—it might mean getting blackballed. That's right. Sometimes, if an enforcer disobeys his coach's wishes to stir it up, then he may have to face the consequences. Of course no coach would admit, publicly anyway, that he ordered his guy to fight, but as fans we all know better. That subtle look or wink or tap on the shoulder is all the information an enforcer needs to know what his coach wants him to do. In many regards, disobeying your coach can be tantamount to breaking the code.

Sadly, more than a few tough guys over the years have been banished to the minor leagues for refusing to fight. For some, the pressure of it all may finally get to them and they may snap. For others, they may have a moral epiphany and decide that premeditated aggression is against their own moral compass. Raw emotion, intensity, passion, and even intimidation or retribution are all grounds for dropping the gloves, but sometimes jumping over the boards to take a guy out just because the coach wants you to is too much to take. If a player feels like he is the coach's puppet, a robot, a tool of destruction, then he has every right to question his reasoning for being there.

One of the most notorious cases of this happened back in January of 1982, when a 23-year-old enforcer for the Los Angeles Kings by the name of Paul Mulvey refused Kings coach Don Perry's order to leave the bench and join in on a fight. Mulvey apparently declined and was subsequently held out of games and practices as punishment. He was then placed on waivers and ultimately banished to the minors. Mulvey later filed a $20

## Shane Churla on the Enforcer's Job

"Growing up I was a skill player, believe it or not, but coming into my first training camp it didn't take me very long to figure out I wasn't going to cut it that way. I figured it out pretty early on that I wasn't going to be on the power play, so I had to go to Plan B. But that is the beauty of hockey: there is a role for everybody, and there was a place for me as an enforcer. My job was to protect my players, play physical, and try to get the other guys off their games. I needed to make it as comfortable as possible for my skill guys to do what they did best. When that happened, then we had a whole lot better chance of winning.

"You know, there is a joke in our line of work that goes something like 'Once they find out that you're really good at fighting, they'll want you to do it all the time and they will even cut your pay in half, too.' What a bargain! But, hey, I was happy to have a job in the National Hockey League and to be a part of some great teams. It was a thankless job and certainly something that wasn't easy to do, but your reward came from the respect you earned from your teammates. Going to war every night was tough, so you had to be strong both mentally and physically."

million lawsuit against the NHL, charging that he was blackballed. The suit was settled out of court, but Mulvey never played another game in the league.

Most players, however, go about their business and make the best of it. After all, at this level guys are making some pretty good coin. And, let's face it, being an enforcer is a voluntary position—you can leave or quit any time you feel like it. Nobody is going to force you to be there and fight for a cause you don't believe in. In the end, it isn't "just a job," it's a career in the league that everyone dreamed about being a part of as a kid. Sometimes being a fighter is like being an offensive lineman in football. It's not the sexiest position on the field—you don't get to score touchdowns and get all the glory—but you have a role on the team and without you, the team would fail. Being a fighter is an important role, and it is one very few people can do effectively. Still, many players just take it day by day and don't get too philosophical about it.

"I'm just happy to get to the next function," said longtime minor league enforcer Doug Doull to ESPN. "I look at the next skate, the next practice, the next pregame warm-up, the next game. That's it. I'm not looking very far ahead. And as for the job, hey, it is what it is. I think of myself as being part of a company, and being a company guy."

It is safe to say that while the vast majority of enforcers are proud of what they do and wholeheartedly embrace their roles on their teams, they all dream of being goal scorers. I mean nobody starts out in this game dreaming of growing up to be a tough guy. As kids, we all loved to just play the game, and we all imagined ourselves hoisting the Stanley Cup for a victory lap around the arena. Who didn't dream of scoring the game-winning overtime goal of Game 7 to win it all?

In one sense it is sad to see how enforcers are used, almost like robots that can be turned on and off and ordered off the bench to pummel the opposition. Sure, enforcers relish their time in the limelight and they are grateful for the opportunity to protect and to serve their teammates. But I am sure that the little boy in all of them wishes that he could take a regular shift with the first line and light the lamp as often as he swings his fists. It takes a special person to come off the bench and fight another behemoth in an effort to get justice for another teammate who he may or may not even like or respect. Talk about selflessness. That is why enforcers are the ultimate team players.

"It's hard for a hockey player to get it through his head that scoring doesn't matter," wrote enforcer Dave Semenko in his autobiography, *Looking Out for Number One*. "Deep down, you want to be a player, to make the big play or score the big goal." Semenko then spoke of his bitter feelings toward Maple Leafs coach John Brophy, whom he briefly played for late in his career. "Brophy expected me to be this atomic bomb, sitting on the bench, ready to explode when he pushed the button."

Being an enforcer is one of the toughest jobs around, so if a fighter can battle through all of the injuries and persevere, he knows that he is in some pretty rare company.

Said McSorley:

> Sometimes you go on the road and you play four games in five nights, in some tough buildings, and you wind up getting into four, five, six, even seven fights. That is a ton, and it takes a huge toll on your body. If you last as a tough guy for eight, nine, ten, eleven years in this league, you have done pretty well. You know that you have won more than you have lost if that is the case because otherwise you wouldn't have been around that long. This job takes a lot of life out of you. I have a lot of respect for those guys; they are the true warriors. A lot of

young kids will come up and have success early on, but most of them can't make it over the long haul. The mental and physical grind of this business eats you up and spits you out, so longevity as an enforcer is a pretty special thing in my mind.

The grind of not only taking a regular shift, but also having to fight night in and night out, without a doubt makes hockey enforcers the toughest athletes in all of sports. Not only did guys like Marty McSorley know that they had to play injured, they also knew that they would have to fight injured. There is a big difference between playing injured and fighting injured, and that is why McSorley was so respected as both a player and a fighter. Adding to the pressure of constantly having to protect their teammates, enforcers also knew that if they had to take time off for injuries a young gun would be called up from the minor leagues to fill in. The enforcer would have to then sit by idly and watch that young gun make the most of his opportunity by fighting as often as he could in order to impress the coaches. Now, that is pressure.

# How League Rules and Officials Affect Fighting

"The code for me was a sort of comfort level of being able to go out and play my game, even though an opposing team may have wanted to get in my face and prevent me from doing so. Even though I was a smaller player, I knew that I had to stick up for myself. But it was certainly nice to know that if somebody wanted to cheap-shot me or get me off of my game that I had teammates who were willing to make that right. There are consequences for doing disrespectful things in this league, and that is the foundation of the code.

"You know, there is a big difference between playing hard and finishing checks and getting in people's faces in a respectable way versus playing cheap and taking liberties with guys or going after knees. Guys who have a history of that, their names get spread around the league pretty quickly because players don't tolerate that crap at this level. Again, anytime a guy plays cheap and threatens to injure another player in this league, potentially hurting his ability to provide for his family, then that guy is going to be dealt with accordingly. That is how the system of justice behind the code works. It goes above and beyond the rules of the game to protect players."

—PHIL HOUSLEY
21-year NHL veteran defenseman

# 13

## The Instigator Rule

Perhaps no rule in the modern era has had more of an impact on the game than the instigator rule. The rule has drastically reshaped the fighting landscape in the NHL, and seemingly everyone has an opinion about it—on both sides of the fence.

According to Rule 56 of the NHL's official rule book on fighting: "An instigator of an altercation shall be a player who by his actions or demeanor demonstrates any/some of the following criteria: distance traveled; gloves off first; first punch thrown; menacing attitude or posture; verbal instigation or threats; conduct in retaliation to a prior game (or season) incident; obvious retribution for a previous incident in the game or season."

Rule 56(a), meanwhile, is commonly referred to as the instigator rule. It was implemented in 1992 and calls for a two-minute minor penalty to be assessed to a player who instigates an altercation (even if his opponent is a willing participant), on top of a five-minute fighting major and a 10-minute game misconduct. In layman's terms, that means that if there is a fight, the guy who started it is going to serve 17 minutes in the box, compared to only 15 for the other guy. Thus, the other guy's team will have a two-minute power play opportunity of four-on-five hockey. Furthermore, if a player receives a second instigator penalty in the same game, he is given a game misconduct and ejected. A third instigator in the same regular season warrants a two-game suspension, and the penalties grow exponentially from there.

To really understand the instigator rule and what its impact has been on the NHL, you have to look at its pros and cons. There are many perspectives and opinions about it and whether it should stay or go. To gain a historical perspective, let's look at the genesis of the rule and see how it has changed the game.

## Back in the Day...

Before the days of Rule 56(a), the policemen, or enforcers, patrolled the ice and kept order. If a player took liberties with another team's star player or perhaps a player who wasn't a fighter, then the policeman stepped in and held him accountable for his actions. The enforcer would go out and have a few words with him and inform him of the consequences he would face should he continue to play that way. If he agreed to behave, the game would be immediately cleaned up and the players would now have space to maneuver freely. If he did not agree, then one of two things would happen.

In the first scenario, the players would mutually agree to drop the gloves and fight like men. Afterward, both players would skate to the penalty box, and usually that would be the end of it. This led to a four-on-four situation, which was considered fair and within the realm of the rules.

In the second scenario, the enforcer would challenge the antagonist to fight, only the antagonist would choose not to. If that was the case, then the enforcer had the responsibility to right what he felt had been wronged by escalating the situation. He now had the right to take a run at the opposing team's top players, getting justice that way.

If that happened, then the other team's enforcers would have to come out and try to keep the peace as well. What started as a simple confrontation may now involve many players and may lead to a much more physical and violent game for all parties. At that point everybody had to be on the lookout, because the unwritten rules of engagement just changed. The referees, for the most part, understood this system of retaliation and allowed the game to police itself.

Where things eventually reached the boiling point with the league, however, was when the enforcers started getting into multiple fights per game, going way above and beyond the call of duty. Those guys were commonly referred to as goons. Goons were big fan favorites, not because

## Dave Schultz on the Instigator Rule

"The rule was put in to prevent some tough guy from beating up a little guy. Well, I got news for you: it never happened and it probably never will happen. Guys fight within their weight classes for the most part in the NHL, unless somebody does something really stupid and totally deserves it. And that guy would get popped with or without the rule, so it is irrelevant. If there is a fight and one guy has to chase the other guy around the rink to catch him, well that guy probably deserved to be slapped around a little bit. This game was meant to police itself, and by taking that away they ruined the game.

"The instigator has taken away one of the most important elements of hockey: honor. Nowadays, instead of guys settling their differences by having a fight, guys run around cheap-shotting guys, carrying their sticks high and playing with absolutely no respect. There is no retribution now other than suspension or fines, which is ridiculous. That doesn't solve any problems.

"Look, nobody wants this wretched rule, especially the players. Sure, the stars need protection, but there is a right way and a wrong way for going about that. This rule is just not the right way. I am sorry, but that is how I feel about it. Nowadays I see two guys out there talking to each other with one trying to talk the other one into dropping his gloves, saying, 'Do you want to go? Do you want to go? Do you want to go?' It is ridiculous. Neither wants to take an instigator penalty, so they are having to discuss their plans with each other like little girls in order for something to happen. It is one of the stupidest things I have ever seen. Get rid of it."

of their skating abilities but because of their fighting, which could turn the momentum around for their teammates.

Other tactics that goons occasionally employed included simply grabbing a skill player and forcing him into a fight. If he dropped the gloves and started pounding on a skill player, the other guy would eventually have to fight back to protect himself, or he'd risk the humiliation of turtling in front of his fans and teammates. As soon as he fought back, though, they would both get off-setting penalties and head to the box. Fair? Hardly.

It didn't take long for teams to figure out that the odds of going four-on-four against a team with their top player sitting in the penalty box were pretty good. They were more than happy to exchange a goon for a goal scorer for five minutes, and this became a big problem. Compounding that was the fact that once a skill player gets picked on, his teammates will usually rush over to offer protection—which may lead to yet another penalty for your team under the "third man in" rule.

Another problem the league wanted to curtail was "intimidation fights," which were the most vicious scraps and most often occurred at the ends of games when there was a blowout. Those types of scrums brought the league tons of bad press.

By the early 1990s, the days of the goon were numbered. Because they were so one-dimensional, they became liabilities. Not only were they liabilities for their own teams with regards to offensive production, but also for the league—which wanted to change its violent image. Eventually, the league, in dire need of mending its reputation, figured that the only way to get rid of this type of player was to create the instigator rule.

In the simplest of terms, the rule gave the aggressor an additional two-minute penalty for starting a fight with an opponent who didn't want to go. It also penalized a player for retaliating against a cheap shot. If player A hacked, speared, elbowed, slashed, or high-sticked player B from behind, then player A should be held accountable, right? Well, under the rules of the instigator, as soon as player B retaliated against player A, to right the wrong, he was penalized. Clearly, the idea behind the rule was to prevent fighting. But the method of doing so prevented the players from policing themselves. It handcuffed skilled players who played a physical game, in a sense taking away a key dimension of their effectiveness.

## A New Game Altogether

With the arrival of the rule, so too came the flood of controversy amidst the players, management, and fans. Those in favor of the rule argued that it put the policing of the game back where it belonged, in the hands of the officials and the league, not with the enforcers. They could then effectively discipline the guilty parties within the guidelines of the rules. Proponents maintained that the rule reduced the number of fights, eliminated vigilante justice and intimidation, and restored civility to the game.

Members of the anti-fighting lobby liked the rule, and rightly so. That, along with the addition of the second referee to patrol the ice, gave the superstars much-needed protection. Those same lobbyists were quick to point out that almost all fighting had been eliminated in the playoffs because the instigator made the stakes simply too high to risk.

As for the opponents of the rule, there were many—starting with the enforcers themselves. The rule handcuffed them from doing their jobs effectively. If they knew that they were going to get an extra couple of minutes in the box and risk their teams having to play a man down, they couldn't properly protect their teammates from dirty play and intimidation. The fact of the matter is that in addition to the extra time in the box, most enforcers weren't going to risk a big chunk of their salaries on fines due to repeat offenses either. In the end, the players who suffered the most were the ones the enforcers were supposed to protect—the goal scorers.

Many argued that what had actually happened since the rule came down is that there had been a shift in power, with too many "little guys" running players and playing dirty, without any worry of retribution. There are supposed to be consequences for your actions on the ice, and the code says that you have to be accountable, but the instigator rule worked against the code. As a result, there were more questionable hits, more stick work, more interference, and more random acts of violence, because the guilty parties knew that they could get away with it without having to face any physical retribution from an opposing team's enforcer.

Opponents of the rule also contend that when the enforcers are out there, the game is cleaned up—ultimately giving more space to everybody and allowing the action to progress unimpeded. In fact, often the enforcer's mere presence on the end of the bench is enough to deter stick work, interference, and dirty play. McSorley puts it this way:

> I don't like the rule. I never have, and I hope someday it is removed for the good of the game. It doesn't allow the players to police themselves, and that is wrong. The NHLPA [National Hockey League Players' Association] did a poll amongst its finesse players one time and the vast, vast majority said that they wanted it to be removed, too. Nobody likes it, nobody. What that shows you is that the tough guys aren't going after the goal scorers. It is just the heavyweights and middleweights that are fighting, that's it. I would also add that it is also a really hard penalty to call by the officials. I think that there is pressure on them to call instigators, and a lot of times they just give one to the winner of the fight. That was the worst, when stuff like that happened, because you were just helpless.
>
> Another aspect of the instigator is that it allowed players to sucker you into an extra two-minute penalty by engaging you and then turtling like cowards. As soon as you dropped your gloves the ref slapped you with the infraction, and then you were screwed. Those types of incidents don't just come from the players, either. They come from higher up the ladder. You know, coaches have a huge impact on

the code. Many of them are former players and they know the rules of the code as well as we do.

One of the worst things that was happening to me in the latter half of my career was when I would go out for a shift and a tough guy, a big 250-plus-pound player, would challenge me to a fight and then cover up. I would drop my gloves like a man, and he would just go down and cover his head. It was sickening. And the reason they were doing that was because their coaches told them to draw me into a penalty. Those guys were coming off the bench with specific instructions to go out and draw me into a penalty, but under no circumstances would they be allowed to fight me. It was such a cheap tactic, totally disrespectful. I understand why they did it and where it came from, and that they were under orders to shake up our lineup, but it was crap.

I remember talking to Bob Probert and Tie Domi one time about this and we all agreed, with the instigator you almost had to wait for the other guy to punch you in the face before you could retaliate, just to make sure he really wanted to go and wasn't trying to sucker you into a penalty. I have had other guys literally come up to me and say, "Hit me, I dare you..." just to get an instigator. If teams have to win by doing garbage like that, then that is pretty sad. I mean, the guys who wanted to play the game right, under the rules of the code, were totally handcuffed. For coaches to orchestrate that stuff was just terrible. I saw things differently after I got into coaching when I retired, and that stuff still makes me sick.

## The Aftermath

The long-term ramifications of the instigator rule are many. For starters, it means that payback and retaliation, both hallmarks of the NHL, are now more premeditated and calculated than ever—giving new meaning to the term *vigilante justice*. You see, those additional two minutes go a long way. And in today's cut-throat world of professional hockey, a two-minute power play in a tight game can be the difference between a win and a loss, or even a spot in the playoffs, so teams have to plan their attacks more carefully.

Another downside of the rule is the fact that there is a lot more pressure on the officials to constantly monitor and manage the physical and emotional levels of each game. Calling infractions is one thing, but to have to police the players from all of the constant obstruction, minor stick work, and intimidation hitting is an entirely different can of worms. The referees and linesmen are more overworked now than

## Mike Peluso on the Instigator Rule

"The new rule where you get penalized for fighting in the last five minutes of a game and your coach gets fined 10 grand to boot might be the worst rule ever put in the books. I mean if two guys want to square off evenly at the end of the game to settle a score, then they should be able to do so. As long as neither is the instigator and they are both willing participants, then I say let them go and then send them to the locker room. Rules like that just ruin the game in my opinion."

ever, and it is only getting worse. You see, while the rule prevents one-sided fights, it also protects the agitators and pests, shielding the hit-and-run artists who need to be kept honest. That job was once done by enforcers, but now, in many instances, it is left to the officials to deal with. Again, before the instigator rule, if there was an incident, such as a high stick or a cheap shot, that didn't get called, the offender would have to fight one of the opposing team's tough guys. It was hockey justice that solved problems right on the spot, before they escalated into altercations involving additional players and further retaliation. After that player who high-sticked someone, or hit someone with a cheap shot, got what was coming to him, it would send a message encouraging his teammates to keep their sticks down and keep the game clean. Sure, there were some flaws, but overall the system worked.

Rob Ray agrees:

> I think the instigator has really diminished the level of respect players have for one another nowadays. It prevents the players from policing themselves and handling their own affairs in a way that forces everyone to be accountable. Once that rule went into place, that is when the game got a lot more violent in my opinion. It just opened the floodgates for guys to do all sorts of disrespectful things, and that is really unfortunate. The cheap shots, the high sticks, the dirty play, and the overall lack of respect are all byproducts of that stupid rule in my eyes. Guys know now that they can do all of that shit without being held accountable. Other than the rare fine or suspension handed down by the league, there is no recourse for players playing dirty and getting away with it.

Combine the instigator rule with the new offensive rule changes that came about in 2005 in the wake of the NHL lockout, and it spells revolutionary changes for the league. Teams can no longer afford to have a goon on their roster, someone who can fight but can't skate a regular shift. Instead, teams have enforcers who can play the game as well as protect their teammates. There is a big difference.

Although fighting is still a pivotal part of the game, it is much different from the pre–instigator rule days. The fighting that takes place nowadays has been reduced to a spectacle between two willing combatants—usually the enforcers, or "designated fighters." In the NHL of the 21st century, fighters have to literally extend an invitation to one another and wait for a response. It can often resemble a sort of twisted wild animal mating dance, enticing and seductive, yet dangerous and risky at the same time. When they agree, they drop their gloves at the same time and get it on. This way, neither player can be deemed the instigator, hence drawing the extra two-minute minor penalty.

## The Three R's: Retaliation, Retribution, and Revenge

Although the instigator does discourage immediate retaliation for on-ice incidents, the problem with the rule is that it doesn't take into account the power of retribution. Hockey players are not only emotional, they have great memories. They are also human, and dirty play to them is nothing less than an act of disrespect that will not and cannot be forgotten. You see, players and teams don't usually forget about those initial slights, or high sticks, or cheap shots, and as a result they let that bad memory fester. They know that they will have to wait until the right moment to exact their revenge; otherwise, they will risk receiving a penalty, leaving their team shorthanded. So the anger builds and builds, which usually makes the inevitable retaliation even worse than what was probably warranted in the first place. When players are forced to carry that frustration, anger, and resentment from game to game, something bad is bound to happen.

This was the case in the Bertuzzi incident. In the pre-instigator days, either Bertuzzi or, more likely, Canucks enforcer Brad May would have come out on the next shift or two and settled the score. They would have challenged Moore to a straight-up fight right then and there for his hit on Naslund and it would have been over with. Moore would have taken his medicine, and justice would have been served by Naslund's teammates, who wanted to protect his honor. Case closed.

## Paul Stewart on Revenge

"Revenge in hockey can be a bitch. I still owe Bob Schmautz for trying to spear me in the eye in Colorado one night. I had hit him with a beautiful elbow right in the chest, which knocked the wind out of him. I could have taken his chin off, but I didn't. So he came back at me with his stick, and we got into a stick fight. It was ugly. I even went after him years later at a celebrity golf tournament up in Pawtucket with a putter one time. Milt Schmidt had to get between us that afternoon, and it was a good thing he was there or that could have gotten ugly, too. I said, 'You haven't got a stick now, how tough are you?' He was a gutless puke. He had no code and no honor. Hey, Schmautz—and you can put this in the book, too—anytime, anyplace. I'm ready for you."

Instead, things brewed for the next three weeks until tempers boiled over. What transpired next was professional hockey's biggest black eye ever. The problem was that the common fans who don't follow the game that closely didn't understand the events that led up to the incident, or the culture of retribution that is the norm in pro hockey. They only saw the last minute of a two-hour movie. To many of those fans it was the usual suspects beating the crap out of a guy. They didn't understand the role that the instigator played in it. Was Bertuzzi right for what he did? Absolutely not. He broke the code, and he paid. But there was more to the story than many fans were aware of.

Hockey is about accountability. Back in the day, guys knew that if they laid a stick on someone, they were going to get smacked in the mouth. That was an effective deterrent for most guys, especially the smaller ones who enjoyed brushing their own teeth versus putting them in a cup before bed at night. The instigator rule has taken much of that accountability away, and that is what the players don't like about it.

The guys who are really capitalizing on the instigator rule are the agitators. Agitators make their living by playing ugly and basically doing whatever it takes to get guys off their games. If that means talking about their mommas, so be it. If it means an ankle slash here or a wrist slash there, so be it. They are relentless, and as long as they are pissing off the opposition and forcing them to lose their concentration, then they are doing their jobs. They are the Claude Lemieuxs and the Theo Fleurys of the world, despised by their opposition and adored by their teammates.

"The problem with the instigator is that there are tons of little guys who are a pain in the ass and deserve to get beat up, but they can hide behind that rule," said Brett Hull. "Guys who have no fear of hurting anyone have no respect for the game, and that is too bad."

Many enjoy taking liberties with the other team's top skill players and then running and hiding after dishing out dangerous hits. With no justice exacted, and the agitator not willing to fight his own fight, the other team's enforcer is then forced to take matters into his own hands. What this means is that he is going to have to exact his revenge on a skill player instead. Now you have skill players being run all over the place, by agitators as well as by enforcers, and the game slows way down. The fans don't like that style of hockey, and it isn't good for the league's bottom line either.

Another interesting comment about the cursed instigator rule came from ESPN's Spider Jones way back in 1996:

> Since the rule's inception, the game has become increasingly more vile, which is opposite of the way it was supposed to turn out. According to league brass, this rule was implemented to curtail fighting and violence. But in cold, hard reality, all it's really created is a more subtle and ugly violence. Now you have guys who wouldn't drop the gloves to go to the washroom committing all kinds of fouls. Pussycats like Esa Tikkanen and Ulf Samuelsson have now become tigers. How many times during the playoffs did you see them yapping at or taking runs at the more skilled players? I can appreciate they have a job to do, but don't mistake their aggression for courage. It's easy to play bad-ass when the threat of retaliation is minimal. For their style of play, the instigator rule is just what the doctor ordered. They can hide under its protection and wreak all kinds of havoc on the opposition. This holds especially true in crucial games where retaliation is frowned upon.
>
> During the days of the Big Bad Bruins and the Broad Street Bullies, this nonsense would not have been tolerated. If someone ran Lemieux or elbowed Gretzky the way Kelly Buchberger of the Oilers did, they'd be dead meat! Teams back then took pride in protecting their bread-and-butter players. While I'm not suggesting we go back to those bench-clearing, stick-swinging brawls of the '70s, I'm also adamantly convinced the instigator rule is not a solution. In fact, since its inception players are being forced more and more to rely on the officials for justice. And, if [this] erratic play is any indication of things to come, the NHL justice system appears to be wielding a white cane.

## Is There a Long Future for the Instigator?

As for the future of the rule, it remains as controversial as ever. While some NHL players, including the likes of Paul Kariya (a Lady Byng Trophy winner for good sportsmanship), have called for the league to eliminate the rule altogether so that the game can once again police itself, others feel that it should remain. Otherwise, they contend, it would be a league of tough guys dictating the rules in a Wild West scenario. The public relations–conscious NHL does not want to go back to the days of the Broad Street Bullies, so for all intents and purposes, the rule is here to stay. Fighting majors are down from years ago, but they still exist and are allowed by the league in what they feel is the proper context.

The league made some major rule changes in 2005 in an effort to clean up the game and encourage more offense. With scoring at an all-time low, it became apparent that the fans were not thrilled by defensive tactics such as the neutral zone trap, which limited scoring to just a few goals a game. They wanted scoring, and they wanted excitement. The new rules, complete with goaltender limitations and the elimination of the red line, were all designed to speed up the game. As a result of a faster game, however, the role of the enforcers drastically changed. Was this an effort to curb fighting or to give more space to the skill players? Either way, the league reacted, and so far the response has been positive.

The league also added a few new conditions to the instigator rule in 2005. The rule now reads as such: "A player who is deemed to be the instigator of an altercation in the final five (5) minutes of regulation time or at any time in overtime, shall be assessed an instigator minor penalty, a major for fighting, a 10-minute misconduct, and an automatic one-game suspension. The length of suspension will double for each subsequent offense. In addition, the player's coach shall be fined $10,000, a fine that will double for each subsequent incident."

The intent of the new rule adjustments is to prevent players from starting fights out of retaliation or sending messages with cheap shots or dirty play in the final minutes of games that might be out of reach. The addendum has some wiggle room, though, and as a result it has had to deal with its share of controversy.

"[That rule] is something I crafted and fought to get with the competition committee and the general managers," said NHL disciplinarian Colin Campbell. "The key to the whole rule was that it would be automatic, no

## Barry Melrose on the Instigator Rule

"When I played, it was entirely different than it is today. When I played if you did something dirty to somebody you had to be prepared to stand up and be accountable. That's really why the game wasn't cheap in those days. Nowadays, players don't have to be accountable for their actions and they don't have to fight. Players can high-stick each other, spear each other, slash each other in the face, run each other from behind into the boards, and do so with the understanding that they can get away with it. That is why there are so many injuries these days, especially in the past 20 years or so, and I think it is terrible, to tell you the truth. That sort of stuff, especially the stick work, is so disrespectful and really has no place in this game. Hopefully the new rules will restore some of that honor to the game, because it needs it.

"I think the biggest reason for this is (a) the instigator penalty and (b) the influx of Europeans [who play a less-physical style of hockey] into the game. Twenty years ago if you ever sticked a guy and then not fought, your own teammates would ostracize you and just wouldn't accept you in the locker room. A guy who turtled after doing something dirty would just not be accepted by his teammates. They would be embarrassed to have him on their team. And let me be clear, it didn't matter if you won or lost your fight, but you had to be accountable. You had to show up. If you did something dirty then you stood up like a man and you defended your actions; players at least respect that. Now players don't even have to show up and that in my eyes is a very sad thing. It is sad because it is just accepted.

"So, all in all, I think the rule should be thrown out. It's awful. It was brought in because of the tough teams that went looking for trouble and tried to intimidate you, the Philadelphia Flyers and the Boston Bruins of the 1970s. Well, there are no teams like that anymore. They needed the rule 25 years ago. Where was it then when they really could have used it? Let the players police themselves. Get rid of it."

appeal by the team, but I would review every instigator in the last five minutes to see if it would pass the litmus test. And that would be, is this guy a two-shift guy who was out to send a message? Was it a tough guy doing his thing and leaving his calling card? So I'm going to assess each and every one when it happens."

In fact, many fight fans feel as though the league has held a double standard for players based on their perceived roles: one set of rules to protect the stars and another to punish the tough guys for trying to do their jobs the way they've been accustomed to doing them for years. In a sense it is telling players that if they play enough minutes and score enough points, they can do anything they want without fear of punishment.

With these rule changes the tough guys are becoming an endangered species. The number of fighting majors is down across the board. While some applaud the move, other traditionalists are not so happy. They do not want to see their favorite players on the chopping block. It is a tough line, especially from a league that is trying to win back its fan base after a year-long lockout. The league's message is clear, though: they want to clean up the game, provide more offense, and hold players as well as their coaches accountable for their actions. Coaches are not going to be too pleased about coughing up 10 grand in the final minute of a game if one of his players decides to go after a guy. No way.

The bottom line is this: the need for policemen to not only protect their star players but also raise the emotion levels of their teammates by fighting will always be there. However, the league's rule changes and emphasis on reducing the amount of fighting has redefined that player's role. Teams can no longer afford to carry a guy who can only punch people. That player must be able to contribute; whether that is by scoring an occasional goal or by serving as a productive member of the checking line, he must become more well-rounded to survive in the new NHL. Guys like Philadelphia's Donald Brashear and Toronto's Tie Domi are prime examples of this. Not only are they productive members of their teams, but they are also well-respected by their teammates and peers for their toughness and heart. Perhaps most importantly, though, they are also huge fan favorites who sell tickets. That is a lethal combination that the league can certainly get behind for its definition of the prototypical enforcer of the future.

### Neil Sheehy: The Original Instigator

It is interesting to note that while the instigator rule was implemented by the NHL back in 1992, the genesis of the penalty can actually be linked to one player whose actions on the ice several years earlier truly changed the game. That player is former Calgary Flames defenseman Neil Sheehy. The International Falls, Minnesota, native is a Harvard University graduate who played in the NHL for nearly a decade and then, after going on to law school, became an NHL certified agent. Sheehy's poignant story chronicles how his agitating on-ice tactics toward Wayne Gretzky caused a major shift in how the game is now played and officiated.

Sheehy made headlines during his tenure with Calgary back in the mid- to late 1980s not so much for his ability to score goals but rather for his ability to get under Gretzky's skin. His methods of distraction against the Great One were the thing of legend. He didn't overtly hack him or slash him, though. Instead, he did it in subtle, discreet ways with an extra push here, an extra hold there, always walking that fine line between what was legal and what wasn't. Sheehy got so good at his job that it often became the most important subplot in the ferocious rivalry between the Calgary Flames and Edmonton Oilers, otherwise known as "The Battle of Alberta."

The Flames dominated the Oilers during this era, and Sheehy's tactics toward the Great One were a big reason why. Knowing how much Sheehy's presence on the ice bothered Gretzky, Flames coach Bob Johnson gave Sheehy the green light to shadow Gretzky around the ice at all times.

"It's tough to put him out of your mind, but I'm going to try," said Gretzky of his nemesis. "He does a good job on me. He stands up and plays the man. I think he plays with more emotion against us than he does against other teams. He keeps pounding away, nothing illegal, but he keeps coming at you to get you off your game."

The key to Sheehy's success was the fact that he refused to fight Gretzky's bodyguards when they taunted him and hacked at him. Oilers tough guy Marty McSorley accused Sheehy of being a coward because he refused to drop the gloves and stand up to the big boys. Sheehy's response was that he was more effective on the ice than in the penalty box, and that he was doing nothing outside the realm of the rule book. Sheehy was not afraid to fight, as he had done many times before, but knew that there was a proper time and place to be drawn into an altercation.

"I'd have to see our team gain some advantage," he said. "The bottom line is to win the hockey game. We have to win on the scoreboard. If I were to fight for myself, I'd just be being selfish."

The method to Sheehy's madness was to study Gretzky's tendencies. He knew that No. 99 liked to skate to open spaces, where he could find room to maneuver and set up his team's potent offense.

"Even though we were taught never to leave the front of the net, I would follow him to the opposite corner," said Sheehy. "I always kept my stick low, I knew the league wouldn't let me get away with much, and I'd push him into the boards, which he didn't like. The Oilers would send out their tough guys to rough me up, but I'd already fought most of them. Instead, I'd take a couple of shots to the face, but we'd wind up with the power play. The Oilers were so good back then, that was one of the strategies you had to use to beat them."

When Gretzky tired of Sheehy's mind games and annoying tactics, he lashed out through the media.

"He said that I turtled, that I was afraid to fight," Sheehy quipped. "I said, here's Wayne Gretzky, one of the biggest supporters of removing fighting from hockey, daring me to use my fists. He needs to make up his mind."

When the press went to Gretzky for his reply, he muttered, "You're right, Neil Sheehy is the single reason fighting *shouldn't* be eliminated from hockey."

Sheehy found a loophole in the rules and he ran with it. While some would say it was cowardly, others concluded that it was brilliant. Either way, Sheehy changed the game. As a cunning and calculating agitator, he certainly paid the price for his team's success, and his teammates loved him for it. He wasn't the first to use those tactics, but he was the first to get noticed, due to his high-profile rivalry with Gretzky. Sheehy had found a kink in the armor of the league's best team, and the other teams quickly took note. Before long, every team was running similar tactics to slow the game's top players down. And sure enough, eventually the whole league slowed down to the point where fans were losing interest in low-scoring games. Sheehy retired from pro hockey in 1992, the same year the league implemented the instigator rule.

While his on-ice legacy may always be intertwined with the rule, an enlightened Sheehy now thinks that it should be eliminated once and for all. In fact, his 2004 Jerry McGuire–like manifesto titled "The Systematic Erosion and Neutralization of Skill and Play-Making in the NHL," on how the NHL needs to change its ways, was right on the money. The opening text of his article reads as follows:

> I rocked the boat. I hit the skilled players and would not fight the tough ones, which distracted them. In part, because I was the recipient of so many cheap shots as pay-back for my tactics, the NHL eventually reacted and implemented the instigator rule, which further encouraged those types of actions and helped neutralize the game's top offensive players.
>
> While I have no regrets about how I played the game back then, completely within the confines of the rules, I have since had a change

of heart regarding the instigator and now feel compelled to express my thoughts. I believe professional hockey is at a crossroads and the future of the game will depend upon decisions that are made now. Most who are involved in hockey recognize that its players are bigger, stronger, faster, and more skilled than ever before. But the game has in fact diminished and is considerably less entertaining.

But, how can that be? I believe it is because the most skilled players are not given the freedom to exhibit their skills. Rather, they are coached to "play the percentages" and...chip it in, chip it out... chip, chip, chip. The "golden age" of hockey, a time when great teams dazzled us all, is a thing of the past. I am convinced we are now at a time when changes must occur. We must discuss and tackle our game's problems, and come up with real solutions, otherwise hockey will never sell in non-traditional markets and the game will suffer. Solving any problem first involves identifying what is wrong, and then the real challenge is finding the right solutions. I hope to offer a perspective that identifies the tactics that began the downturn of skill and play-making in hockey, and then to offer possible solutions.*

---

* The full text of Sheehy's article can be found in the appendix.

# 14

## Divers

While goading opposing players into penalties, particularly retaliatory ones, is frowned upon, it is an accepted and legal part of the game. Diving, or pretending to be fouled in order to draw a penalty, on the other hand, is both a foul and a blatant violation of the code. Taking a dive to trick the referee into calling a penalty, or "dressin' it up" as it is sometimes called, can have consequences.

The NHL started cracking down on the diving perpetrators after the lockout of 2004, and the results have been a mixed bag. The league has been trying to limit the amount of hooking and holding that goes on, and diving relates directly to those calls. The rules currently state that a player who is penalized for diving or suspected of doing so can be sent a warning letter by the league. A second offense garners a $1,000 fine while also "outing" the accused by putting his name on a list of known divers, which is then sent to all the teams. It is a humiliation tactic that has worked. The penalties get worse from there.

The problem with diving is that it is usually a package deal. Rarely called as a stand-alone penalty, it is often bundled with a hooking or tripping minor for the other team. The diving penalty is then thrown in as an offsetting call for the guy embellishing the foul.

The NHL isn't the first major sports league to have to deal with dramatics. Soccer players have prided themselves for years as being great divers and fakers of injuries. Watching them writhe in pain after being touched by an opposing offender is borderline revolting, especially when you see them miraculously jump to their feet after the ref hands out a yellow card to the sucker who got called for doing absolutely nothing. Basketball has its version, too, which usually results in an opponent drawing a charging foul. Wide receivers in football often pretend to be interfered with in hopes of drawing a flag for pass interference, and baseball players have been known to fake being hit by a pitch that actually struck their bat so they can draw a free pass to first base. So, faking in sports is nothing new, to be sure.

Many feel that because sports are so subjective, with referees making spur-of-the-moment calls with so little margin of error, that there is a sense of gamesmanship involved with the athletes as far as trying to get away with whatever they can. Others feel that all is fair in love and war. In most sports, the referees, umpires, and officials are older men trying to run along and keep up with the action while still being able to make tough calls that they can't even see half of the time. Heck, even instant replay gets it wrong some of the time.

The NHL wants to clean up its act, though, and it has taken a stand against diving and its best divers. Take a player like Peter Forsberg, for instance, one of the best players in the league. Well, because Forsberg gets whacked and hacked so much every time he touches the puck, and rarely gets penalties called against him, he has made embellishing almost an art form. In fact, he is so good that it is not uncommon to see signs in opposing arenas that read "Forsberg for Best Actress," for his Oscar-like performances as a diver. The guy is good, no question about it. And in his defense, that is how he draws penalties to give his team a power-play advantage. If he can get away with it, more power to him. But rest assured, the players know when guys are diving, and those types of things have a way of working themselves out on the ice.

The biggest problem for referees is determining just what really happened when there is a dive. Did he dive or was he tripped? Is the victim hurt? Did he get cut during the act of being tripped, which would warrant a stiffer penalty, or was the cut already there? The refs have to make tough, spontaneous decisions during those situations, which can send an already infuriated crowd into hysterics. It just makes their jobs that much tougher. A good diver knows this, and just like a perfectly timed open-ice body check, so too can a diver get away with a perfectly timed leap of faith. He knows that if he is on a breakaway and a guy is pulling him from behind, or if he is behind the play and out of sight of the referee, or in traffic with a bunch of lesser-skilled players clutching and grabbing him to slow him down, there will be a window of opportunity to go down. Good divers put themselves into positions where they can get away with it.

The bottom line with diving, however, is this: the players and officials view it as disrespectful. While a trip or even a slash can be cheap, they are an accepted and sometimes necessary part of the game. The worst-case scenario is that it costs your team a goal in a power-play opportunity. Diving, meanwhile, is disrespectful to not only the player who was falsely accused but also the referee. And referees don't like to be made fools of. They don't like it when a punk assumes he is smarter than they are and rubs it in their faces for all to see.

In fact, humiliate a ref and you can guarantee that he will not forget about it anytime soon—which means there will be a microscope on your hide every time you step on the ice. Maybe you won't get the next penalty call you legitimately deserve; or maybe the next fight you are in, that official will wait just a few extra moments before breaking it up, to make sure you get what's coming to you. Plus, once you cry wolf with something like this, no one will believe you, even when you aren't faking. You get the picture.

Lastly, it is safe to assume that players who take shortcuts to gain an illegal and immoral advantage out on the ice will eventually get what's coming to them. That is all part of the code.

# 15

## On Bench-Clearing Brawls

When some people think of hockey, they immediately think of bench-clearing brawls. And although movies like *Slap Shot* keep those visions fresh in our minds, the fact of the matter is that there hasn't been one in nearly 20 years. The league discouraged bench-clearing brawls in 1978 when it instituted a rule making it an automatic ejection for the third player to join in a scrum, the "third man in" rule. Five years later, the league added fines and game misconducts for players who dropped the gloves during a stoppage in play resulting from another altercation. Then, in 1987, to get rid of them once and for all, the league imposed a 10-game suspension for the first player off the bench to join a fight, as well as a possible suspension and fine for his coach. It was formally called Rule 72, "Leaving the Players' or Penalty Bench." In fact, the last bench-clearer on the books came when the Boston Bruins and Quebec Nordiques had a yard sale on February 26, 1987. This spectacle got so ugly that the league finally had to take action. Amazingly, there hasn't been a bench-clearer since, proving that harsh penalties really do work.

Bench-clearing brawls are synonymous with the "old-time hockey" and tough-as-hell teams like Philadelphia's Broad Street Bullies, who made the tactic of fighting and intimidation into their own twisted art form. They would usually start out harmless enough, with two guys dropping the gloves and everybody else pairing off like dance partners. Pretty soon everybody would jump over the boards and join in to make sure nobody was getting double-teamed or just plain pummeled. It made it almost impossible for the officials to regulate what was going on, though, because as soon as they would break up one fight, three more would be starting behind their backs.

One of the most notorious bench-clearers of all time came on April 20, 1984, during a game between the Montreal Canadiens and Quebec Nordiques, in what is now known as the "Vendredi Saint Brawl," or "Good Friday Brawl." The arch rivals squared off against each other in a playoff tilt for more than an hour that night, fighting nonstop in what was later called the "Game of Shame," complete with 198 penalty minutes and a whopping 10 game misconducts. Incidentally, Montreal eliminated the Nordiques that night, 5–3.

Three years later, in 1987, arguably the worst bench-clearer in international competition went down when Canada met up with Russia in the championship game of the World Junior Tournament. This mêlée started with a scrum and evolved into a full-blown donnybrook unlike anything seen before. The officials couldn't keep up with the more than 15 simultaneous fights going on at one point, so the arena simply turned off the lights. Incredibly, they still went at it, with horrible consequences. Players were pounding away while their opponents were down on the ice and defenseless. It was truly a sick sight to behold. The game was ultimately canceled with both teams being disqualified. It is still considered one of the worst brawls in the history of the game.

Although the bench-clearer is pretty much extinct in the NHL, it still rears its ugly head from time to time in the minor leagues and in junior hockey. Most guys will tell you that the scariest part of being in one is simply not knowing who is coming at you, especially if you are a little guy. Former NHL player and current ESPN analyst Ray Ferraro talked about the mayhem he witnessed firsthand during his days in the junior and minor leagues:

> While the days of the true bench-clearer have come and gone, junior hockey was a different story. I was 14 when I played my first game in junior and wound up in the middle of a bench-clearing brawl. Everyone was pairing off and I was grabbed by an older guy. As I stood there looking around to see what was happening, he broke my nose. I learned my first lesson about fighting that day: always keep your eye on the guy who has a hold on you. It was not uncommon to have two or three fights a year like that.

One of the scariest brawls I was ever involved in also happened in junior. Former Flyers, Nordiques, and Islanders goalie Ron Hextall was the netminder for our team, and before the second period started he instigated a fight in retaliation for something that took place earlier in the game.

I was the last guy on the ice, and when I arrived on the scene it was total mayhem. Former NHL tough guys Stu Grimson and Lyndon Byers were also part of that fight, and it was a little frightening to be out there with such players because they got pretty busy in situations like that.

Heading onto the ice during a brawl is a huge adrenaline rush at first; everyone is scrambling around, not really knowing where they're headed but just trying to get out there and grab someone. The scary part is that you never know who you'll be paired up with. For a smaller guy like me who was not a very good fighter the idea was to find a guy my size before someone else got to him so I could at least have a chance. And I was always a popular opponent in those brawls precisely because I couldn't fight.

There are no rules or etiquette when it came to bench-clearers. Anything could happen. My strategy was to keep my back to the boards and my head on a swivel so I could see who or what was coming at me. I wasn't looking for a fight, but I was looking to protect myself and my teammates.

The last brawl I took part in happened during pregame warm-ups before a minor-league game in Binghamton, New York, just before I got called up to the [Hartford] Whalers. We were playing the Nova Scotia Oilers, and in the previous game against them one of our defensemen, longtime NHLer Ulf Samuelsson, had gotten his stick into the face of an Oilers player.

Nova Scotia had legendary minor-league fighter Archie Henderson on their roster at the time, and before that next game even started the Oilers came after Samuelsson. Things got ugly in a hurry. No one could break it up, the coaches fought off the ice and police dogs were eventually brought onto the ice to restore order. Each team started the game with about nine skaters apiece.

The same story was true for defenseman Phil Housley, who played for 21 seasons in the NHL. "Being in a bench-clearing brawl was both terrifying as well as exciting for a guy like myself," said Housley. "I just hoped to God a heavyweight never paired up with me. As a little guy I was over the boards pretty quickly searching for somebody at least close to my size, otherwise you never knew what was going to happen to you. When those things broke out everybody was fair game, so you had to really be careful."

Sometimes bench-clearers are more for show than anything else. In most instances it comes down to everybody just pairing off so that the one or two guys who really do want to scrap can do so cleanly, without the fear of anybody else jumping in. For the most part, guys just hold on to each other until it's over. What happens out there during that time between the nonfighting lightweights who may get matched up with a heavyweight, however, can range from horrifying to hilarious, depending on who you talk to.

Chris McAlpine had the following to say of bench-clearing brawls:

> For people who wonder what really goes on out on the ice when a bench-clearing brawl is going on, I've got the inside scoop. It was early on in my career when I was with St. Louis and we were playing Edmonton one night. Well, a big mêlée breaks out and I wind up tying up with Edmonton's tough guy, Kelly Buchberger. We are locked up and I am just praying he is not going to connect with me. Meanwhile, our fighter, Kelly Chase, comes over and says, "Hey, Cow Pie, I got him, let him go." Let me preface this story by explaining that he and Brett Hull had given me this ridiculous nickname that somehow derived from saying McAlpine real fast, which sounded like "McCow Pie." Well, they eventually dropped the "Mc," and just went with "Cow Pie." Hey, who was I to argue with those guys, right? Anyway, Kelly comes skating over to me while I am locked up with this guy and wants to take him, because he was a fighter and he had my back. So, as he says this, "Cow Pie," Kelly Buchberger just starts laughing hysterically and can't stop. He is just dying out there. He looks right at me and says, "Cow Pie?" He thought that was the funniest thing he had ever heard. So, here I am in the middle of this bench-clearing brawl, tied up with this notorious goon who I think is going to kill me, and he is laughing so hard I probably could have pushed him over. The worst part about it was afterward, whenever I would skate past the Edmonton bench they would all yell out "Hey, cow shit! Come back over here, cow shit." At least it got me out of an ass-whooping.

# 16

## Facial Protection

P art of the code is not only looking tough, but presenting yourself in a manner of toughness and readiness. Since the inception of the game, players have detested wearing helmets, visors, and face masks. In fact, had it not been for the tragic death of Minnesota North Stars forward Bill Masterton back in 1968, players may still not be wearing helmets. Masterton fell and hit his head on the ice during a game and sadly later died, forcing the league to take a hard look at the issue.

Back then wearing a helmet, or "brain bucket" as it was called, meant you were a pussy. A man's reputation on the ice was more important than any injury in those days. Slowly but surely, helmet usage steadily increased into the 1970s, especially with more college players joining the pro ranks. Behind the scenes, however, debate over making them mandatory got heated. The old guard argued that wearing helmets might be merely exchanging one set of problems for another. Despite the obvious added protection they would provide, they argued that as the helmets went on, the sticks would invariably come up and a whole host of other injuries would take place from all the dirty play instead.

In 1979 the NHL finally made helmets mandatory. All current players from that point on were grandfathered in, though, meaning they didn't have to wear a helmet if they didn't want to. It wouldn't be until 1997, when Craig MacTavish retired, that the league's collective heads would be completely covered. Fittingly, Masterton's memory lives on through a league trophy named in his honor that is given annually to the player "who best exemplifies the qualities of perseverance, sportsmanship, and dedication to hockey."

The next great debate in pro hockey would be the visor, or half shield. Again, there is a stigma in the league that if you wear one you are some sort of sissy or are soft. In the NHL, enforcers don't wear visors for the most part. They feel that if they need to get into a fight in the heat of the moment that it would be disrespectful and an unfair advantage over an opponent. But with the growing number of players who have had serious eye injuries over the years, more and more players are putting them on to protect their faces from all of the flying sticks and pucks. The reluctance of players to wear them reflects the independence players have in choosing how they wish to protect themselves.

According to *The Hockey News*, 38 percent of NHL's 640 players wore visors as of October 2005, up from 14.2 percent in 1995. As for the NHL, they are firmly "pro-choice." Commissioner Bettman confirmed the league's position that although they are not mandatory, players should wear them nonetheless. Other leagues got the picture a long time ago. In fact, all major Canadian and U.S. junior teams are required to wear half shields. European professional leagues require them for players under the age of 30. College and university teams, meanwhile, have been required to wear full face masks since the late 1970s. Serious eye injuries in the college ranks are unheard of. There is a question, however, of whether the full face mask affects players' chances of making it to the next level.

"With the college guys, it is a big adjustment for them to play at the next level," said Marty McSorley. "For them to come in without that face mask on, that changes everything big-time. I saw so many young guys come into training camp over the years pretending that they were tough and gritty, but most of those guys really didn't have a clue. Those guys got weeded out pretty early."

Fighting still exists at the junior levels, but in a much different form. Gone are the spontaneous glove-dropping ceremonies at center ice, and in are players mutually agreeing to first drop their gloves and then remove their helmets. When an opposing fighter removes his own helmet in a challenging gesture, it's "game on." At that point the opposing player can either take off his helmet and join him, or simply turn and skate away. The choice is his.

While the safety of one's face is paramount, many argue that the use of protective facial coverage at the youth and collegiate levels has produced a

### Glen Sonmor on Visors

"I do like the visors, absolutely. And I can tell you this from firsthand experience because I am one of the only players in the history of the league to lose an eye during a game. It happened back in 1955 when I was just 25 years old and playing pro hockey with Cleveland. Ironically, it came on a deflected shot from an old childhood friend of mine from back home. So, you just never know in this game what can happen. My career was over at that point and luckily I was able to get into coaching after that. So, yes, the visors are a wonderful thing and really do protect these kids. Hell, if the fighters are worried about them, then just take the damn helmets off and fight that way; nobody will mind a bit. It would probably save them a lot of broken knuckles from hitting those helmets anyway. So, yeah, visors are a positive step in keeping guys safe from sticks and pucks. I look back and just wish that they would have been around when I was playing. I most certainly would have been able to play pro hockey for a lot more years."

generation of players who not only play as if they are invincible, but who are also much more disrespectful with their sticks. They contend that the amateur game is much dirtier because the masks protect everybody from any form of retribution, à la a punch in the face.

Lawrence Scanlan, author of the book *Grace Under Fire*, writes, "Ophthalmologist Dr. Tom Pashby of Toronto has been looking at eye injuries in Canadian hockey since 1972. His data show 1,906 incidents, with 309 losses of sight in injured eyes. In every case, the injured wore no visor or full-face mask. Eight eye-injured players wearing half-visors, Dr. Pashby strongly suspects, wore loose chin straps that allowed too much movement. Since 1972, 40 NHLers have been forced into retirement because of eye injuries. In the year 2000 alone, 12 players in the NHL sustained eye injuries."

Columbus Blue Jackets defenseman Bryan Berard nearly lost his eye from an errant high stick during a game in 2000. Berard, who was able to come back but now wears a visor, still doesn't support mandatory usage.

"We're professional athletes, and we need to have that choice," said Berard. "We all know that as soon as we step on the ice, there's a chance we can get hurt. It's something we accept as professional athletes. ... It's part of our job, our life. It's easier to play without a shield, and a lot of guys will want to play without one."

The big debate with visors and masks has always been that when they are on, the stick work runs rampant, especially from suddenly brave little guys who have no business playing that way. Regardless of that, the NHL should adopt a mandatory visor policy because players only have two eyes, and odds are pretty good that they are going to need them for their lives after hockey.

One player with firsthand knowledge of the topic was former Phoenix Coyotes winger Joe Dziedzic, who suffered a career-ending eye injury during a fight after just three seasons in the NHL. He had the following to say:

> I was with the Phoenix Coyotes in 1999 but was down with their minor league team at the time, the Springfield Falcons. I wound up getting into a fight which seemed pretty harmless at the time, but when the guy went to grab onto my jersey his thumb went straight into my eye. He didn't mean to do it, but it was pretty bad. At the time I thought that he just hammered me with a left, because I couldn't see out of my eye and it just hurt like hell. The worst part about it was that he didn't know that he did it and kept on swinging. I just tried to hold on for as long as I could, but I was really hurt. It was really scary. I knew it was bad when the linesmen broke it up and just gasped at the sight of my eye. I wound up having a bunch of problems with it, and after some surgeries I eventually had to retire. It really sucked because I felt fine physically but couldn't risk ever getting hit in the face again. I could have lost my eyesight permanently, so making a comeback at that point wasn't even an issue. Seeing was way more important than ever hoisting the Stanley Cup in my book, so I just had to hang 'em up. You just never knew when your time was up in this game.

As for the enforcers, they don't care for the visors. Many feel that they are disrespectful to the code.

"Look at a guy like Claude Lemieux," said longtime enforcer Jack Carlson who played 11 years of pro hockey. "He was one of the biggest agitators out there and now he wears a visor. The code is about respect and the threat of retaliation if you disrespect another player. I mean, as a player it was always in the back of your mind that you could get your teeth knocked out, your nose broken, or stitches on your face. But now, with the face shield, what fear do players like Lemieux even have? He can do whatever he wants without the fear of taking a punch in the face."

# 17

# The Official's Influence

It is safe to say that the code would not exist were it not for the on-ice officials, the referees and linesmen. They have, arguably, more influence with regards to how a game flows than any of their officiating brethren from the other major sports. In deciding whether to make a call, hockey officials play a pivotal role, and that, more than anything, can directly affect the outcome of games, seasons, and even careers. Their discretion and subjectivity in calling penalties and managing tempers has to be nonwavering, and for that they should be commended. These guys have a tough, tough job. To watch them work when chaos breaks out on the ice is amazing. There is so much they need to watch out for and so many different infractions and rules to enforce.

When it comes to the code, officials have to closely watch the drama and story line of each game so that they can follow how justice will be meted out by the players. They need to know when to let things transpire, and when to "swallow their whistles." It is always a balancing act to make sure things don't get out of hand.

And then there are the fights. Officiating them is an art form all its own and requires a great deal of patience and discipline. Respect is such an important thing for officials, because they are right there on the front lines with the tough guys. Over the years, linesmen, who are responsible for breaking up fights, have suffered broken bones, black eyes, mangled hands, and more than their fair share of errant haymakers while trying to maintain order.

They use discretion, too, allowing certain players to go while quickly breaking up others. A man's life can literally hang in the balance during a brawl, and they need to know when to step in so that no one gets injured. The league schools its linesmen on the art of separating two crazed heavyweights, but plain old experience seems to be the best training of all.

Officials know the intricacies of the code and understand how the game polices itself. They know just how long to let fighters go and when to come in and break it up so that they can escort the players to the penalty box. That is just part of the job for these guys, and they relish the close bonds that they foster with the various enforcers they work with on a daily basis. They know when they are hurt, when they are tired, when they are truly pissed off and dangerous, and when they really don't want to fight after all.

A good linesman can sense when an enforcer has had enough and wants to call it quits. He can read his body language and the subtle nuances of how intense the situation is. When the time is right, he will move in and separate them. There will be a lot of foul-mouthed trash talking going on at that point between the two brawlers, and there will be plenty of adrenaline flowing as well, but the linesmen wade through all of that to make sure both parties are safe and secure from each other, committed to going to the penalty box or locker room without incident, and declared the winner. That's right. Linesmen have to be amateur psychologists, too, constantly reassuring each player that he won and definitely came out on top. He has to massage their egos a little bit to calm them down. It's all part of the gig. If not, then the players have rematches lined up before they even get to the box, making the officials' job even tougher. They also run the risk of having those situations escalate, involving more players and more chaos.

Hockey is guilty, however, of allowing its officials to make non-calls (putting the whistles in their pockets) at certain points in a game in order to let the teams play. For instance, a trip or a hook is most definitely a trip or a hook early in a game, whereas it might not be in overtime. And as for the playoffs? Many would claim that they have their own set of rules entirely for the postseason. Officials don't want to determine the outcome of a game over a penalty, so they oftentimes figure that a non-call is more appropriate than a controversial one. When the league allows for this double standard of "looking the other way" at certain times of the game as well as certain times of the season, the fans lose faith in the entire system.

### Rob Ray on Linesmen

"The linesmen were a big part of fighting. They understood the code and they knew when and why we fought out there. They knew that when two enforcers wanted to go, to let them go until they were all tired out. They know what their roles are and what they each need to accomplish, and they accommodate that. As long as nobody had the upper hand or nobody was hurt, they would let us go. There is a lot of respect with those guys, too. If you treated them right then they would treat you right in return. That was important. Hell, after 16 seasons of doing what I did for a living, I was on a first name basis with just about every one of them."

And yes, there is even an officials "code," which is all about preserving their integrity. According to former NHL referee Vern Buffey's book entitled *Black and White and Never Right*, there are all sorts of things we never knew about our zebras. For starters, the reason they skate backward after a whistle is so that they can watch for any unsportsmanlike gestures or comments from disgruntled players. On top of that, did you ever wonder why they point their entire hand at a penalized player to signal his infraction? Apparently, it is so he won't point a single finger at him, which might be deemed disrespectful or antagonizing. Go figure.

Officials take their fair share of abuse, too, from the players, coaches, and especially the fans. Hockey is such a subjective sport, with infractions that are shades of gray instead of black and white. Seemingly everyone has an opinion on how penalties should be called, and they are rarely shy to let the refs know exactly how they feel. That all comes with the territory, though, and a good official expects to hear boos every time he calls a penalty against the home team. What isn't acceptable, however, is when a referee or linesman gets physically abused. That is where the line is crossed.

Physical contact with an official may warrant a long suspension or possibly even criminal charges, depending on the severity of the incident. Players also know that if they lash out at an official verbally, then they are pushing their luck and could receive additional time in the box for unsportsmanlike conduct. It is usually the captain who can address a referee, to plead his case regarding an incident or to get a rule clarification. That is a privilege that the person wearing the "C" is afforded. Again, that relationship between players and officials is all about respect. Both are professionals, and both have a job to do.

Stories of officials getting attacked are sickening, especially in youth leagues. Angry parents and coaches are so emotionally and financially invested in their kids these days, and by God they want a return on that investment. Sometimes the officials are in the cross-hairs of those wackos and wind up getting physically assaulted. We hear stories about those incidents all too frequently. Even short of actual contact, the verbal taunting, threat of physical harm, and overall hostility toward officials has gotten way out of control in certain areas of the hockey world. From refs being spat on in peewee games to a ref being held down and attacked by a player in a junior game, it is insane.

In the NHL, the code would never tolerate garbage like that. Players who violate that sacred covenant are punished severely either by the league or by the teams themselves behind closed doors. The league feels bad enough about the fact that kids try to emulate the fighting that they see in the NHL in their own youth league games. The last thing they want is for kids to treat officials disrespectfully because they see them doing that on TV, too. Therefore, the players in the NHL take it very seriously and know that there is a lot on the line when it comes to their officials.

McSorley explained:

> Some officials just have a great hockey sense for how a game is being played out. I remember this one game where Matthew Barnaby kept jabbing me with his stick every time I got near him. I just figured he was trying to goad me into a penalty, but he would never challenge me. He just kept whacking me. Finally, the referee, Terry Gregson, comes over and says to me, "Hey, knock it off." I was like, "I'm not doing anything. Barnaby is just agitating me and trying to get me riled up." So I said, "Watch him, keep your eye on him." He does, and sure enough Barnaby comes back over and tries to start a little scrum with me. Gregson then comes back over and says to Barnaby, "Okay, if you do that again I am going to tell my linesman to turn around and leave so that McSorley can beat the hell out of you." Barnaby turned as white as a ghost and he said, "You can't do that!" And Gregson said, "Yes I can. Watch me!" Needless to say, Barnaby stayed about three steps behind me for the rest of the game.
>
> It was a very veteran move by a well-respected official who knew the game. I had a very good rapport with most of the linesmen, and that certainly helped my cause from time to time throughout my

career. If you showed them respect and listened to them when they wanted to break things up, they were very easy to work with. Some referees were tough, though, like Paul Stewart. That guy just had it out for me. Maybe it was because he was a former tough guy in the NHL or just an ego thing, I don't know, but he used to call a penalty on me in the first period of every game I think I ever played with him out there. He just had my number.

Sometimes I would go up to a ref and tell him that I was having a problem with a guy and that I was going to fight him, just to let him know what was coming. Some of them really appreciated that and would thank you for it. Again, the code is all about respect, and if you treated the officials with respect, you would get it back. Each set of officials had their own way of doing things and own way of keeping order, so you had to kind of feel them out to see how they were going to call each game as they happened.

One official with an extremely unique perspective was referee Paul Stewart, a former NHL tough guy. Stewart's antics—both on and off the ice—are as legendary as his stories. Said Stewart:

Sometimes guys would just talk tough, and as an official, the best way to see what pussies like that were made of was to simply stand back and let them go. There is nothing worse than seeing a guy talk shit and not back it up. Paper tigers, they would run around like assholes, talking smack to other guys, thinking that they could just hide behind the officials. Well, I knew better, so when I saw guys doing that I told my linesmen to go stand out on the blue line and let that guy get his ass kicked to teach him a lesson. That was fun, it really was. The expression on their faces when we wouldn't step in was priceless. Another time two kids were shadow boxing in an AHL game I was reffing, so I went over to them and said, "If you two assholes don't stop wasting my time and start throwing some punches, I am going to take my whistle off and kick the shit out of both of you."

The greatest fight I ever saw was up in Saskatoon, during a Western Junior Hockey League playoff game I was refereeing one time. Two future NHL tough guys, Shane Churla and Wendel Clark, went at it like nothing I had ever seen before. It was so good that they just literally fought until they couldn't lift their arms up. The linesmen of course tried to rush in and break it up, but as the referee I held them back and just let those two warriors go. I said, "I'll take care of this one." So I finally went in to break it up after they were just hanging on to each other in utter exhaustion. They weren't cat-calling each other or anything; you could tell that they each had a lot of respect for each other. Well, I skated them both over to the penalty boxes and as I was going along I took both of their hands and raised them up over their heads, to signify that they were both the champs that night. The crowd just went crazy; they loved it. I really appreciated what those guys did and what they were doing for their teams. As a former tough guy, I got it. A lot of other officials didn't have that perspective.

Sometimes, though, being a former tough guy is hard to get out of your system. I remember refereeing a game in Edmonton one time when a fight broke out. Well, after a while the Edmonton guy started to look like he was getting worked over pretty good, so I stepped in to prevent him [the Oilers player] from hitting him again. Well, just as I put my arm in there, he wound up hitting me in the back of my head with an overhand right. It stunned me. Incredibly, though, my hockey fighting instinct just took over and without even thinking, I reached up and grabbed his throat with one hand and then grabbed his crotch with the other. So, as I was falling I got a hold of him and just pile-drove him into the ice. On the way down, though, I hit him with two quick lefts just for good measure. I mean, I was seeing stars at that point, but it was good to know that even after so many years of being retired that my natural instincts were there when I needed them. I wasn't even aware that I hit him, to tell you the truth. Luckily, people fell on top of us to break it up; otherwise, I might have kept nailing him. The funny part about that whole incident, though, came afterward when the Oilers threatened to have me fired for hitting their player. Their coach, Glen Sather, and I used to play together, and there was no love lost there. So I went right back to the league and said, "Sure, you can discipline me, right after you hand out a 25-game suspension to that kid for hitting an official." Needless to say, that was the last I heard about the incident from Glen.

Officials are on the ice for many reasons, most importantly to enforce the rules and to facilitate the game itself. They are also there, however, to keep the peace and to prevent the games from getting out of hand when the players get frustrated. But they know that the game polices itself, and they know that the code is there for a reason, so they play their role accordingly. They are a big factor in the success of the code and the game itself, and the players respect that.

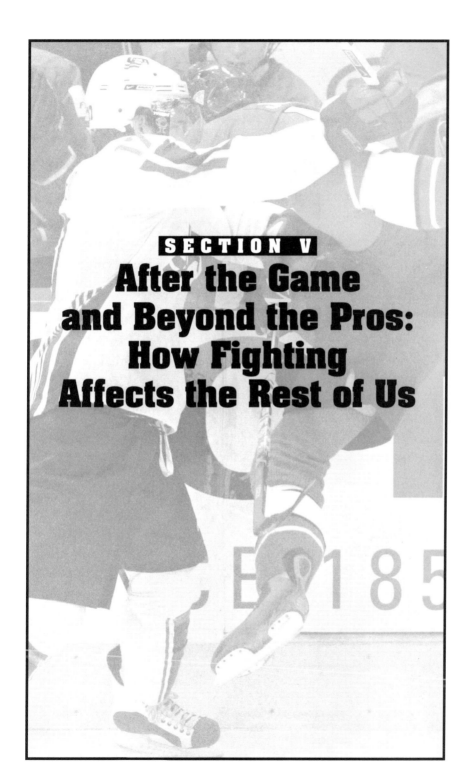

# SECTION V
# After the Game and Beyond the Pros: How Fighting Affects the Rest of Us

"Every guy on the team has a role. I was a goal scorer and because of that, I didn't ever have to fight. Other guys did that on my team; that was their role. … I had respect for every guy's role on my team because collectively we were all in it together, whether you were a first-liner or a fourth-liner.

"While I was certainly a guy who was protected by the code, I would not say that I needed protecting, because I didn't mind getting dirty in the corners or out in front of the net. There was a price to pay to make your living in front of the net, and believe me, I paid it. I have the scars to prove it. I tell you what, though, having a guy like Tony Twist on your team sure made life a lot easier. Having a feared tough guy on your bench made sure the other players had to play you straight up. On one hand it was nice to know that I had guys like that watching my back, but conversely, it was also nice for them to know that I wasn't skating around like an asshole out there, either, provoking people. I never took advantage of that privilege. …

"I appreciated my tough guys a ton and I let them know it whenever I could. … I would never have been able to have any success out there if it weren't for those guys all doing their jobs and looking out for me."

—BRETT HULL
21-season veteran of the NHL

# 18

## Junior Hockey

Most fighters in the NHL will tell you that they learned and honed their craft in junior hockey up in Canada. Kids often leave home in Canada when they are as young as 14 or 15 years old to play what's known simply as junior. The top kids then advance on to play major junior, which is for many the final proving ground en route to the NHL. It is the best of the best for kids ages 15 to 20, with all of the top players being drafted. There are three major junior leagues in Canada: the Western Hockey League, the Ontario Hockey League, and the Quebec Major Junior Hockey League. The players live with host families and attend high school while they are playing. Players also receive a modest monthly stipend, which provides them with spending money that they cannot otherwise earn in part-time jobs due to the time commitments of school and hockey.

The pressure on those kids to perform is incredible, especially if they are big kids and know that the only way they are going to make it at the next level is by being an enforcer. Think about it: teams carry only one or maybe two enforcers out of 22 players. Those are tough odds. So the kids do whatever they can to get exposure and to get noticed by the scouts. They play physically, and they fight whenever they can to show the scouts what they are made of. If you are a fighter, your measure for success is not registered in goals and assists but in penalty minutes—usually laced with blood and swollen knuckles.

## Tony Twist on Junior Hockey

"I tell you what, when you take your helmet off in junior, man, that is an eye-opener. Those were some of the most vicious fights I ever had up there because you could really just go at it with a guy. When you don't have to worry about what angle you are going to punch a guy from, so you don't break your knuckles on his helmet, you can just swing away."

Fighting in junior hockey is much different nowadays, though, because visors are mandatory. Now when a pair of willing combatants wants to drop the gloves, they also have to unstrap their helmets before throwing the first punch. Some players even take off their elbow pads and really ham it up. As many critics will contend, it can be more of a show in junior.

Regardless of the showmanship, some of the most ruthless, meanest, nastiest SOBs patrol the ice at this level. Players have to skate with their heads on a swivel in junior because unlike the pro game, where tough guys fight only tough guys, anybody is fair game down there. Some of the ugliest bench-clearing brawls in the history of the sport have the distinction of coming out of the junior ranks.

And remember, these are just kids living and playing in a man's world. They grow up pretty quick riding the bus from Thunder Bay to Moncton, getting in fights and living like rock stars. Sometimes their youthful exuberance can be both good and bad. Stories of kids in fights, with girls, in bars, and on the road are legendary in junior. There have been more than a couple of players over the years who have gotten into gnarly scrums on the ice and have then had to hitch a ride home in their team bus's luggage bin to evade the local authorities.

Just like in the pros, however, there is great pressure to succeed. This is the training ground for the toughest of the tough, and they know that if they don't make it by the time their draft year comes around, they will have to play in any number of minor leagues and start all over again. An injury or a poor scouting report can be a death sentence for some of these kids, because many have nothing to fall back on.

Whereas football, baseball, and basketball players in large part come through the college ranks, the majority of professional hockey players go through the junior route—or as some critics call them, the "puppy mills of the Canadian junior"—and skip college altogether. Getting an education for life after hockey can be a difficult proposition. These kids live virtually the same lifestyle that the professionals do, being on the road all the time and living away from home, yet they are just teenagers. College is not an option for many, which drives them to succeed at their chosen profession even more. That desire and grit is what separates them from their typical American counterparts.

Peter Hankinson, a former University of Minnesota player who went on to play in both the AHL and the IHL, had the following to say about junior hockey:

> I think that for a lot of Canadian kids there is no fall-back option. I mean college kids have a degree to fall back on if things don't work out, whereas the Canadian kids just go for broke because for many of them it is all or nothing. So they have more incentive to work their tails off and make it at all costs. I played three years of minor league hockey, including one year up in Canada, and I definitely saw that hungry attitude from a lot of those guys. Even the guys who weren't that skilled were willing to make it as fighters, just to make it. A lot of college kids wouldn't do that.

In junior the kids fight because it is expected of them. And there is a whole bunch of dog years' difference between a kid who plays where fighting is allowed and an American kid who doesn't. It is an entirely different game after that face mask comes off, that is for sure. Coaches in the junior ranks want to make sure that their kids are tough, and they

### Derek Boogaard on Junior Hockey

"As a kid growing up in Canada, all you think about is making it onto a junior team. I knew pretty early on that I was going to be a good fighter. I can still remember my first fight. I was a bantam. There were some major junior scouts at my game and I wanted to impress them. Well, I wound up getting into a fight with a kid and just beat the piss out of him. I took my mask off and then got his mask off and just went to town. He had done something really dirty to one of our players and I was really upset. I was so mad that I dove into their bench and started fighting their entire team. Most of the kids just threw up their hands like they were under arrest or something. It was pretty funny now that I look back on it. Needless to say, nobody ever messed with us again after that. And I got listed, or signed, by the junior team from Regina because of that fight right after that as well. I was on my way."

## Gordie Roberts on Junior Hockey

"I learned the code while I was playing junior hockey out of the Detroit area against teams from Canada. Those guys would test us, and you learned pretty quickly how the nuances of the code worked. They were tough on us American kids for sure. I went on and played major junior that next year, and I may as well have been from Alabama as far as a lot of guys were concerned. In fact, I think many of them confused my first name, Gordie, with 'You f*cking Yankee!' which sort of told you how a lot of them felt about us playing up there. I got through it, though, and learned a ton. You learn things up there that you aren't exposed to in the States, and that was important for me as I made the transition to pro hockey."

reward those kids with ice time. If kids work hard and mix it up out there, then they will get a regular shift. A regular shift might make the difference in getting noticed by a scout and being drafted. There is a lot at stake for these kids, no question.

"When I was younger it was very hard to gain a spot on a junior team," explained Al Secord to Ron Spence of Hockeyenforcers.com. "There were dozens of guys willing to fill every possible role. In fact, one year, there were probably around 40 different guys wanting to make the team as an enforcer. There were a lot of brawls, even in intra-squad games or practices. Those were very wild fights. I played a physical game in juniors and it was an advantage for me and my teammates. Because of my reputation, I got a little bit more room to operate on ice and it also created more room for my line mates."

It is a test of courage when the coach taps a young guy's shoulder and sends him out to stir it up with another player. That is when they see what those kids are made of, just how hungry they really are. It can be brutal. Those young men know that if they get drafted and get called up to the "show," their lives will change overnight. They also know that as fighters, they will have to prepare themselves for battle like never before, because they will have gone from squaring off against 19-year-olds to squaring off against 30-year-olds, and that is a huge leap. It is survival of the fittest down there, and only the toughest survive.

Marty McSorley explained the difference between junior in Canada and college kids in the United States:

When a kid plays junior in Canada, he has to be able to fit in. If he isn't doing what is needed for that particular team to win and just isn't fitting in chemistry-wise, he will simply be traded or cut. In college, meanwhile, kids come in on four-year scholarships and have a lot of job security. The coaches have to pamper them and oftentimes build their system around the players that they've got. In junior, players are forced to fit in just to survive. If they don't they are gone. Sure, they will develop kids and bring them along, but up there they don't cater to the top kids. The kids figure out pretty quickly what their roles are going to be and they either go with it or they get the hell out. That may sound brutal, but that is just the way it is up there. They'll fight if they have to and they just suck it up. No one is forcing them to be there. They all want to be there, and they all hope to advance on from there to the next level.

# 19

## Southern Cookin'

Hockey has always been a product of its environment. In the days of old, extremely cold weather was a barrier that kept the game north of the Mason-Dixon Line, and then some. So when hockey began expanding south into nontraditional hockey markets, many wondered if it would catch on, or if it would just be looked at as some sort of circus freak show. Not surprisingly, it has done well, especially at the NHL level. With franchises now in L.A., Phoenix, Dallas, Atlanta, Raleigh, Nashville, Tampa Bay, and Miami, the league has spread its web across the country in hopes of further growing the game from the grass-roots levels.

The league knows that if it is going to acquire lifelong customers, it needs to have a fan base of knowledgeable people who understand the game. With a scarcity of arenas throughout the Sunbelt, however, it has been an uphill battle. Although many transplants and retirees from the north and east have relocated to those areas, there is still a great need to build that core base of locals to come out and support their teams. Much of that starts with kids playing youth hockey, and because of the limitations with regard to the number of rinks, that has been tough. In-line hockey has helped fill the void, but it will never be like it is for kids in Massachusetts, Michigan, Minnesota, or Manitoba.

Because of this, many in the hockey world speculate that fighting has become a bigger factor in those markets for the sole purpose of selling tickets. As one player put it, "They may not understand hockey, but they understand fighting." Others were more blunt, comparing the novelty of hockey down South to that of the antics of pro rassling or even NASCAR, which provides its fans with not only violent crashes but also death, which is sadly not too uncommon for its brave drivers.

In fact, in many ways hockey is similar to auto racing. What are the two things they always show for both sports on the 10:00 news? In racing it is the checkered flag, followed shortly thereafter by a horrific crash. In hockey, meanwhile, it is the game-winning goal, followed by two toothless thugs pounding on each other. Many wonder if auto racing were to magically announce that it had somehow eliminated crashing, would anybody show up to watch it? Surely the die-hards would, but beyond that is anybody's guess. The same is true for a certain percentage of hockey fans, who come for the fights. As for just how many, we will never know.

"I would say there are some circumstances where fighting can be for show, such as in the East Coast League," said McSorley. "I know that there have been coaches in the ECL who have pretty much said that they wanted four to five fights per night, minimum. That is just another world out there, though, because they have to sell tickets or they're all out of jobs."

The fact of the matter is that violence sells. It always has. Does it need to be more prevalent in those markets? The answer, at least at the NHL level, is not necessarily. It sure helps, that is for sure, especially for a non-playoff team struggling to fill seats. At the minor league levels, however, that answer gets much more complicated. The bottom line for many organizations at that level is to sell tickets, no matter what. It is a simple matter of economics, and for many, they have chosen to highlight their "assets."

Many teams market their product with what are known as "blood ads," billboards and advertisements that get right to the point, such as the AHL's Tidewater (Virginia) Red Wings, which once used posters that read: "Brutal, fast, brutal, exciting, and brutal" and "If they didn't have rules, they'd call it war."

Some have even taken it a quantum leap beyond that, offering "Guaranteed Fight Nights." In 2000 the IHL's Orlando Solar Bears held one against the Houston Aeros. The Cape Fear (North Carolina) FireAntz of the now defunct Atlantic Coast Hockey League also had one, against the St. Petersburg Parrots, shortly thereafter. Then, two years later, the Aeros, who had been drawing poorly on Thursday evenings, decided to host a couple of their own against the Milwaukee Admirals and the Wilkes-Barre/

> ## Joe Micheletti on Fighting in Southern Leagues
>
> "A few years back when Nashville first came into the league, I think that a lot of people figured that there were going to be a lot of fights in their games in order to draw fans from that nontraditional hockey market of Tennessee. Well, they were right in one sense, because they either led the league in fighting majors or were pretty close to leading that first year or two. What people don't realize, though, is that the Predators organization had made a decision to build through the draft and was going with a lot of young skill players on their roster. As a result, they had to bring in some tough guys to prevent other teams from making runs at those guys, which was all well and good in my eyes. Once those guys got established, their fighting majors went way down. In fact, in 2006 I don't think they even had a single fight in their first 20 games. If you look at them now, those kids have matured and they are one of the top teams in the league. So, while a lot of people thought that they were just fighting to attract fans, it couldn't have been further from the truth. Protection is key in situations like that, but a lot of fans don't realize that. Now, do some fans enjoy fighting? Absolutely. But in this instance that wasn't the intent whatsoever."

Scranton Penguins. They thought it was going to be a win-win. If there was not at least one five-minute fighting major issued, then every fan in attendance would get free tickets to the next home game.

"It's not like we were promoting something that isn't part of the game," said Houston P.R. man Sandy Kirk. "To us, 'Guaranteed Fight Night' isn't any different from 'Guaranteed Goal Night' or a 'Guaranteed Sack the Quarterback Night' in football."

Not everybody saw it that way, though, and when league president Dave Andrews ordered the Aeros to cancel their promotions or risk a huge fine, the Aeros called it off.

"We try to promote the integrity of the game in everything we do and something like this promotion doesn't fit well in our plans," said Andrews. "It was an ill-conceived idea. It is disrespectful to the game itself, and it is disrespectful to the players. It suggests that gratuitous violence is a big part of the sport, and that's just not the case."

Of those types of antics, Paul Stewart said:

> That stuff is a crock, it really is. I remember playing for Vince McMahon, the famous wrestling promoter, who owned a minor league team in Cape Cod back in the early '80s. He used to always try

to get me to go out and fight for no good reason, and I told him no way. I said I didn't do that crap. I wasn't going to go out and pretend to be Hulk Hogan out there and make an ass of myself. No way. A lot of minor league teams do that shit to sell tickets, but I think it is a real crock of shit. It belittles what the real professionals have to do out there to protect their teammates and help their teams.

Lou Nanne, who played for 11 seasons with the Minnesota North Stars back in the 1960s and '70s and then served as the team's long-time general manager, feels that they don't need to fight in the South to sell tickets:

I disagree with a lot of people who think that they need fighting in order to sell tickets down south. If anything, I think it hurts it. You have to remember, first and foremost the southern part of the country doesn't know hockey that well. And the game doesn't televise that well either, which makes it even tougher for them to follow it. So, unless you get pockets where you get kids who play the game or have a lot of retirees from up north or out east, it is tough to sell tickets. The thing that sells in hockey is speed and contact. You don't need fighting to achieve that. Look, when they have minor league teams down there pulling stunts like "Guaranteed Fight Night" and bullshit like that, those aren't the fans who are going to be coming to an NHL game anyway. Minor league games are very inexpensive, like seven to 10 bucks per ticket, whereas NHL games run anywhere from $40 to $60. Is it a tough sell down there? Sure, but most of the teams down there now have made investments in their communities to educate their fan base and they are doing all right.

Taking it one step further than guaranteed fight nights was the "Battle of the Hockey Enforcers," held at the CN Centre in Prince George, British Columbia. Held on August 29, 2005, the event gave hockey fighting an entirely different meaning. The event, or tournament, featured a couple dozen current and former hockey fighters squaring off in full gear at center ice to compete in one-minute bouts. As soon as the gloves came off, the clock started. (The combatants had to wear martial arts gloves to get around a ban on bare-knuckle fighting for prize money.)

Like in the NHL, no fighting on the ground was permitted, and the officials separated the combatants if the fight turned too one-sided or if someone got badly injured. Other rules included no hitting below the belt, no spitting, and no hair-pulling. If a fight went on past the designated time and was a draw, then a panel of judges determined the winner. The group hosting the event took several safety precautions prior to the event, including having each participant get physicals complete with CT scans and blood tests. Two doctors and two ambulance crews were on site as well.

The controversy surrounding the event scared away a lot of arena owners in the beginning. Initially, the event was supposed to take place in Minneapolis, but squeamish arena owners backed out, calling the spectacle a "goon show." The Prince George mayor welcomed the show, however, comparing it to the pro wrestling and ultimate fighting contests.

As for the actual event, it was considered a moderate success. The arena was one-third full with about 2,000 spectators in attendance. The pay-per-view numbers were also reported to be encouraging. The favorite going in was former San Jose enforcer Link Gaetz, but "the Missing Link" had to withdraw after suffering a concussion in the first round. Dean Mayrand from Windsor, Ontario, wound up beating Mike Sgroi in the finals, earning a cool $62,000 and the title of hockey's toughest enforcer.

"Hockey fighting has been around for decades and decades," said Manitoba promoter Darryl Wolski, the mastermind behind the event. "For 100 years it's been part of the game. Maybe not at the college level, but at every other level of serious hockey. So, we've taken one aspect of the game and made it an All-Star game."

# 20

## To Fight or Not to Fight

There may be no other issue in professional sports that has been as hotly contested as is the one of whether fighting should remain in hockey. Every time a controversial event such as the Bertuzzi incident goes down, it stirs up the knee-jerk reaction from the masses for the league to "clean up its sport." Both sides are passionate about what they feel is right for the game, and it has been that way for more than a century.

### The Case for Keeping Fighting

While everybody agrees that fighting has no place in any level of youth hockey, here are the proponents' arguments as to why fighting should remain a part of professional hockey.

Pundits and pugilists alike agree that fighting has been a part of hockey since the game's inception. Therefore, in keeping with history and tradition, they believe it should remain as a manageable, yet punishable, aspect of the game. It is legal, and when used properly, they argue, fighting can be an effective tool teams can use to swing the momentum when they are down.

Said ESPN analyst Barry Melrose:

> I once broadcasted a game between the Rangers and Hurricanes in Carolina. The 'Canes came out flat and trailed 1–0 after the first period. Just 39 seconds into the second, Carolina's Jesse Boulerice got into a scrap with Rangers enforcer Chris Simon, who looked to be winning the fight. But Boulerice would not go down and got stronger

as the fight went on. The building erupted. The crowd, teams and the game were different after the fight. The Hurricanes tied the score a little more than two minutes later and eventually went on to a 3–2 victory, thanks in part to the emotional boost they got from Boulerice. There is no way they win that game without that fight.

Fighting also serves as an effective deterrent, allowing teams to police one another and hold each other accountable for their actions. Getting punched in the face is something we can all understand: it hurts. Players know this, and a big reason they aren't allowed to wear face masks is so that they can be held accountable for any dirty or cheap shots that they may dish out. If they play dirty, then they will have to face retribution for those actions, which may deter them from doing them the next time.

It also protects the league's star players, because if someone wants to go after them and take liberties with them, they will have to pay the price for it afterward. This threat of violence cleans up the game, especially the slashing, elbowing, checking from behind, and illegal stick work, which ultimately allows for more offense and excitement. It is also necessary, they contend, because of all of the better safety equipment that has been adopted by the players through the years. They believe the new equipment

### Glen Sonmor on Why Fighting Should Remain

"I am a fan of fighting in pro hockey, absolutely. You know, a lot of fans really do enjoy that aspect of the game. The league is probably not that sure just how many fans they would actually lose if they got rid of it, either. The fact of the matter is that they may lose a lot more fans than they think if they ever did. And once they took it out there is no way in hell they could ever put it back in. So I don't think they will ever eliminate it, to tell you the truth. Yeah, I like fighting in hockey. Hell, a lot of people like to see a good scrap every now and then. It is a part of the game. Sure, we can live without the bench-clearing brawls and the unnecessary stuff, absolutely. But the emotional, in-the-heat-of-battle fights are important for the game, I think. Look, this is a very physical game played by very tough, physical players. They need to let off some steam out there every now and then and fighting is a good way of letting them do that. The bottom line with fighting is that it actually cleans up that game, but most people don't realize that. Without it, guys could high-stick other players or cheap-shot them with no fear of any retribution. Fighting promotes accountability. It also is what earns guys respect not only from their opponents, but from their teammates."

has led to looser play with the sticks, and fighting, they feel, levels the playing field in that regard.

Proponents believe that if fighting is taken out of the game altogether, many players simply won't be afraid to hack away at the opposition's star players because there would be no recourse from anybody. Even a harsh penalty wouldn't deter all the cheap and dirty stuff, they contend, and the game would come to a standstill ruled by bullies and pests. Look at European hockey, for instance. Across the pond there is very little fighting and as a result the players have no fear of being held accountable for their actions. However, there is much, much more stick work and dirty play over there. Removing fighting would be as if you took sharks out of the oceans. Without sharks, the other fish would overpopulate, corrupting the entire ecosystem. Enforcers are the sharks in this scenario, and they keep the other fish honest.

Many feel that the league's attempts to sanitize the game through penalization, by creating such rules as the instigator penalty, for instance, have contributed to more injuries being suffered by players. The instigator penalizes a player for retaliating against a cheap shot and in theory is designed to prevent fighting. While it may cut down on fighting, it also prevents the players from policing their own—which ultimately leads to more dirty play and injuries.

Legendary Philadelphia enforcer Dave Schultz had the following to say:

> When I played, cheap shots were handled by the players, not the officials. If an opposing player dared to dish one out on one of our guys, I would get his number, force him to confront me, and then everyone would see what we're both made of. It's the essence of sport. It's respect, showmanship, and civility in competition. Let's face it: respect is worth fighting for. Players are supposed to stand up for something, build something, and protect what is theirs. As far as I'm concerned, fighting is one of the more celebrated traditions of hockey. It is what keeps things civil, on a basic human level of understanding and respect in competition. We need to remember the game's past, embrace it and shape the game more in the likeness of what it was meant to be. Fighting has always had its place in the game. I hope it always will.

On March 5, 2004, in a game between the Philadelphia Flyers and the Ottawa Senators, continuous brawling led to a new league record for combined penalty minutes in a game, with 419.

## Barry Melrose on Why Fighting Should Remain

"I love a good fight every now and then. I don't see anything wrong with that whatsoever. I don't ever want to see fighting legislated out of the game. Now, I also don't want hockey to go back to the days of the old Broad Street Bullies either. But fighting is a part of the game and should remain a part of the game. It is a tool like anything else, and when used properly by a smart coach it can change the flow and momentum of a game. Look, it should never be there for gratuitous reasons; that is just for show. But it definitely has a place in this game. It is exciting as hell, the fans appreciate it, and it serves a very important purpose."

"While many cite this as evidence for more legislation," added Schultz, "I saw this as an example of players responding to a cheap shot and settling matters right then and there. That's partly what the game is all about."

On the lighter side, many fans absolutely love fighting and the human drama surrounding it. Many of them simply enjoy watching two grown men battle in the purest sense, bare-knuckle brawling. The warrior-like atmosphere of up to 20,000 screaming fans rooting for their guy can be intoxicating. That is why some fans come to hockey games, quite frankly, to see the contact, the violence, and the fighting. In fact, a 2004 *Hockey News* reader survey reported that 75 percent of hockey fans "love" or "like" fighting.

When a fight breaks out between two heavyweights, one adored and one loathed, you will be hard pressed to find a single rump in his or her seat while its going down. The fans live for that type of excitement; that is the escape and guilty pleasure of attending a professional sporting event. A good fight often draws a louder reaction from the fans than a good goal.

"When I go to a hockey game, I look forward to seeing a fight, and I enjoy it immensely when one happens," confessed legendary sports journalist Frank Deford. "I know I shouldn't, but I do. It brings out the worst in me. Apparently, this makes me a very typical hockey fan. The NHL won't give up fights to please critics for the same reason that strip shows won't give up naked ladies. You gotta play to your constituency."

Most fans, however, come to games to watch the entire package. They want to see goals scored, great passes, great checks, great fights, and great players leading their teams to victory. That is what is so unique about the sport at this level—there is something for everybody. However, enforcers, not skill players, are often the most popular players on the roster, and the large number of sweaters they sell with their names on the back will support that.

"Those who say fighting is just gratuitous violence don't understand the game, and they also fail to see the entertainment value in it," said Barry Melrose. "I've never seen anyone get up and leave an NHL game during a fight, so why do away with something exciting that can keep fans in the seats? These are the same people who are simply opposed to violence of any kind and think boxing should be outlawed, too."

Fighting can be very entertaining. The fans go crazy when they see their tough guys go to work, and that is good for business. Entertained fans are happy fans, and happy fans buy season tickets, hot dogs, and souvenirs. And when you have an arena full of happy fans, along with countless more happy fans watching at home on TV or listening on the radio, you've got happy corporate sponsors. Happy corporate sponsors buy TV and radio advertising, dasher-board signage, luxury suites, and stadium naming rights. All of that adds up to a healthy bottom line for everybody. Which leads us to the philosophy of "if it ain't broke, don't fix it."

The game has been cleaned up quite a bit over the years. The days of the bench-clearing brawls are gone, and the instigator penalty has cut down on fighting. And since the league bumped up its security detail by adding a fourth official on the ice several years back, the game is cleaner now than it ever has been. Plus, for various reasons, players don't typically get seriously injured in fights. Sure, injuries happen, but the players are watched closely by the officials and strict guidelines are enforced with regard to the rules of engagement. The NHL devotes several pages of its rule book to "fisticuffs," ensuring that if it is going to go on, it goes on as safely as possible.

The bottom line with fighting in hockey is this: it's more than likely here to stay. The league acknowledges it, accepts its role in the game, and stresses that it makes up a very small part of the entire package. It's true, in a game that takes three hours to complete, a fight might comprise a minute or two. Look, hockey is a game of emotion, and sometimes that emotion can overcome good judgment and lead to a fight. Fighting provides an outlet for that emotion and allows the players to police themselves. Some say that if fighting were eliminated, the game would lose its edge, its character, its personality, the very essence of what defines it. Others contend that if it weren't for fighting in hockey, more serious injuries would be dished out

### Darren Pang on Why Fighting Should Remain

"What I don't like, and I am sure a lot of people will agree, is a gratuitous fight that means nothing and is a waste of time. But a fight that has meaning and is about something that was done which was disrespectful, or in the heat of the moment between two players who might be battling for position, then that is different. That has a place in this game in my opinion. If it is a playoff game between the Avalanche and the Red Wings and a fight breaks out between two first-line players, that is compelling. As a TV analyst I love that. There is a story line developing about players establishing their territory and about a team making a statement. On the flip side, if I am broadcasting a meaningless 7–0 game and player X steps out on to the ice for his first shift with nine minutes to go in the game and gets into a meaningless fight, I have no interest or enthusiasm in that."

by frustrated players using their sticks instead of their knuckles to exact revenge.

Remember, even if fighting were eliminated, that doesn't necessarily translate to clean play, especially in the international hockey ranks where stick work runs rampant.

"They [the Soviets] were pretty violent as far as stick work," said Al Sims, a veteran NHL defenseman who played against the dominant Soviet teams of the 1970s. "In the back of the legs and in different, sensitive areas where you don't have padding. And you hit them—they were like tanks. They didn't even feel it because they were used to it."

Other popular Soviet tactics of that era included skate kicking or "slew footing," where a player kicks his opponent's skate from behind, causing him to lose balance and fall backward. There were also some nonviolent dirty tactics, including "skate cutting," whereby a player would very subtly kick his sharp skate blades across an opponent's skate laces, cutting them and forcing the player to take a couple of shifts off to replace them. It becomes a case of pick your poison. If you don't want fights, then dirty play is what you will get.

It is interesting to note that while we may have taken a big step toward cleaning up the violence in the NHL with the new rule changes following the lockout, in Europe they are dropping the gloves more than ever, especially in the Russian elite leagues, where brawling was almost unheard of as recently as the 1990s. But the NHL is a global game now, and kids in Russia watch TV the same as the kids here do, and they too want to be like the big boys. Eventually, those kids grow up and before you know it, there is a new attitude about how the game should be played. Many American and Canadian players who have played in Russia come home with horror stories of not only two-on-one fights, but excessive stick work, cheap shots, and even fans who go at it in the crowds. So, the argument that "hockey across the pond is a cleaner game" is true for the most part, but has certainly lost some of its luster in recent years as players' attitudes change.

Like all sports, hockey has its critics. But many fans feel that to even entertain the thought of outlawing fighting in hockey is both absurd and naïve. The physical element of the sport, they contend, is woven into the fabric of the game and should not be touched.

Former player and current Minnesota Wild GM Doug Risebrough weighed in on the subject:

> The bottom line for me, as an NHL general manager, is this: I would be very nervous without fighting in professional hockey. First of all, it has been dramatically reduced as a result of the new rule changes. There is no organization at this level that is going to be successful with anything more than putting a focus on winning. If a physical component to your team helps you win, then you will embrace it, but if it is a distraction then it will be eliminated pretty quickly. I am fearful for a game that has no recourse for players to be held accountable for their actions. The officials in the National Hockey League do a great job, but they are human and there are only four of them out there in any one given game. They can't see everything that goes on. So, if a guy whacks another guy over the head and gets away with it, there needs to be some level of accountability for that guy or otherwise this game would be utter chaos. And even if he is penalized for doing something like that, two minutes in the penalty box does not always warrant the appropriate retribution. Again, players need to be held accountable for their actions so that players are not seriously injured out there.

And there are some who want fighting but are a little torn nonetheless. One of them, Harry Neale, who coached in the WHA and NHL for eight seasons back in the 1970s and '80s and currently serves as a TV analyst on CBC's *Hockey Night in Canada*, explained:

You know, I am not against fighting in hockey, but I do have a hard time justifying it sometimes. Fighting is a contentious issue, though, and is really more about entertainment in my eyes. When sports and entertainment collide, at the pro level anyway, the entertainment keeps the fighting alive. Hey, the fans seem to enjoy it when it happens and even the players themselves enjoy it, too. So it has its place, I suppose. I know that the league has cracked down on it recently, but I still think there is a ways to go. I am okay with the heat-of-the-moment fights, but when a guy has 30 or 40 fighting majors in a season, that is over the line in my mind. They are doing it for other reasons. I mean, you don't get mad enough to drop the gloves that many times. I should also say that I am firmly opposed to fighting at all other levels of hockey, especially at the amateur level. There just is no place for it there.

Another school of thought is that it should never be legislated out because then they could never bring it back in if they later decided that the game just didn't work without it. I mean, how would they go about reinstating fighting after already having made a rule to ban it? It would never happen. What makes hockey so unique is the fact that bare-knuckle brawling is flat-out legal. What an amazing concept. That fact alone truly separates the boys from the men. Fans enjoy that type of entertainment the same way they support boxing, mixed martial arts, and ultimate fighting. It is real, it is legal, and it is exciting.

Furthermore, fight proponents believe that eliminating it would not only have a devastating effect on the ice but also on the bottom line of the business. The league does not want to alienate its core fans, but at the same time it walks a fine line between how much fighting is too much and how much is not enough. While the NHL has always adjusted its rules to both accommodate and contain fighting, the rule changes that came into effect following the lockout of 2004 have forced the fighter of the 21st century to evolve into more of a well-rounded player. As a result, a different kind of fighter along with a different kind of fighting have emerged. That, most will agree, is a good thing.

Most likely, until somebody dies from a blow to the head, fighting will be a part of the game in some form or another. The owners like it and the fans love it. It's like legendary Maple Leafs owner Conn Smythe once said of fighting more than a half century ago: "We've got to stamp out this sort of thing or people are going to keep on buying tickets." Old Connie was right on the money with that one.

## The Case for Eliminating Fighting

Just as there is a pro-fighting lobby in professional hockey, there is also an anti-fighting one—hockey's "tree huggers," as their critics have labeled them. Here are their arguments as to why fighting should be eliminated from professional hockey.

While many fighting opponents were glad to see the addition of the "third man in" rule, which eliminated bench-clearing brawls, some remain conflicted over the effectiveness of the instigator penalty. Is it enough of a deterrent, they wonder. Others would like to just ban fighting altogether, for good. They look at the Canada Cup, the World Cup, the Olympics, or international hockey in Europe and Scandinavia as examples of models that work, as well as the college game, which has virtually no fighting either. Nobody turns off the TV or stays home just because there's no fighting in those games, they contend.

Arguably the best case for the anti-fighting lobby is the Olympics. After all, they are 99.9 percent altercation-free and extremely successful in the TV ratings—a pretty good indicator of success. Take the 2002 Winter Games in Salt Lake City, for instance, when Team USA made a riveting run to beat the hated Russians in the semis only to wind up losing to rival Canada in the gold medal game. The Herb Brooks–led Americans were attempting to become the first gold medal winners since Brooks' fabled "Miracle on Ice" team of 1980. They came up short, but the interest was there on the home front.

In fact, the gold medal game was rated three times higher than any Stanley Cup Final in history (10.7 versus 3.6 share), with some 38 million people tuned in to the action. What is even more amazing about this story, though, is that not one player from Team USA dropped his gloves during the entire tournament. There was tons of excitement, drama, and action—all hallmarks of great games—yet not one fight. The players knew that if they fought they would receive a game misconduct plus a one-game suspension. The stakes were simply too high.

Opponents of fighting look at movies such as *Slap Shot*, a satire of hockey's culture of goonery, and they want to clean up their game. They will all agree that it has come a long way since those raucous days of the 1970s, but it's not yet where they want it to be. They plead to the guardians of the game to provide positive role models for their children, but to no

## E. J. Hradek on Why Fighting Should Be Eliminated

"The game has changed so much over the past few decades. I think fighting has become more of a coaching strategy for many teams. Personally, I have sort of had it with fighting in general because when I was a kid growing up, hockey fights were more a result of two competitive players dropping their gloves in the heat of battle. Nowadays, fighting in hockey has become more about swinging your team's momentum when you are down by two goals. It is a tactic and really unnecessary in that regard. Then the league expanded into some nontraditional hockey markets and before long the game had really changed. I think it is to the point now where guys pick and choose when they will fight and who they will fight with. That is not what the code is about in my eyes. You also see more and more guys turtling up after provoking a confrontation, refusing to be held accountable. They just don't follow the etiquette which had been a part of the game for so long. That is too bad. Hopefully things will change in the future."

avail. Opponents want to create a new culture of hockey, one that they can feel proud to take their families to on a Saturday night.

Some say that if the powers that be won't eliminate it altogether, then the next best thing would be to make the penalty much harsher. If you fight, you're ejected and you sit out the next game with no pay, they suggest. And if you play dirty or hit someone with a cheap shot, you're ejected, followed by a suspension with no pay if it happens again. Eventually, they contend, it will be cleaned up. Teams will no longer need to stockpile nuclear weapons like we did back in the Cold War era. The enforcers will go the way of the dinosaur, and a new, faster, cleaner style will arise. The reality is that fighting makes the owners a lot of money via fan interest. Would they go for a ban on fighting if the players suggested it? Probably not. In 1975 the National Hockey League Players' Association (NHLPA) came up with a proposal for the league to consider a one-year trial with no fighting. Each time a player got into a scrap he would be suspended for that game plus one more. Although it sounded like a good idea, the owners rejected the deal.

Another argument that the abolitionists have raised is that the league would flourish under a system of no fighting because of potential television revenues. They contend that with fighting, the major networks won't give them a high-profile platform, currently reserved for the likes of the NFL, NBA, MLB, PGA, NCAA, and NASCAR. Is this the ultimate catch-22? On one hand, if the league eliminates fighting, they might get a lucrative TV deal, but on the other, they might just alienate the core of their fan base who have been so loyal to them for years. They know how many fans tune in to watch the game with fighting, they just wonder how many would be willing to tune in *without* it. Fighting has simply outlived its usefulness, say members of the anti-fighting brigade, and has stunted the sport's growth. They feel that even though TV ratings are high in Canada, for the sport to truly grow and prosper the ratings have to rise in the United States—especially in the North and the East, where the game is most popular. But because so many viewers don't take hockey seriously due to its tolerance of fighting, that may never happen.

Debate over the issue has raged on for decades, and is usually cyclical, based on a big event that triggers a public outcry. For instance, the Bertuzzi incident drew all sorts of reactions from mainstream media back in 2004, and the overwhelming message was for the league to clean up the game before someone got killed. Even some of the old sacred cows chimed in, including Canada's national newspaper, the *Globe and Mail*, which carried the headline "It's Time to Ban Fighting in the NHL" for a huge four-part editorial aimed at saving the league.

Hockey icons such as Hall of Fame goalie Ken Dryden had an opinion, too, saying at a recent symposium that the game was "at risk of becoming an extreme sport" and that it needed "a complete, ambitious, and fundamental review."

It wasn't just the players who spoke up, either. Even the winningest coach of all time said that he was open to "limited" change.

"It wouldn't bother me if they took fighting out," said Hall of Fame coach Scotty Bowman. "If two people need to settle something between themselves, that's where it's probably needed. But doing it to protect someone or to fire up your team, that's really not necessary."

Noted ESPN hockey writer Terry Frei summed up his position quite eloquently:

> Fighting, at least in the traditional fashion, does not belong in the game. I can summarize my stand in three words: It's just stupid. Here's the deal: Ninety percent of NHL fights are moronic your-slug-vs.-my-slug sideshows. What does that have to do with "protecting" star players or with accountability? The ONLY argument that makes any sense at all is that some fans love it and it can be an attempt to swing momentum. Those are low-rent reasons. Accountability and

deterrence? Stick work and such? OK, if it worked that way, this would be a reasonable argument. But deterrence and retribution and accountability too often are not what NHL fighting is about. At least not often enough. And even if it were, it's still silly.

Some contend that one potential solution would be for the owners to adopt the larger Olympic-size rink, like they have in Europe and in many college hockey arenas. Olympic ice sheets are 200 feet by 100 feet, compared to a standard-size ice sheet, which is 200 feet by 85 feet. That extra 3,000 square feet of real estate on the Olympic sheet gives the quicker skaters an extra 7.5 feet of room on each side to go around a slower defenseman, which is significant. It makes for a much faster, more exciting game. The NHL-sized sheet, meanwhile, makes for more of a "read and react" style of play that is more conducive to big hits and obstruction. That is why the bigger, more physical players typically come from North America, while the smaller, faster, better stick-handlers come from across the pond.

Not everyone likes the faster style of play, though, including one of the game's best ever: "I say to hell with the Olympic-size rinks," said Brett Hull. "In fact, I think we should go to smaller rinks, to have even more excitement and even more action out there. It would be like having more kinetic energy instead of more stagnant and dull hockey."

Added former NHL goaltender and longtime ESPN TV analyst Darren Pang, "You know, whenever an Olympic year comes along a lot of people jump on the bandwagon about how we should sell this game as an Olympic-style game, with the larger ice sheet. Well, the Olympics are what they are because of how short that tournament is, and how much is at stake in that two-week window between the best players from each country around the world. For them to think that that could happen in the NHL for 80 games is absolutely naïve."

Anyway, the Olympic ice sheet solution would reduce violence and collisions and make it too difficult for many one-dimensional tough guys, who can't skate well, to keep up. It would be addition through subtraction by virtue of the fact that the enforcers would be weeded out of the game. The downside to this argument is threefold: First, the owners would have to spend millions on retrofitting all of their arenas with a larger ice surface. Second, they would then lose millions in revenue from the first three rows, which would have to be eliminated in the process. Third, the owners want violence and collisions; it sells tickets.

## Lou Nanne on Why Fighting Should Be Eliminated

"Look, they don't need fighting today in the NHL; it serves no purpose. They could get by in a heartbeat without it. Look at the Olympics or the world championships, or even the playoffs. Look at the college game, too. Why couldn't the NHL get by without it? The reason it still exists today is because the old guard in the league, the older owners, think that it would hurt them at the gate if they took it out. That is the only reason. They'll come up with these stories about how players will get hurt with high-sticks and what not, but that is just bullshit. I mean, fighting doesn't exist in any other sport except hockey. Players just have to learn to be disciplined, like in anything else in life. If a guy hits you with his stick, then he gets thrown out of the game. If anybody wants to sell you on the idea that we 'need fighting' because of this and that, that is just utter bullshit."

Abolitionists also hope that the league will further market its players as gifted athletes, and not as tough guys. Case in point: the NHL recently began selling a DVD called *Honor and Courage: Tough Guys of the NHL*. "They are loved, feared, and respected," screams the tagline. Some question why the league would choose that message to sell their product to kids.

Another argument debates the role of the designated fighter, which, in today's new NHL, is not a goon but a hybrid enforcer who protects his teammates. Many fighting opponents could live with fighting by players who drop the gloves in the heat of the moment, as long as the guys who make their livings just fighting each other are eliminated. They don't view it as justice when the thugs fight each other instead of the actual guilty parties who are too afraid to do so themselves.

This isn't a new concept either. Well-rounded players who could score goals as well as hold their own in a scrap, guys like Gordie Howe, Cam Neely, Mark Messier, and Chris Chelios, are the epitome of how the game is supposed to be played. Today, ironically, we call them "throwbacks."

Each of the 30 teams in the NHL typically has at least one designated fighter out of their 22 roster players. That represents less than 10 percent of the league's total number of players. This means that pretty much the same 30 to 60 guys are constantly fighting each other, representing more than 90 percent of the total number of fights in the league. That, in the eyes of the anti-fighting lobby, is more of a sideshow than a form of justice for the actual offenders.

Hockey has also created a culture, they contend, that promotes violence and fighting as a way of life. Players are rewarded for that type of behavior at every level; from fan appreciation, to respect from teammates, to increased salary. They are applauded for "sending messages," "taking guys out," and "making them pay dearly." They are rewarded for "playing the game the way it was meant to be played," old-time hockey. They know that upper management condones fighting and until they change their stance, the fighting will continue.

Another argument against fighting is the idea that it dumbs down and cheapens an otherwise beautiful sport. When arenas turn fighting into sideshows, abolitionists contend, we all lose. They cringe when accompaniment songs, such as the Village People's "Macho Man," are played during fights, as happened when Dallas Stars enforcer Shane Churla dropped his gloves. Even wholesome Disney got into the act, putting its animated characters up on the video screen to get the crowd fired up when one of their Mighty Ducks was about to engage in battle. Is that intimidating, or just plain silly? Sure, it gets the fans out of their seats, but it also put hockey just a notch above pro wrestling in many people's eyes. And, maybe most importantly, it sends a horrible message to kids who emulate hockey players as role models.

Finally, many opponents believe that if the league is ever going to ban fighting, it will probably be forced to do so as the result of wrongful death lawsuit. That is a horrible hypothetical scenario, of course, but one that is not too far-fetched. Death in hockey is not a new concept. It has happened at all levels of the game and probably will happen again in the future. Sadly, tragedy usually has to intervene in situations like this before something changes. Hockey has enjoyed a unique "shield of amnesty" for a long time, and that could certainly change if the doomsday scenario, God forbid, ever plays out. For hockey's sake, let's hope it never does.

# 21

## The Effects of Fighting on Youth

### On Parents Explaining Fighting to Kids

Most professional hockey players have been called out or taken to task at least once in their careers by an upset or concerned parent over how they have had to explain the role of fighting to their kids. Professional hockey has always struggled with the fact that it not only tolerates but promotes something kids know they are not supposed to do. Hockey's response to parents over this issue has always been the old "do as I say, not as I do" approach, which puts the responsibility squarely where it belongs—with the parents. Playing hockey and watching hockey are all about choices, and those choices need to be made by the families of young kids, nobody else.

Kids will occasionally see fights throughout their adolescence, not only on TV and in videogames but on the playground, the school bus, and even in their own backyards. For parents, the best way to deal with what their kids might say to them if they see fighting on TV or at a sporting event is to be honest and straightforward. Kids are smart; they can handle the truth if it is told to them in the proper context.

Parents need to explain the different kinds of violence that their kids see, whether it is in an action movie, on a TV program such as *ER* or professional wrestling, in the heat of battle on the sports field, or in real life between two people. In boxing and other martial arts, there are rules that must be followed and referees to make sure the combatants fight fairly. When it comes to hockey, however, fighting is a way to resolve conflicts and release frustration. Hockey is a sport filled with emotion and passion, and that's why people snap sometimes out on the ice. But officials are there to make sure they fight cleanly and to prevent anybody from getting seriously hurt. Those are positives to take out of a bad situation if you are a parent.

To compound children's confusion is the fact that the fans go wild and really enjoy fighting at hockey games, sending mixed messages to kids. The lessons here are to explain why the players are fighting in the first place. It may be about a player defending the honor of a teammate who is too small to fight a bigger bully; it may be about retaliating for a dirty hit; or it may be about frustration in the heat of the moment between two professional athletes. Parents need to reinforce that fights are rare and for a reason. There are ways to spin lessons about honor, respect, and good sportsmanship in there; getting them out appropriately is up to Mom and Dad.

The bottom line is that fighting, of course, is not acceptable for kids except as a last resort. Parents should also teach their kids about the real world, and about just what that last resort is. Fighting in some rare instances might not necessarily be a bad thing for kids. If they are being bullied, at some point they will need to stand up for themselves. And if they are in an emergency or if they are being attacked, it is an effective tool or deterrent in defending themselves. Kids should be prepared and know the basics of self-defense so they can react appropriately during a crisis. They should also know that punches are real, and they hurt. People can get seriously injured from fighting, and kids need to understand that as well.

Hockey at the professional level is not a game for the weak of heart, and it makes no bones about that. Hockey at every other level, though, is all about athletics, sportsmanship, fun, and excitement. There is a huge difference between the two, and hopefully children will understand that.

Parents also need to remind their kids that even though professional hockey is a business, the people are real and they feel real pain and bleed

## Rob Ray on Explaining Fighting to Kids

"I used to get people all the time that would come up to me and say stuff like 'What kind of an influence are you on my kids; fighting is wrong and you are setting a terrible example for them.' I used to just look at them and say, 'Look, it's not my problem to teach your kid what's right and wrong. If you can't explain that to them as a parent, then that is your fault. That is your job and this is my job.'"

## Willie Mitchell on Explaining Fighting to Kids

"You know, when I explain fighting in hockey to people who aren't that familiar with the game I usually use this analogy. I tell them that if society didn't have policemen, then there would be chaos. So in hockey each team has a policeman, and they keep the peace. They enforce the laws, or the code, and the players abide by that. Sure, the officials call the penalties and regulate the game, but the enforcers make sure that guys play honest. They make sure that if a guy cheap-shots somebody or high-sticks them, then he will have to be held accountable. Nobody wants to get hurt in this game; it is our livelihood, and sometimes guys who play dirty have to be dealt with accordingly. That keeps things on an even keel. Hockey is such an emotional, intense sport played by people with such passion, and sometimes in the heat of battle things happen. Fights happen in hockey for a reason, and hopefully the end result of them is so that the game can be played in a much better, fairer, safer environment for everybody."

real blood when they get hit. The players have families back home with kids just like them, and business is left on the ice when they leave the rink. Tell them that, believe it or not, Dave "the Hammer" Schultz, one of the toughest, meanest hockey players in the history of the game, has never been in a fight off the ice. In fact, most fighters will tell you that they never dreamed of being a fighter when they were kids. They dreamed of scoring goals. Some will even say it is just a job.

"I don't even like to talk about fighting," said Edmonton enforcer Georges Laraque to *The Sporting News'* Kara Yorio. "When I was a kid, I was Wayne Gretzky. I was Mario Lemieux. I didn't fight guys when I was a kid. Is there fighting in the playoffs? No. Tough guys don't even play in the playoffs. If all they see is me fighting on the ice, what are they going to assume? It's not the perception that I want to give to the kids or the community."

## On the Subject of Youth Hockey Violence

When it comes to fighting in youth hockey, this is an entirely different can of worms. Kids can definitely relate to the concept of "monkey see, monkey do," and hockey at the professional level has a lot of things in it that are clearly inappropriate for youngsters. Parents need to remind their kids that professional hockey is a business with its own set of rules and laws and that it is a game played by adults. It is much different from the amateur game, which is played by kids and should be treated as such. Kids need to know that if they sucker punch someone in school or on the ice the same way the pros do, they are going to get suspended, kicked off their teams, or even worse if their victim gets really hurt. Kids need to remember that when they get frustrated or angry out on the ice, that there are ways to deal with those emotions without violence. Parents need to reinforce that, too.

Many critics say that the problem with youth hockey is the parents themselves. We all know the negative connotation associated with the term "hockey mom" or "hockey dad." Why? Because hockey parents are passionate. They are also extremely emotionally and financially invested in their kids' hockey careers and they want a return on that investment. The sport of hockey is unique in that, compared to a sport like football, kids start playing the game at an extremely young age. The pressure is there right out of the gates for kids to advance to the A team or the triple-A traveling team. Parents want to give their kids every opportunity to make those teams and will do whatever it takes to give them that advantage. That will likely entail buying expensive equipment or sending them to expensive summer camps. The average pair of skates nowadays will set you back anywhere from $200 to $500, and a one-piece composite stick will cost you $100 to $150. It is not a cheap sport, and if you are a hockey parent reading this, you can certainly relate.

Sometimes the pressure of it all can be overwhelming for parents. They want their kids to do well, and they get upset when coaches don't see things their way. They also get upset at referees and other parents. In fact, sometimes they just lose it altogether and get into fights with other fanatical hockey parents in the stands, humiliating their kids as well as themselves in the process. And it is not just parents who are doing it. Plenty of coaches have gotten into fights with other coaches at the youth levels, and more than a handful of referees have been assaulted over the years as well. When kids see all of this, they follow suit, eventually getting into fights themselves. Pro hockey may be guilty of creating a culture of violence, but that only goes so far. It is up to our parents and coaches to teach kids right from wrong and how to be a good sport.

Some parents are so invested that they too join the fight, only instead of fighting with their fists, they bring in their lawyers to fight for them. One father of a nine-year-old in Canada sued the coach of a rival team who he said threatened to "put a bounty on his son's head." Another father from New Brunswick actually tried to sue a local league for $150,000 in damages over the fact that his 16-year-old son didn't win his team's MVP award, despite being the leading scorer. Then there was the family from Ottawa who sued over the fact that their 15-year-old was publicly humiliated over not getting enough ice time. Of course, all of those things pale in comparison with what happened several years ago in Massachusetts, when the dads of two 10-year-olds on rival peewee teams got into a fight at a game. One died after being assaulted, and the other got 10 years in the joint for manslaughter.

It seems as if the culture for hockey violence is fostered at a young age. While body checking is introduced at the bantam level in the United States, for kids aged 12, it is allowed in some peewee levels in Canada, for kids even younger. Fighting, meanwhile, is first allowed at the junior level, with kids as young as 15 years old, all the way up to 20. Kids who play hockey at the age of 15 have no business fighting, but in Canada, where the junior leagues are most prevalent, it is all about getting on to the next levels. Kids who learn the game with fighting play much different from the other kids, for sure. It is a much more physical game when the specter of fighting is involved, and those kids are tough.

Someone with a great perspective is former Minnesota North Stars and WHA Fighting Saints tough guy Bill Butters, who now coaches kids:

> I think our youth players put too much of an emphasis on playing league games. I mean when peewees and bantams are playing 55 games, plus the playoffs, that is too much. The European kids don't do that stuff. They work on skill development instead. It is no coincidence that 13 of the top 20 goal scorers in the NHL are from Europe. I think our society is so intent on winning at a young age that we don't take human growth and development into the equation. We cut some kids because they don't go through the pylons in 6.4 seconds or whatever, and we don't give them a chance to develop. Size is another huge thing. The NHL doesn't want guys who are 5'9", so those guys don't stand a chance unless they are like guys like [New York Islanders forward] Jason Blake and can scooter around the ice a million miles per hour.
>
> Then you look at high school football and basketball and you've got tons of 6'2", 6'3" kids just standing around on the sidelines who don't have a prayer to ever even make a Division III program. Well, if a lot of those guys didn't get cut from hockey early on, because maybe they were uncoordinated as a peewee, they might have had

the opportunity to really develop out on the ice. Who knows? The smaller communities as well as the European communities develop more kids because they spend more time with them. They don't cut them early on; they stick with them and let them develop. That is so important. Our coaches need to look at those things. It is a win-at-all-costs society and sometimes that isn't right.

When it comes to youth hockey violence, some communities are fighting back and trying to change the game one program at a time. Attorney Chuck Blanaru is the president of the minor hockey association in Nanaimo, British Columbia. In 2003 his association implemented a "no-violence code" for its players, coaches, and fans, regarding checking, fighting, and stick work. So successful was the program that several programs in the United States have called to obtain copies of the "Nanaimo Rules."

"I think people are looking for help," said Blanaru. "It's very difficult when the kids that we're talking to turn on the TV and see their professional idols doing everything we told 'em not to do."

Blanaru said his program addresses issues for talented but less physical Canadian players who are leaving the sport when hitting is introduced.

"He can be playing with kids a foot taller, 40 or 50 pounds bigger than him, and getting creamed," he said. "The kid drops out. By 14 or 15, he may have grown bigger than the kid that was creaming him, but he's out of the game now."

Stories like Blanaru's can be found throughout the hockey world: individuals trying to make a difference by doing the right thing. The pro scouts nowadays are much more interested in the size of the kids than their skill levels. It has become a case of "you can't teach 6'4", 220 pounds," meaning you can teach big kids how to play hockey, but you can't make even the best kids any bigger. The scouts want to see the player's parents and look at how big his dad is. They will look at the size of the kid's feet and hands and try to predict how much he will grow. For the scouts it is all about getting kids into the major junior programs and then onto the professional ranks. It is a business even at that level, and the kids will do whatever it takes to make it.

One person with an interesting perspective on the subject is 15-year NHL veteran J. P. Parise, who is the director of hockey at the prestigious Shattuck St. Mary's prep school in Minnesota, a midget Triple A powerhouse that has had 15 of its kids drafted into the NHL from 2003 to 2005. He had the following to say:

> As for kids, I would never condone fighting for young kids, no way. But we do play physical hockey here at our program. We also teach our kids to play clean and to play with respect. We get a lot of parents who are concerned about their kids getting hurt. It is just inevitable that every kid will get bumped and bruised from time to time if he plays long enough. If parents don't want their kids to be exposed to any physical contact, then they should encourage them to play Ping-Pong or bingo. I will say this, though: we prepare our kids to be able to defend themselves should that situation ever arise. Kids need to be prepared, and they need to have that confidence out there. Again, fighting has no place at the youth levels, but you never know when you might run into some other kid on some other team who doesn't share your same philosophy. We have tough kids, most of whom go on to play Division I hockey or junior hockey in Canada, including Sidney Crosby a few years ago, but we play the game the right way here. That is very important to teach our kids the right values about how the game is supposed to be played.

Although hockey's popularity at the youth level continues to grow, particularly in the southern states, many critics believe that the game is losing youngsters to other activities due to the ever-increasing level of violence. More and more kids are playing baseball, football, soccer, and even the extreme sports, which they may view as more "hip and cool." There are no coaches or parents yelling at them on the skateboard half-pipe, and to a lot of kids that is very appealing. Heck, a lot of kids just don't want to wake up at 4:00 in the morning for practice and go through the physical exhaustion to do "whatever it takes." It may be a sad social commentary, but it is true nonetheless. While the cost of the game, from ice time to equipment, has scared some away, for most it is the fear of injury and the violence that deters them from getting involved. That is a shame.

Violence and injuries are and always have been the great paradox in hockey, at all levels of the game. Whenever somebody gets cut after an accident or altercation and bloodies the white ice red, the referee comes over and uses his skate blades to scrape up the pinkish goop and whisk it away with a shovel. It is like removing the evidence from a crime scene in a sense, "out of sight, out of mind." But the violence does exist, and we can't hide that; it is just a part of the game. Heck, it's cool to get cut in hockey, to take stitches, and to look tough. On one hand we loathe it while on the other we quietly condone it. That's hockey to the core.

Another aspect of hockey violence for kids is that it can be a "gateway" for bigger and badder things down the road, both on and off the ice. If violence is condoned for kids playing junior hockey, for instance, then that attitude can carry over into other things, such as hazing rookies and conducting freshmen initiations. A bad situation can create a culture of violence that trickles down and permeates not only other aspects of the game but also other areas of that young person's life.

Kids need to be strong enough and confident enough to say no to things like that. Peer pressure is huge at the youth levels, because the threat of being beat up is very real. Kids need to be able to take a stand and speak up about these things when they come up, or they can be scarred emotionally for life. Even the great Bobby Hull once sat out for a game to protest a cheap shot his teammate suffered following a high-sticking incident. He said no to violence that day and he was heard. Kids can and should do the same if they feel strongly about it, and their coaches and parents should be there for them when they do.

For those who do play the game, sadly, the number of injuries from excessive violence are also on the rise. Many attribute that to the fact that face masks and highly protective equipment have made kids fearless. With face masks being mandatory at the youth levels, kids can swing their sticks with no fear of retaliation. So, there is no deterrent to cheap play.

The worst of the worst when it comes to cheap play, however, is checking from behind. Spinal-cord injuries have skyrocketed over the past several decades because of this, not to mention the boom in broken bones and blown-out knees as well. To prevent kids from doing it, youth players now wear a bright red "STOP" (Safety Towards Other Players) patch, in the shape of a big stop sign, on the backs of their jerseys. This reminds them in the heat of the moment to not hit people from behind and risk injuring them. In addition, many players, parents, coaches, and officials have to sign a fair-play pledge, acknowledging their commitment to promote nonviolent causes in hockey and clean up the game.

Respectful youth hockey players grow up to be respectful junior, high school, college, and professional players. That is a fact. It is always a battle, though, to win the hearts and minds of our kids. According to the *Pediatric*

*Emergency Medicine Journal*, 16 percent of all youth athletes say that they would purposely injure someone for retaliation. And those are just the brave souls who admitted it. Scary.

According to Lawrence Scanlan, author of the book *Grace Under Fire*, a 1995 study by three Minnesota health professionals looked at 117 hockey players with spinal-cord injuries and determined that the most common cause was a shove from behind into the boards. "Even so," the study reported, "26 percent of surveyed peewee and bantam players, who well understood that checking from behind could cause serious injury or death, reported that they would be willing to do so if angry or to get even."

The study also determined that among Canadian peewee teams, the incidence of bone fractures was 12 times higher in checking leagues than in noncontact ones. According to Scanlan, overall, hockey is the most dangerous team sport in the world, with the highest injury rate: 37,000 injuries per 1 million participants, compared to football (18,000) and skiing/snowboarding (11,000). Scanlan also confirmed another report from the *Canadian Medical Association Journal*, which found that 243 players have suffered severe spinal injuries in the past three decades, while six players have died.

For parents, it will always be tough to talk to their kids about fighting. Kids are kids, and they will always try to emulate their heroes. The last thing the sport needs, though, is a generation of kids dreaming of becoming the next great goon. Hockey has created a culture of violence, but hopefully that cycle will shift now that the NHL has instituted its rule changes. The game has opened up, and there is no room for those who can't skate. Skating is where it all starts for the kids. Young players need to learn the fundamentals, be creative with the puck, and have fun. That is the bottom line, because once you have that, then the sky is the limit.

# SECTION VI

# The Lockout and Its Aftermath

"The code to me was how I conducted myself out on the ice. For me, I just wanted to be a good professional. I wanted to play the game with respect and do things the right way. It was a dream come true for me to play professional hockey, and I never took that for granted. As a player you have an obligation to your teammates; you have an obligation to your coaches; you have an obligation to your organization; and you have an obligation to your fans. I always wanted to give them their money's worth and give them a good show. If that meant scoring a goal, great, or if it meant getting into a fight, then that was great, too. I just wanted to do whatever it took to help my team win; that was my obligation. That whole attitude is sort of what the code embodies to me, just playing the game the right way, with respect. If guys took liberties with my guys, then I was going to have to do the same to theirs."

—KELLY CHASE
11-season veteran of the NHL

# 22

## On the Events That Led Up to the 2004 NHL Lockout and Its Aftermath

The 2004–05 NHL season was lost due to an impasse between the players and owners, which led to the league declaring a lockout. It is interesting to look back at the events that led up to the work stoppage, as well as the rule changes that followed. One thing is for sure, fighting and retaliation in hockey will never be the same.

Although the league did experience a 103-day labor-related work stoppage in 1994, nothing compared to the disaster that came a decade later. The entire 2004–05 season was canceled in what would later be referred to as "hockey Armageddon." NHL commissioner Gary Bettman and the team owners locked out the players, demanding that a salary cap be negotiated into the new collective bargaining agreement. The owners were hemorrhaging money and needed to stop the bleeding. Their only solution was to force the players into submission. The players put up a united front and hung tough for an entire year, but finally conceded to not only a cap but also a significant reduction in pay.

So, how did the league get into that situation in the first place? Many critics speculate that it was because the league simply did not have the necessary television revenues to support the rapidly escalating salaries that were being thrown around to all of its players. Take a look at this: the NFL, which boasted a $17.6 billion TV deal in 2004, divvies out around $80 million a year to each of its teams. NHL franchises, meanwhile, make

## Tony Twist on the New Rules

"As for the new rules, I think they are okay. Look, I understand that they want to get rid of the goons, the guys who can't skate, but there will always be room for guys like me in the league because I protect my team's top players. You can't afford not to have a guy like me on your roster, even if I didn't play that much, because otherwise teams would run your top guys all night long. Sure, it will clean it up somewhat and it will eliminate some guys, but when you are one of the top heavyweights around, that is a pretty valuable commodity for a team to have.

"You know, the league has really changed in other ways, too. I mean, nobody is passing the torch anymore. I think that there has been a slow disintegration of hockey at this level, I really do. Do you know why there aren't as many guys telling good stories about the old days and whatnot? Because nobody has any to tell. And do you know why they don't have any? Because what it took to become a national hockey player is going out the window. Today the kids get these big signing bonuses; they are not riding the bus anymore; and they are out of touch. Gone are the days of the guys like Al MacInnis or Craig MacTavish or Brett Hull or Brendan Shanahan, guys who had to fight to get where they are. We used to go out drinking together, fighting together, screwing around together, and having fun together.

"Well now, with the growing dollars, combined with European influence, you don't have that team camaraderie anymore. Back in the day when you were out on the road you would all go out as a team. Now guys pair up in twos and fours to go out on their own. The classic old-school stories that used to be told way back when while we were all sitting around on the team bus aren't being told anymore because there aren't any to be told, and that is sad. When you don't have that chemistry together, your team really suffers both on and off the ice."

around $2 million each for their respective television deal. Despite that fact, top-tier players in both leagues had comparable salaries.

It was an orgy of spending by the NHL's owners, and the players were living high on the hog. Bidding wars ensued for the top players, and teams threw ridiculous amounts of cash at marginal players, too. Everybody was trying to keep up with the Jones'. The average NHL salary soared from $572,000 in 1995 to $1.64 million in 2004, a 187 percent increase. Total team payrolls during that same period rose nearly 260 percent, going from $12.2 million to $43.9 million.

To make up for that shortfall, the league expanded like wildfire and relocated several franchises over that decade, which resulted in hundreds of millions in new revenue coming from "expansion fees" from new ownership groups. So, the league put a team in San Jose in 1991, followed by Tampa Bay and Ottawa in 1992. The Mighty Ducks of Anaheim and the Florida Panthers were added in 1993. Then came the relocations, with the Minnesota North Stars going to Dallas; Quebec transferring to Colorado; Winnipeg heading to Phoenix; and Hartford moving to Raleigh, North Carolina. In 1998 the league expanded again, adding a team in Nashville and then in Atlanta in 1999. Columbus and Minnesota, this time as the Wild, were then added in 2000. It was dizzying.

With that, the league had swollen to 30 teams. As a result, the talent pool was diluted, which meant lesser-skilled players who were more prone to physical play. It also opened the flood gates for European, Scandinavian, Eastern Bloc, and Russian players, who had good offensive skills but lacked good English-speaking skills—which resulted in fan apathy toward many of them. In addition, a major realignment of divisions took place, erasing many good natural rivalries. Before long the attendance was down league-wide, which meant even less revenues would be coming in.

A huge part of the problem was that scoring was way down across the league during that decade, the "dead puck era" as some would call it. Stifling defenses, neutral zone traps, and paralyzing obstruction had turned

### Doug Risebrough on the New Rules

"I like the new rules a lot. It certainly puts a new emphasis on players' roles. You know, I think it is disrespectful if you, in management, view fighting as the only thing a guy can do. First of all, that is not fair to that individual who wants to play the game. So you have to be able to work with role players of all skill levels and bring them along so that they can help your team in different ways. If you have a physical guy who is not comfortable with the puck, then you as an organization had better find a way to get guys around him who will get him the puck and build his confidence up. You have to be respectful that this player wants to do more out there and, more importantly, should be doing more to help your team win. We want to get the most out of every player's ability. That is why we pay their salary, and that is why we have such high expectations for success. Players want to play this game. Everyone wants a taste of success and they all want to be an integral component of that success. Nobody wants to just sit on the bench and do only one role, regardless of what that role is. As a general manager I don't want one-dimensional players on my team, I want guys who can contribute and wear many different hats."

## Paul Stewart on the New Rules

"Hopefully the new rules will force teams to work with their tough guys so that they can showcase their talents and get some more ice time. Enforcers oftentimes get typecast into that role and never get to do anything else. Some coaches would work with the tough guys, like a Terry O'Reilly, and they would develop their skills to complement their tenacious ability to fight. I was jealous of guys like that because that wasn't me. I was the guy sitting at the end of the bench, waiting for my turn to go out and beat the hell out of somebody. I will never forget my last game in the National Hockey League. I was with Quebec and we were playing in Montreal. I didn't even get a single shift in the entire game. Finally, with six seconds to go my coach, Jacques Demers, says to me, 'Get out there and get your shift.' Back then you had to at least touch the ice during the game so that it would count toward your pension. I just turned to him and said, 'I would love to, Coach, but look.' I pointed down to my feet; I didn't even have my skates on. I mean I knew that I wasn't going to play so I didn't even bother. That's the way it was in those day, but maybe that will change now."

the game into utter boredom for many die-hard hockey fans. The scoring drop-off was so painful that Tampa Bay's Martin St. Louis led the league in scoring with just 94 points in 2003–04, less than half of Gretzky's 215 in 1985–86 or Lemieux's 199 in 1988–89. In just 10 years, the NHL had seen its combined goals-per-game average drop from seven to five, nearly a one-third decrease. It was becoming dangerously close to being soccer-like in the eyes of many.

When you combined all of those factors—higher payroll; a diluted talent pool that translated into fewer skill players scoring fewer goals; less-skilled players using more obstruction and intimidation tactics to slow down the skill players; overexpansion into nontraditional hockey markets; fewer marketable superstars from across the pond; and a bad TV deal with NBC and ESPN—the writing was on the wall. Add in the fact that corporate sponsorship was down, as were ticket sales, and it's no wonder the league was having financial troubles.

To make up for revenue shortcomings, the NHL traditionally had some of the highest top-end ticket prices in pro sports. But as prices rose, many middle-income fans simply couldn't keep up and got out. Many couldn't justify paying $10 to $20 for an upper-level seat to see the Boston Celtics, and then turn around and pay $50 to $60 for that exact same seat to see the Bruins. No way.

Eventually, the economics didn't make sense and the owners realized that they couldn't keep up with their ever-increasing payrolls. According to an independent audit of the NHL conducted by Arthur Levitt, former U.S. Securities and Exchange Commission chairman, all 30 franchises lost a combined $273 million during the 2002–03 season. In addition, several teams, including the Ottawa Senators, Los Angeles Kings, and Pittsburgh Penguins, had filed for some sort of bankruptcy protection over the past several years as well. It was a mess.

Many fans were turned off by what had become of their beloved league. From Fox TV's glowing puck experiment; to the tearing down of all of the classic cathedral arenas in favor of the newer, corporately named luxury palaces; to the way free agency had made it too easy for their favorite star players to just pack up and leave; to the way the stifling defense and unnecessary obstruction employed by many players had killed the creativity in the game; to too many of the league's top stars getting injured because of the violence—something had to be done. Many felt that Commissioner Bettman, who had been trained in the glitzy world of the NBA, was out of touch. The resulting backlash was in actuality a long time in the making.

The owners had a desire to achieve cost certainty, and that ultimately pushed them over the edge. Owners were spending nearly 70 percent of their revenues on players, something that had to change in a "new" economic system. So they issued an ultimatum to the players, but the players called what they thought was a bluff. They weren't going to be bullied. After months and months of bitter negotiations, as well as the specter of a shortened 2004–05 season, the league begrudgingly decided to pull the plug on February 15, 2005. The result was the first professional North American sports league in history to cancel an entire season. It was a sad day for hockey. Talks of contraction, irrelevancy, and utter pandemonium ensued shortly thereafter.

Desperate to rebuild its fan base and increase national TV ratings that had fallen lower than that of arena football, women's basketball, and poker, Bettman promised drastic rule changes designed to bring back the speed, flow, and creativity that had sorely been missing from the game.

## Lawrence Scanlan on the New Rules

"While I am glad that the new rule changes were put into place, I think the league still has a long way to go, too. Historically, if you look back to the old days of the game, refs in the NHL were more like consultants. They really weren't empowered with any real control of the game. They were never given that power by the powers that be. The first referees actually never called a goal. They would sort of consult over it and either approve or disapprove of it. They wore these great white coats and they rang a bell—it was a joke, it really was. And when the players got upset with them they would just haul off and cork them. It was a kind of anarchy, and what ultimately prevailed was a kind of prison justice where the players made the rules.

"There is a great quote from Scott Young, a reporter with the Toronto *Globe and Mail*, where he says something like, 'Some provisions of the league's rule book are enforced; others sometimes are enforced; while others never are enforced. If one took the Ten Commandments and decided to ignore the ones on theft, murder, and adultery on the grounds that they are extremely popular and too hard to stop anyway, one would have an exact definition of the way the NHL regards its rule book.' For years and years people like Scott have said that the rule book was there, so why don't we just enforce it? If it was the third period or in overtime of a playoff game, a sort of mayhem prevailed where players could seemingly do anything they wanted to out there. So that is why the code became so important, and that is why it will always be a part of hockey. There need to be rules, and there needs to be some sort of system of justice.

"The biggest rule change of them all, I think, was not about the red line, or the shootout, or about the goaltender restrictions; it was about the fact that the league was finally going to have the power to call the game the way it says it should be called in the rule book. That, more than anything, will be the defining factor of the new rules following the lockout. As for the fallout? Well, up here in Canada, people love the new rules. They love the speed of the game and how the smaller, quicker guys now have room to play. Nobody is 'skiing' anymore, where, when the play turns over and the defender just locks his stick onto the belly of the other forward and drags him down the ice. The obstruction is being cleaned up and that is great for the game. The fighting is still there, but it has been reduced significantly. So overall I am pleased."

"The very future of our game is at stake," said Bettman. "We do apologize to our fans, and this is truly unfortunate that they have to go through this, but we've got to correct this situation in the right way and not with Band-Aids."

With the league shut down, the players were forced to play elsewhere: in Europe, Russia, the AHL, and even in some backwoods bar leagues. Some just wanted to play, while others needed the money. During that time, however, the league discussed making some fundamental rule changes that would allow it to reinvent itself when they finally did return to the ice.

With that, the league began figuring out a plan to resuscitate itself. After conducting exhaustive research among the players, general managers, owners, and fans, the league realized that it had to make some radical adjustments. They looked at every aspect of the game and asked themselves how they could make it better.

At the heart of it all was the basic premise that they needed more scoring. Period. They wanted the league's best and brightest to be able to showcase their creativity and talent. So, they looked at goalie equipment, and how players such as Anaheim's Jean-Sebastien Giguere were somehow able to cover nearly the entire net. They looked at cracking down on obstruction, which had almost single-handedly ruined the flow of the game. They remembered the glory days of watching players like Bobby Orr skate from one end of the rink to the other, like poetry in motion,

### Joe Micheletti on the New Rules

"With the new rules, the NHL is now a skating game. Teams now have to stock their fourth lines with guys who can kill penalties, who can play a checking role, who can play the power play, or who can maybe get into a scrap—but they all have got to be useful players. The goons are gone. Teams can't afford to just have a fighter on their bench, that is too much of a liability. So yeah, I like the new rules. I was one of those guys who complained for the last 10 years that because of all of the obstruction that was going on, we weren't seeing just how good these great athletes really were. Now we are seeing better skating, passing, and shooting, and that is what hockey is all about in my eyes. As for what they could do even further in the future, I would love to see the rinks get bigger. Maybe not to Olympic size, but bigger. And I say that because the players have gotten so much bigger and stronger. We have just run out of room out there, it seems like. I know that will be a long shot to get that done, but I think it would make the game even better. Overall, though, the new rules are great and I can tell you from being around the league, there are more people excited about the game right now than there has been in a very long time. That is just fantastic in my book."

## Willie Mitchell on the New Rules

"The game has certainly changed as a result of the new rules. But, while fighting is way down, there are a lot more high-sticks now, too. They wanted to take some of the physical stuff out because they felt that it was slowing down the pace of the game. So you have to sacrifice one to get the other, I suppose. The game is evolving, though, and that is ultimately a good thing. As for fighting, between the no red line rule and the instigator stuff, the numbers are way down. Teams can't carry guys who are just one-dimensional now, and that is probably a good thing. Back in the day the physical players could get away with a clutch or a grab here or there in order to slow a guy down just enough so that he could get back into the play going the other direction. Not anymore. They are calling obstruction penalties, and guys have to be able to skate and keep up. Players need to grow and evolve, which is good for the game. It just raises the bar for everybody. I think overall the new rules clean it up for everybody and make the game a better one to play and to watch."

and without the sticks of three opposing players hacking, hooking, and holding him as he flew by.

They also looked at the obstruction in front of the net. Sure, teams want the slot to be a dangerous place for opposing players, but the slashing and interference had become brutal. It was nonstop clutching and grabbing followed by boring dump-and-chase hockey. Something had to give.

So, the league took that year off and began testing some new ideas down in the AHL. Finally, when the two sides came back to the bargaining table, things were able to get resolved in time to hit the ice for the 2005–06 season. They agreed on a fluctuating salary cap that everybody could live with, and they agreed that the rules needed a thorough shake-up. Both parties negotiated long and hard on how the proposed rule changes should be implemented, and the results were extremely positive. In what was described as "changes that would emphasize entertainment, skill, and competition on the ice," the following major rules were added to the books.

First and foremost was the crackdown on obstruction, which was now going to be called much more liberally by the officials. Next was the elimination of the red line, which brought two-line passes back into play and opened up the ice. The goal line was then moved out while the blue line was moved in from the end boards, resulting in the shortening of the neutral zone from 54 feet to 50 feet. In addition, not only was goaltending equipment downsized by 11 percent, but restrictions on the goaltender playing the puck outside of a designated area behind the net were also introduced.

In addition, fighting was further deterred by the fact that anyone starting a fight in the last five minutes of a game or in overtime would now be assessed an instigator minor, a fighting major, a misconduct, and an automatic one-game suspension. Other rules included such things as when a team ices the puck they would not be allowed to make a substitution on the ensuing faceoff. The tag-up off-sides rule was also reinstated, adding more flow to the game by virtue of having fewer whistles to stop the action. Furthermore, a shootout would be introduced if the game remained tied after a five-minute overtime.

When the players finally hit the ice that next season, the impact of the new rules was immediate. The players, for the most part, liked the new changes, and the fans loved the fact that the game had improved exponentially both offensively and defensively. As for the enforcers, however, things got decidedly more difficult. With two-line passes now legal since the red line no longer existed, speed became a huge factor in defensive strategy. Quicker, smaller skaters now had space to get by larger defenders, and that exposed many players' liabilities.

And with the crackdown on obstruction, skaters can skate much more freely through the slot without the fear of being pummeled every time. Gone are the days when a player would have a stick in his ribs the entire

### Barry Melrose on the New Rules

"There are a few things I would like to see eliminated. The zone defenses, such as the neutral zone trap and the left wing lock, all those things just slow the game down too much and stifle offense. Basketball eliminated the zones in the '60s and it helped a lot to open things up. It lets the players get back to one-on-one situations and allows for more free-flowing offenses. I also think that knee-to-knee hits are a big problem, too. I think if one is delivered in a game, the player needs to be severely penalized when it happens. Not a two-minute call, but a four-minute call. If the player does it again, suspend him. To take the point further, I think the hip check should be banned. The hip check is an old-time kind of hit. Any time a hip check is delivered, there is a strong chance for a knee injury. I don't think we should keep a hit in the game that isn't officially in the playbook, but can still hurt a player."

## Darren Pang on the New Rules

"I have two issues on ways to improve our game. First—and as a TV guy I may step on some toes here—is to figure out a way where we aren't showing so many commercials. The only time you get no stoppage in play is when you are in overtime during a playoff game. The amount of commercials that we have, and the frequency to which they are constantly being shown, has sucked the enthusiasm out of the crowd. There are just far too many breaks in the action and people lose interest. And, it takes the players out of the flow of the game as well, with all of the TV timeouts. That is the problem.

"Of course it is a catch-22, because you have to have commercials in order to pay the bills. But soccer has figured out a way to do it. They have a sponsor for each period. Why couldn't hockey do that, too? Maybe Labatt or Molson Beer is the sponsor for that period, and you would see their signage on your TV screen, or something like that. I don't know, but they need to at least look at that to make the game flow better. Or maybe you would only have two commercial breaks per period instead of having so many of them and so often. I mean hockey is such a fast, beautiful, free-flowing, change-on-the-fly type of a game, and all of the stoppages just kill it.

"Secondly, I think there is too much protective equipment in the game right now, I really do. Players are fearless because they are so well protected and that level of respect has gone right out the window. Do I think visors are good for safety? Absolutely. But they also give guys a green light to keep their sticks up high. I remember playing with Doug Wilson, who was one of the last guys to play in the NHL without a helmet. He commanded respect because he played the game the right way. And I will tell you what, when opposing players went into a corner following Doug Wilson to get a puck, they kept their hands and sticks down. They did that out of respect.

"Nowadays, the players have visors that cover their whole faces, huge elbow pads that cover their forearms, huge shin pads, huge shoulder pads with stomach protectors to block shots, mouth guards, the works. So when they go into a corner they have their hands and their sticks way up high. They are fearless about being injured and they play like it. So, while some injuries are down, other more serious ones are up. It is just a matter of time before a player is paralyzed in our league from being hit from behind. It is scary. The code used to be about honest hitting, not shoving a guy into the boards from behind when a guy is in a vulnerable position. The league should penalize players much more severely with five-minute majors for playing like that, no question. I mean, the players have gotten so big and strong over the years now, too, that the hitting is just unbelievable. We still have a lot of work to do."

time he skated into "no-man's land." Defensemen can't risk penalties for holding players up, or clearing them out of the slot, and as a result the game opened up immensely.

"Whatever they learned all their life goes straight out the window," said New Jersey Devils goalie Martin Brodeur. "You can't do the pin and hold, you can't do the old can opener, you can't do anything anymore. It's definitely hard for the defenders, especially if mobility is not one of your assets."

In the new NHL, speed trumps intimidation, and that means big changes for fighters and for fighting. While the pure heavyweight isn't about to become extinct, he is certainly going to have to change his ways in order to survive.

"For the most part, the fourth-line enforcer/tough guy has been eliminated because of the amount of ice time they can get," said Mike Murphy, the NHL's vice president of hockey operations. Murphy contends that the league never wanted to eliminate that role, but that the evolution was a "byproduct of a faster, better NHL that rewarded skill."

"With the strictness by which hooking, holding, interference have been called," Murphy continued, "a lot of times this type of player's role is to clog up, block, make contact, bump, and reel people in. When they're not able to do it, they're less effective because they end up in the box."

Several big-name enforcers were let go by their teams, sending shock waves through the league. Teams had to be accountable for every weak link in the chain. Enforcers typically aren't very fast skaters, so they could easily be beat with no red line. They are also a liability when it comes to obstruction, because slower players tend to clutch and grab those around them to slow them down—not to mention cross-check them in front of the net to clear them out. Coaches also couldn't risk wasting a roster spot on a guy who can't contribute on special teams or be used in a shootout. Perhaps the biggest factor in all of this, however, were the ramifications for instigating a fight in the waning moments of a game. This used to be "sending a message" or "settling scores" time, but not anymore. The one-game suspension is simply too severe to risk.

Of the new rules, Marty McSorley said:

> I like them. It was unfortunate that they had to lose an entire season in the process, but I am okay with how it all turned out. The new rule changes are forcing teams to be more patient with their tough guys

and to work with them on the fundamentals of the game. If they want them to be able to be effective players nowadays, then they know that they have to bring them along slowly and get them some extra help. A prime example of this is a guy like Georges Laraque, who Edmonton really invested a lot of time into. He came in as a pretty raw player and now he has developed into a solid two-way threat. It is great for the players, it really is. I mean, no tough guy likes to just be a fighter, no way. They all want to play the game and to score goals and be a part of all of that. We all did as kids and that never changes. So, if the new rules make the league produce more well-rounded players as a result of all of this, then I say fantastic.

You know, the goon, or the guy who was so specialized that he never played, was only a recent phenomenon. In fact, it was only during my era of the 1980s and '90s that these types of players were let into the league. If you look back historically at enforcers like John Ferguson or Teddy Green, they were players first and tough guys second. So, I think it is great for the league to take this philosophy and to force teams to get rid of those guys. If they can't keep up with the no red line rule, then I say good riddance, it's about time. It's a lot tougher for teams to develop big tough players who can play hockey at this level than it is to just develop big tough fighters who come off the bench and can't skate. The new rules in that regard are long overdue.

Quite honestly, the guys I felt most sorry for were the tough guys who only got 30 seconds of ice time a game. That would be hard. To get prepared, to train, to go through all of the same things the other guys went through, and to only get one shift would be brutal. And to know that you were only going out there for that one shift to fight, that would be pretty demoralizing. I played against a lot of those guys and it was sad to see. Even if you were fighting against one of those guys, you felt for them. That is not how hockey is supposed to be played. Their job was much tougher than mine, that was for sure. The emotional stress for those guys was huge because after a while their teammates never even looked at them as players, but as fighters, as robots, and that was not right. Sure, they were happy to have a job and to be in the NHL, but at what cost? Seeing those guys made me work even harder on my game to make sure I was never in their shoes.

The league didn't want to legislate out the spontaneous fights, which result from a genuine eruption of emotions. Not a chance—that is what makes hockey special. They just wanted to get rid of the "goonery," and force players to become more well-rounded and not so one-dimensional. The fighters who remain today have to be able to contribute. If they can't

### Phil Housley on the New Rules

"The new rule changes have really made the game much more fun to watch, both live as well as on TV. It's not like a tennis match anymore, where both teams just volley and wait for one to make a mistake. Guys can attack with speed through the neutral zone because teams are not able to hook anybody up anymore to slow them down. It is just a better game now and is much more appealing. It has evolved, and that is great to see. The goons slowly got weeded out as the rules changed and that is good for the game. Players have to be able to skate and contribute much more than just being able to fight; otherwise they are just going to be a liability. Those players who can do both, guys like Tie Domi for instance, they are very sought-after commodities. The new rules have really curbed fighting, too. It is way down, and that is probably good for the game, too. You know, between the faster pace of the game as well as the scheduling of all of the back-to-back games, teams need depth and they need to be able to play four lines. No teams nowadays can go with just three lines; they would get way too diminished and burned out. So, enforcers need to have stamina and they need to be able to carry their own weight out on the ice by doing different things."

score goals, then they need to be able to do the dirty work: get the puck out of their own end, take a hit, take out the trash in the slot, crash the net, play defense, kill a penalty, work the corners, and force turnovers, among other things. Their ice time will have to be earned one shift at a time.

As for the results, it has been mostly positive through the first season of play, 2005–06. Scoring is way up, nearly 25 percent, as are scoring chances and shots on goal. The new composite sticks also had an impact, adding as much as 10 percent more velocity to their shots. The goalies, with 11 percent less padding, felt 89 percent worse about the entire situation. Oh well, somebody had to suffer. The speed and excitement are there, too, which fans enjoy both in person and on TV.

The changes have made a big impact and the resulting offensive explosion was just what the doctor ordered: the fans are back. The salary cap gave everybody the peace of mind that eludes other sports, such as Major League Baseball. One questions how it is fair that the Yankees can spend $150 million more on its players than a small-market team. That's ridiculous. Even though it was painful, hockey did the right thing.

It's not as if physical play is gone from the new NHL, however—no way. The big hits are still there, as are the fights. They are just managed better and not abused. Now more than ever, teams cannot afford to be short-handed, so fighters have to choose their spots and not be selfish. According to the NHL and Elias Sports Bureau, fighting majors were down a whopping 45 percent in the first few months of the 2005–06 season. That number steadily rose throughout the season, but still remained much lower than in years past.

Not all of the players like what has transpired, though, and many miss the days of old. They feel that there are too many "ticky-tack" fouls being called, which ruins the flow and intensity of the game.

Colorado Avalanche veteran right winger Dan Hinote said the following to the *Denver Post*:

> There's no testosterone in the game right now. They've taken a lot of the physical aspects out of the game. It's predominantly special teams now. There's no more battling in the corners. I won't say there's none, but there's a lot less. There's no scrums in front of the net.
>
> There's far less hitting. You play a more tentative style because you don't want to put your team down. On the other side, I think it is more entertaining for people to watch. From my point of view, the type of game I have to play, they've taken a lot of that part away.
>
> Now, is the league better because of these new rules? Perhaps. Maybe the fans like it more. And if that's what we're geared toward, then they're doing their job right. But there's a lot of hockey fans, fans who have been watching a long time, that are going to miss that part of the game.

As for the enforcers themselves, not all have been too thrilled with the changes either. While many current players won't air their opinions on the matter publicly, one prominent alumni of the tough guy fraternity, Tiger Williams, did weigh in:

> They can sell this [garbage] to anyone else, not me. Tell me, with all these rule changes, how many more five-on-five goals are there now over last year? None—maybe even less. The stars are too tired because they've been on the power play for five minutes. How can anybody say this is more exciting—explain it to me? You can't.
>
> They're going to kill all the goalies and most of the good defensemen. And some snot-nosed little [punk] that isn't going to break a nail is going to score 50 goals and he's never driven to the net in his life. He's never stood in front of the net with Moose Dupont giving him 89 cross-checks in the back of the head.

> Whether cross-checking a guy in front of the net like we did was right or wrong [we] played through that. And now to have today's players score 400 goals in a no-touch pond hockey league is garbage. Getting in another guy's face is part of the character of the game.

Another interesting perspective came from long-time enforcer Tim Hunter, who accumulated more than 3,000 penalty minutes over his 16-year NHL career.

"The fighters today are bigger and tougher, but it is harder to get the job done these days," said Hunter. "There is less respect today than there once was. I have never believed there was or is a code. I have been sucker punched a number of times, jumped from behind, had my eye nearly gouged out, and kick-kneed. Saying that, today's players seem to be under greater pressure and the stakes are so high they are reckless and have no respect for the damage they can do. The day is coming where a player is going to be killed in a fight."

Most will agree, however, that the NHL is a much better product for not only its players but also the fans. Every aspect of the game is still there,

### Mike Peluso on the New Rules

"The new rules have made fighting a lot more infrequent, no question. I think the vast majority of fans like to see fights. Many of them wouldn't admit that, but it's true. Look, I think fighting is great for hockey. It is a rush for the fighters, a rush for the fans, and it serves a purpose by keeping the game clean. I say embrace it and celebrate it. As long as it is done properly by people who want to do it and who are clearly protecting their teammates and providing them with a spark, then I say it's great.

"I think the entire environment in professional hockey has moved away from fighting. I mean look at all of the old classic arenas which are now gone: Chicago, Boston, Toronto, and Philly. Those were all really intimate places which were built for the fans to be right there next to you on those small ice surfaces. Now, these giant palaces have replaced all of those buildings and everything is moved away and everything focuses on the box seats. It's all corporate now, and you can feel that change in all of these new environments. That is too bad in my opinion. I understand new buildings are necessary to grow the game from the business end and all of that, but I miss the old places which had so much character. The blue-collar guy can't even afford a ticket nowadays, either, which also bums me out. Those are the people who can relate to tough hockey, not the corporate fat cats up in the luxury suites."

but it has been "cleaned up and sanitized" significantly. The future of the league seems to be headed in the right direction. Despite losing its TV deal in the aftermath of the lockout (ESPN declined to pick up its option, so the league went with little-known Outdoor Life Network), the fans are tuning in and showing up to see their heroes once again.

The franchises are healthier, too. In fact, according to a January 2006 Bloomberg News report, the increase in NHL franchise values since the lockout was settled has skyrocketed upwards of 50 percent. According to Curtis Eichelberger, it is estimated that the Mighty Ducks, which sold for $75 million in 2005, are now worth between $130 million and $150 million. One franchise was recently offered a 60 percent premium over its pre-lockout valuation, while another party was apparently willing to offer $250 million for the right to purchase an expansion team as well.

From the looks of it, the ship has been righted, at least for now. So far so good. Yes, change can be a good thing, just ask goalie Jacques Plante, who defied tradition when he decided that he had taken enough stitches and put on a mask. Certainly, hockey, not to mention Jacques' mug, is better for it. This seems to be just what the game needed to get back on track, both financially and entertainment-wise, to end the complacency that had plagued the league for so long. (Let's just hope the league doesn't find a way to self-destruct before the next collective bargaining agreement, which, by the way, is only a few short years away. Stay tuned.)

As for the future of the game? I think it looks brighter than ever. Now that some of the old guard has moved aside and embraced change for the new millennium, we are all much better off for it. Should fighting remain as a part of the fabric of this beautiful game? I say yes, but with the caveat that the game get rid of the goons once and for all. No more premeditated brawls for the sake of entertainment or intimidation. Fighting should remain as a release valve reserved for two emotionally, adrenaline-charged players who want to settle their differences right then and there like men. It should also remain to serve its essential purpose as a deterrent to not only cheap, dirty play, but also the absurd taunting and disrespect that so often manifests itself in the form of false bravado in other major sports. Players with heart and courage can stay, too, but they need to clean up their acts and get rid of the cheap stuff, the obstruction, and especially the stick work.

As for the growth and future of the game with regards to expanding south? It looks better than ever. In fact, the last two Stanley Cups were won by teams south of the Mason Dixon Line: Tampa Bay in 2004 and the Carolina Hurricanes in 2006.

Perhaps this game's most frustrating dilemma is that its toughness, its brutality, its violence is so appealing to some, yet so despicable to others. As one writer put it, hockey is a "strange mixture of grace and disgrace," depending on your morals and ethics. That is where the code comes in, to protect and to serve, no matter what.

# Appendix

## Neal Sheehy on the Aftermath of the Rules Changes

It is important to note that Sheehy made the following comments while the league was in lockout mode back in 2004. Neil would later be vindicated, though, when a high-ranking member of the NHL told him that nearly every member of the league's competition committee read his thoughts on the subject, and that it made a "profound impact" on their decision to implement the rule changes that were rolled out the next year.

"Hearing that certainly made me feel good," said Sheehy. "I only wish the league would have been able to reconcile with the players earlier, so that the entire [2004–05] season wasn't lost. I still stand by my thoughts regarding the instigator, though, and am hopeful that they [the league] will come around on that sometime soon as well. It is such a great game, and you hate to see it cheapened in any way."

### The "Original Instigator" on the Genesis of the Instigator Rule

"I rocked the boat," said Sheehy. "I hit the skilled players and would not fight the tough ones, which distracted them. In part, because I was the recipient of so many cheap shots as pay-back for my tactics, the NHL eventually reacted and implemented the instigator rule, which further encouraged those types of actions and helped neutralize the game's top offensive players.

"While I have no regrets about how I played the game back then, completely within the confines of the rules, I have since had a change of heart regarding the instigator and now feel compelled to express my thoughts. I believe professional hockey is at a crossroads and the future of the game will depend upon decisions that are made now. Most who are involved in hockey recognize that its players are bigger, stronger, faster and more skilled than ever before. But the game has in fact diminished and is considerably less entertaining.

"But, how can that be? I believe it is because the most skilled players are not given the freedom to exhibit their skills. Rather, they are coached to 'play the percentages' and...chip it in, chip it out...chip, chip, chip. The 'golden age' of hockey, a time when great teams dazzled us all, is a thing of the past. I am convinced we are now at a time when changes must occur. We must discuss and tackle our game's problems, and come up with real solutions, otherwise hockey will never sell in non-traditional markets and the game will suffer. Solving any problem first involves identifying what is wrong, and then the real challenge is finding the right solutions. I hope to offer a perspective that identifies the tactics that began the downturn of skill and play-making in hockey, and then to offer possible solutions.

"Many discussions regarding 'What is wrong with our game?' revolve around the way the game was played in the '80s by the great Edmonton Oilers' teams. I was fortunate enough to play for some great Calgary Flames' teams, and I always considered myself lucky to have even been on the same ice surface as 'Gretzky and Company.' Although it may have appeared otherwise, I had tremendous respect for them.

"The Battle of Alberta was hockey at its finest, with two of the best teams in hockey going to war nearly 20 times per season, including exhibition and playoff games. It played at a time when the game was wide-open and highly offensive. And then it happened, the beginning of the systematic erosion and neutralization of skill and play-making in the NHL.

"Wayne Gretzky warned against not protecting the NHL's best players and was dubbed by some as 'Whine Gretzky.' Mario Lemieux warned against it and he was discounted as a baby who felt he deserved special treatment. And 'why not?' I ask. Players like Gretzky, Lemieux, Hull, Yzerman, Federov, Sakic, Modano, as well as the NHL's future stars such as St. Louis, Kovalchuk, Heatley, Richards, Thornton, Leopold, and Gomez, among others, should be treated differently because these players make the NHL the greatest league in the world.

"The NHL is steeped in history and tradition and therefore rarely makes radical changes to the game. Therefore, I am not advocating for radical changes to the rules, but rather for focusing on the league's interpretation of the rules, instruction of the rules, and the league's commitment of more resources for officials. In order to fully understand my perspective, I believe it is important to briefly outline the history of the NHL as I experienced it.

"I have distant memories as a boy in the 1960s watching *Hockey Night in Canada*, and I witnessed expansion in 1967. I watched great Montreal Canadiens teams with Yvan Cournoyer, Jean Beliveau, and Jacques Lemaire. I vividly remember when Bobby Orr arrived on the scene, and in his break-out season with the Boston Bruins, won the Stanley Cup in 1970 and again in 1972. The Bruins dazzled us with their skill and their hard physical style of play on the small rink of the Boston Garden. Orr and Company received the nickname, 'The Big Bad Bruins,' but not one player was bad, nor really that big. However, they were a great team that bonded together and played with tremendous overall team skill and toughness.

"Philadelphia responded with 'The Broad Street Bullies' and won two Stanley Cups in 1974 and 1975. Dave 'the Hammer' Schultz glamorized the role of the goon, and the Flyers changed the make-up of the game with players like Gary Dornhoefer, Don Saleski, Dave Schultz, Andre Dupont, Ed Van Impe, and Bob Kelly. The evolving game in the NHL then influenced the minor leagues and the minor league style of play became the impetus for the movie *Slap Shot*.

"The Montreal Canadiens continued their dynasty of skill and team toughness in the late 1970s with the likes of Guy Lafleur, Pete Mahovlich, Lemaire, Guy LaPointe, and Larry Robinson. The New York Islanders responded with their own skill and overall team toughness in the early '80s with Bryan Trottier, Mike Bossy, Denis Potvin, John Tonelli, Bobby Nystrom, Clark Gillies, and Billy Smith. These dynasty teams could win however any other team wished to play them, with skill or toughness.

"Then in 1984, in a Stanley Cup rematch with the New York Islanders, the Edmonton Oilers' players came of age and created the NHL's most recent dynasty. The Oilers were dominant with Wayne Gretzky, Jari Kurri, Mark Messier, Glenn Anderson, Paul Coffey, and Grant Fuhr. The Oilers successfully intimidated other teams with their youth, speed, and skill.

"Edmonton not only had the fastest and most skilled team in the league, but [coach] Glen Sather had taken a page from Fred Shero's Philadelphia Flyers' playbook and had one of the toughest teams in the league with Dave Semenko, Marty McSorley, Kevin McClelland, Don Jackson, Ken Linseman, Dave Lumley, Dave Hunter, and Wayne Van Dorp. The Oilers could play whatever game a team wanted to play and dominate. There was no team as fast, as skilled, or as tough.

"In the 1980s, as a tactic, the Oilers created scrums and pushing matches so that players from both teams would be put in the penalty box. Four-on-four, there was no better team than Edmonton, and with that advantage, the Oilers feasted on all other teams in the league. That was until the NHL decided the Oilers' style of play was unfair, and neutralized Edmonton's game by implementing the coincidental penalties rule.

"Edmonton was the best in the NHL and every team dreamed of finding a way to beat them. Bob Johnson, the coach of the Calgary Flames, worked day and night looking for ways to beat them by trying to neutralize their speed and skill. To do this he needed players who could skate well and who were also tough.

"I played an important role within Badger Bob's system and my role as a member of the Flames was the same as in guerrilla warfare. I was unpredictable at a time when most players were predictable. I kept players guessing by distracting them and keeping them off their game. It was a time in the game when tough guys fought tough guys, and a tough guy would never turn away from a fight. The 'goons' protected the skilled players, and no one touched the skilled players unless they wanted a fight, a line-brawl, or even a bench-clearing brawl, of which Calgary and Edmonton had many. This was the way the game was played until the NHL implemented rules that awarded a 10-game suspension (without pay) for the first player over the bench in a brawl.

"I pushed and prodded Gretzky to get him thinking more about me than about scoring goals. Consequently, I had to face Semenko, McSorley, Jackson, and McClelland every night. But I would not fight them. I took several hits to the head and was challenged to fight every shift. I told these tough guys that I would get fined if I fought them and Kevin McClelland eloquently quipped, 'I'll pay it,' because he and his teammates so desperately wanted a piece of me.

"The officials didn't call many penalties against the Oilers until we [Calgary] used the media to highlight that fact. We got the story out that our players were being mugged and challenged to fight, and the Oilers were not being penalized. A couple officials even said to me, 'Don't worry, you'll get yours!' Eventually the league cracked down on that type of behavior and started calling interference and unsportsmanlike conduct penalties. While the instigator rule wouldn't go in the books until a few years later, the wheels were in motion even then.

"So, I continued to rock the boat. I hit the skilled players and would not fight the tough ones, which distracted both of them. I was now allowed to annoy Gretzky to distraction and was able to keep Edmonton's tough guys off-center by drawing penalties, and this was at a time when Calgary had the number one power-play in the NHL. This was one of the ways which enabled the Flames to have consistent and continued success against the Oilers during that era.

"I retired from the game in the early '90s, and then watched it systematically change when the instigator rule was put into effect. Players were now not being held as accountable for their actions as they had before, because the new rule protected them. They could neutralize their opposition's top skill players, knowing that if the other team retaliated, they would receive an additional two-minute minor penalty.

"This began a shift in how the game was played throughout the NHL, a process which has continued to evolve over the years. Coaches studied the great Oilers' teams and the tactics the Flames successfully used against them. Players were then expected to implement similar tactics. Unfortunately though, because the NHL allowed such tactics without individual player accountability, an increasing number of players adopted this style, which legally shuts down the best offensive players, but which also eliminates a great degree of skill from the game.

"Incidentally, I believe the Todd Bertuzzi incident never would have happened if the instigator rule didn't exist and if players were better able to police themselves. I do not condone what Bertuzzi did and his actions have absolutely no place in the NHL game. But in the old days, that situation would have been dealt with long before something like that took place, and a star player like Bertuzzi probably would not have been involved. Incidents like this do more to hurt our sport throughout the United States, where the league is in quest of an elusive television contract, than periodic fisticuffs among its players throughout the regular season.

"Since the mid-1990s, the NHL has promoted speed and high-impact body contact in hopes of attracting a national television audience. What effect has that had on the game? It has encouraged high-impact body contact with reckless abandon, which is often overlooked by officials, and has also further eroded skill in professional hockey.

"Coaches nowadays want their players to agitate opponents and draw penalties. 'Agitate, but don't fight,' they say. This was a novel idea back in the '80s, but now it is the norm and our overall game is suffering because of it. It neutralizes skill and frustrates the very players who make hockey the greatest game in the world.

"I agree that the NHL should protect its most skilled players. I believe the instigator rule should be eliminated. The officials should not be forced to call more penalties with new rules, but rather focus on calling fewer penalties and allow players to police themselves. If this were to happen, the tactics of trying to draw more penalties would be diminished.

"If a player is held accountable for the way he plays, by facing retribution without the prospect of drawing a penalty, in most cases he will likely stop his tactics. Therefore the role of the tough guy should remain important in the NHL, to make players accountable and to keep the game under control. This would help open up the game and give it back to the skilled players.

"Officials do the best they can given their direction from the league. Another focus of the NHL should also be on working with its officials to protect the league's most skilled players. If the NHL would allow the players to police themselves within reason, and give the officials the leeway to control it, the tactics players use to draw penalties would eventually lessen and skilled players would again be able to fully showcase their abilities.

"Indeed, there are numerous possible remedies that would help fix our ailing game, and I have highlighted a few. But I believe the NHL's number one focus should be to insist that its officials understand the critical fact that NHL players are not created equal, nor should they be treated as such. Yes, it's time for the instigator to go, for the good of the game."

# Notes

## Chapter 1

"Did these targets go to the dressing room..." Lawrence Scanlan, *Grace Under Fire* (Toronto: Penguin Books, 2002).

"If some of the longhairs..." Lawrence Scanlan, *Grace Under Fire* (Toronto: Penguin Books, 2002).

"For 20 years, man and boy..." As cited in Lawrence Scanlan, *Grace Under Fire* (Toronto: Penguin Books, 2002).

"If I hadn't learned to lay..." CBS Sports Online, "The Top 10 Hockey Violence Lowlights" (March 9, 2004).

"Steve, I just want to apologize..." Jim Morris, "NHL Reinstates Bertuzzi, Disappoints Victim," *Canadian Press* (August 8, 2005).

"The attack has been bad..." Associated Press, "Bertuzzi, Canucks Sued by Moore," CBC (February 17, 2005).

"inflicted significant permanent..." "Moore Files Writ against Bertuzzi in B.C." CP/TSN. ca (March 7, 2006) http://www.tsn.ca/nhl/teams/news_story/?ID=157544&hubname= nhl-canucks

"I'm glad the NHL has finally..." Associated Press, "Bertuzzi Reinstated, 17 Months after Attack," (August 10, 2005).

"You've got only one brain..." Tim Dahlberg, "Does NHL Need Death to End Violence?" MSNBC.com (March 12, 2004).

"The fact is, it's very much a part..." Jim Kelley, "Bertuzzi a Product of Hockey's Culture," ESPN.com (March 11, 2004).

"They should stay out forever..." Scott Burnside, "Should Courts Look More Closely at Sports?" ESPN.com (March 11, 2004).

## Chapter 3

"Someone in my shoes has to know..." Stan Fischler, *The Ultimate Bad Boys* (Toronto: Warwick Publishing, 1999).

"'Doc,' he asked as he..." Lawrence Scanlan, *Grace Under Fire* (Toronto: Penguin Books, 2002).

"You might change three…" Derrick Goold, "Bertuzzi Breaks the Code," *Post-Dispatch* (March 13, 2004).

"If we can, we'll intimidate…" Lawrence Scanlan, *Grace Under Fire* (Toronto: Penguin Books, 2002).

## Chapter 4

"I'm well aware of the enforcers…" Kevin Allen, *Crunch* (Chicago: Triumph Books, 1999).

"Fighters talk amongst themselves…" Lindsay Berra, "NHL Fighters Motivated by Fear," ESPN.com (January 19, 2004).

"Domi, he just stands in there and punches…" Lindsay Berra, "NHL Fighters Motivated by Fear," ESPN.com (January 18, 2004).

"The important thing is that…" Ron Spence, "Darren McCarty: Enforcing by Committee," www.hockeyenforcers.com (2003).

"The guys that are really tough…" Ron Spence, "Sandy McCarthy: Doing His Job," www.hockeyenforcers.com (2003).

"I was coming off the end…" David Singer, "Q & A: Troy Crowder," Hockeyfights.com (March 23, 2005).

"We met at a golf course…" David Singer, "Q & A: Troy Crowder," Hockeyfights.com (March 23, 2005).

"That happened to me once…" Stan Fischler, *The Ultimate Bad Boys* (Toronto: Warwick Publishing, 1999).

## Chapter 5

"When you do something to…" Derrick Goold, "Bertuzzi Breaks the Code," *Post-Dispatch* (March 13, 2004).

"I don't regret anything I did…" Michael Russo, "Sometimes Being a Leader Means Getting into a Scrap," *Star Tribune* (January 26, 2006).

"Sometimes he's got to, not…" Michael Russo, "Sometimes Being a Leader Means Getting into a Scrap," *Star Tribune* (January 26, 2006).

## Chapter 6

"That was the perfect match-up…" Terry Frei, "Rivalry Fueled by Many Motives," ESPN.com (January 18, 2004).

"I respect him for what…" Terry Frei, "Rivalry Fueled by Many Motives," ESPN.com (January 18, 2004).

## Chapter 8

"You know a guy has a broken wrist…" Punch Imlach, *Hockey Is a Battle: Punch Imlach's Own Story* (Halifax, Nova Scotia: Formac Publishing, 1969).

"I've broken my nose five…" "Bad Face Day," *Maxim Magazine* (April 2006).

"I stitch better when my skin…" Lawrence Scanlan, *Grace Under Fire* (Toronto: Penguin Books, 2002).

"People see us fight and think…" Lawrence Scanlan, *Grace Under Fire* (Toronto: Penguin Books, 2002).

"I think it's time that I kind..." Associated Press, "Concussions Prompt Deadmarsh to Retire" (September 22, 2005).

## Chapter 10

"I was afraid every time..." Lindsay Berra, "NHL Fighters Motivated by Fear," ESPN.com (January 18, 2004).

"It's like the playground..." John Buccigross, "Kids Understand, Sometimes More Than Adults," ESPN.com (January 19, 2004).

## Chapter 11

"It's always an interesting situation..." Scott Burnside and Jim Kelley, "The Dos and Don'ts of Fighting," ESPN.com (January 18, 2004).

## Chapter 12

"I'm just happy to get to..." Lindsay Berra, "NHL Fighters Motivated by Fear," ESPN.com (January 19, 2004).

"It's hard for a hockey player..." Dave Semenko, *Looking Out for Number One* (Toronto: General Paperbacks Publishing, 1989).

## Chapter 13

"An instigator of an altercation..." "NHL Official Rules," NHL.com (2006).

"Since the rule's inception..." Spider Jones, "As Entertaining as the Scoring of a Goal," *NHL Sports Forecaster* (1996).

"A player who is deemed to be the instigator..." "NHL Official Rules," NHL.com (2006).

"[That rule] is something I crafted..." Douglas Flynn, "National Hypocrisy League?" *Boston Herald* (November 27, 2005).

"It's tough to put him out..." Eric Duhatschek, "Beauty and the Beast?" *The Hockey News* (Winter 1987).

"I'd have to see our team..." Eric Duhatschek, "Beauty and the Beast?" *The Hockey News* (Winter 1987).

"Even though we were taught..." Adam Proteau, "Sheehy, Gretzky Had Fierce Battles," *The Hockey News* (May 23, 2003).

"You're right, Neil Sheehy..." Adam Proteau, "Sheehy, Gretzky Had Fierce Battles," *The Hockey News* (May 23, 2003).

"I rocked the boat..." Neil Sheehy, "The Systematic Erosion and Neutralization of Skill and Play-Making in the NHL," www.sheehyhockey.com (2004).

## Chapter 15

"While the days of the true bench-clearer..." Ray Ferraro, "Empty Benches Equal Total Mayhem," ESPN.com (January 19, 2004).

## Chapter 16

"Ophthalmologist Dr. Tom Pashby of Toronto..." Lawrence Scanlan, *Grace Under Fire* (Toronto: Penguin Books, 2002).

"We're professional athletes, and..." Brian Murphy, "Visor Debate Intensifies in NHL," *Pioneer Press* (October 22, 2005).

## Chapter 18
"When I was younger it was..." Ron Spence, "Al Secord: On His Way to the 30/300 Club," www.hockeyenforcers.com (2004).

## Chapter 19
"Brutal, fast, brutal, exciting, and brutal..." Ken Dryden, *The Game* (Etobicoke, Ontario: Wiley Publishing, 1983).

"It's not like we were promoting..." Ron Spence, "Guaranteed Fight Night," www.hockeyenforcers.com (2004).

"We try to promote the integrity..." Ron Spence, "Guaranteed Fight Night," www.hockeyenforcers.com (2004).

"Hockey fighting has been around..." Ron Spence, "Guaranteed Fight Night," www.hockeyenforcers.com (2004).

## Chapter 20
"I once broadcasted a game..." "Does fighting belong in the NHL?" ESPN.com (January 19, 2004).

"When I played, cheap shots..." Dave Schultz, "Players Need Fighting to Police Themselves on the Ice," *The New York Times* (March 21, 2004).

"While many cite this as evidence for more..." Dave Schultz, "Players Need Fighting to Police Themselves on the Ice," *The New York Times* (March 21, 2004).

"When I go to a hockey game..." Frank Deford, "Goon Be Gone," SI.com (April 14, 2004).

"Those who say fighting is just..." "Does Fighting Belong in the NHL?" ESPN.com (January 19, 2004).

"They [the Soviets] were pretty violent..." Jeff Miller and Mike Heika, "The Raging Debate over Fighting in Hockey," *The Dallas Morning News* (May 9, 2004).

"In 1975 the National Hockey League Players' Association..." Lawrence Scanlan, *Grace Under Fire* (Toronto: Penguin Books, 2002).

"at risk of becoming an extreme sport..." Jeff Miller and Mike Heika, "The Raging Debate over Fighting in Hockey," *The Dallas Morning News* (May 9, 2004).

"It wouldn't bother me if they took fighting out..." Jeff Miller and Mike Heika, "The Raging Debate over Fighting in Hockey," *The Dallas Morning News* (May 9, 2004).

"Fighting, at least in the traditional fashion..." Terry Frei, "Does Fighting Belong in the NHL?" ESPN.com (January 19, 2004).

## Chapter 21
"I don't even like to talk about fighting..." Kara Yorio, http://www.insidehockey.com/openicehits/2003_09_22.html

"put a bounty on his son's head..." "Hockey Violence Cuts No Ice," *Guardian Newspapers* (November 21, 2002).

"I think people are looking for help..." Jeff Miller and Mike Heika, "The Raging Debate over Fighting in Hockey," *The Dallas Morning News* (May 9, 2004).

"He can be playing with kids..." Jeff Miller and Mike Heika, "The Raging Debate over Fighting in Hockey," *The Dallas Morning News* (May 9, 2004).

"Even so, 26 percent..." As cited in Lawrence Scanlan, *Grace Under Fire* (Toronto: Penguin Books, 2002).

"The study also determined that among..." As cited in Lawrence Scanlan, *Grace Under Fire* (Toronto: Penguin Books, 2002).

## Chapter 22

"The very future of our game..." NHL Media Conference Call, September 15, 2004.

"Whatever they learned all their life..." Associated Press, "Players Showing Their Creative Side Again: New Rules Opening Up Game Better Than Almost Anyone Imagined" (December 10, 2005).

"For the most part, the fourth-line..." Michael Russo, "R.I.P. the Pure NHL Fighter," *Star Tribune* (November 27, 2005).

"There's no testosterone in the game..." "Where's the Black and Blue NHL?" *The Denver Post* (December 24, 2005).

"They can sell this [garbage] to anyone..." Eric Francis, "Tiger Takes Jabs at Rules," *Slam!* (November 10, 2005).

"The fighters today are bigger..." Martin DesRosiers, "Q & A: Tim Hunter," Hockeyfights.com (February 10, 2005).